THE BRONTËS AND THEIR BACKGROUND

THE BRONTËS
AND THEIR
BACKGROUND

Romance and Reality

TOM WINNIFRITH

Lecturer in English
University of Warwick

MACMILLAN

First published 1973 by
THE MACMILLAN PRESS LTD
London and Basingstoke
Associated companies in New York Toronto Dublin
Melbourne Johannesburg and Madras

SBN 333 14582 8

Printed in Great Britain by
WESTERN PRINTING SERVICES LTD
Bristol

FOR THOMAS

Contents

Acknowledgements

THIS BOOK was originally written as a doctoral thesis during two years as William Noble Fellow at Liverpool University. I would like to thank Liverpool University in general, and the Department of English in particular, for the opportunity thus provided.

I am glad to acknowledge indispensable help generously given by Professor Kenneth Allott, Mr John Carter, Miss Diana Crawfurd, Mrs Inga-Stina Ewbank, Miss Amy Foster, Miss Ann Griffin, Professor Barbara Hardy, Mrs Jennifer Harrison, Mrs Joanna Hutton, Professor Kenneth Muir, Dame Daphne du Maurier, Sister Margaret Needham, Mr John Nussey, Miss Cassandra Peterson, Mrs Isabelle Pigot, Mr Roger Prior, Professor Norman Sherry, Miss Pamela White, Mr Ioan Williams and Sir John Winnifrith. I am especially grateful to the supervisor of my thesis, Dr Miriam Allott, for the time she selflessly devoted to discussion, improvement and correction of errors.

I would like to thank the following libraries for supplying books, manuscripts, and information about manuscripts: The Bodleian Library; The British Museum; The Brontë Parsonage Museum; The Brotherton Library, Leeds; The Fitzwilliam Museum, Cambridge; The Harold Cohen Library, Liverpool; The Harvard College Library; The Henry Huntington Library, San Marino; The London Library; The Wrenn Library, Texas.

Finally I would like to thank my wife, whose company has made the writing of this book such a pleasure, and my children, who have made the writing of it such a challenge.

Bibliographical Note

ALL REFERENCES to the text of the Brontë novels and to Mrs Gaskell's *Life of Charlotte Brontë* have been taken, unless otherwise stated, from the Haworth edition of *The Life and Works of Charlotte Brontë and Her Sisters*, edited by Mrs H. Ward and C. K. Shorter (London, 1889–90).

The following abbreviations have been used in the notes:

BST   *Transactions of the Brontë Society*

PMLA   *Publications of the Modern Language Association of America*

SHCBM   *The Miscellaneous and Unpublished Writings of Charlotte Brontë and Patrick Branwell Brontë*, edited by T. J. Wise and J. A. Symington, 2 vols (Oxford, 1936–8)

SHCBP   *The Poems of Charlotte Brontë and Patrick Branwell Brontë*, edited by T. J. Wise and J. A. Symington (Oxford, 1934)

SHEA   *The Poems of Emily Jane and Anne Brontë*, edited by T. J. Wise and J. A. Symington (Oxford, 1934)

SHLL   *The Brontës: Their Lives, Friendships and Correspondence*, edited by T. J. Wise and J. A. Symington, 4 vols (Oxford, 1932)

TLS   *The Times Literary Supplement*

In some of the above, the prefix SH means the Shakespeare Head edition.

Introduction

AFTER STRATFORD Haworth is England's most visited literary shrine, with over 100,000 pilgrims to the Brontë Parsonage Museum in 1970, but scholars and critics have generally failed to follow the popular lead in examining the achievements of the Brontë sisters. No doubt the extravagant adulation of amateur writers has acted as a deterrent to professional investigators, but other factors have played their part in preventing us from seeing the Brontës in a true light. It is the first task of this book to reveal some of the obstacles in the way of a proper study of the Brontës; the unreliability of the primary evidence is shown to be equalled only by the fallibility of secondary authorities. It is the second task of this book to examine some of the religious, literary and social ideas of the Brontës, and to criticise the way they expressed these ideas in their novels.

Most Brontë biographers, critics and scholars have paid insufficient attention to the unreliability of the primary evidence on which they have based their theories. The Letters of Charlotte Brontë and the juvenilia were both owned and edited by T. J. Wise; a detailed examination of some of the manuscript evidence shows Wise to have been both dishonest and inaccurate. Thus much of the biographical evidence and the juvenilia are unreliable sources for theories about the Brontës, but we need not, as some literary critics do, build theories on no evidence at all, as we can examine closely the text of the novels, with which Wise did not interfere, and consider evidence on the background of the Brontës which has been insufficiently related to their writings.

Most writers have either given a false account of the Brontës' religion, by for example confusing a belief in eternal punishment with a belief in predestination, or have paid no attention to the religious element in the works of the Brontës. Yet not only did the Brontës have an obviously religious upbringing, but the country as a whole was vitally concerned with religion. Hell was an ever-present reality in Haworth. But the Brontës had the courage to break away from the almost universal belief that sinners merited eternal punishment. Of the three sisters, Anne is the most obvious and crude in her exposition of her Universalist creed; Charlotte is more tentative and negative; Emily boldly states a problem, but does not offer any easy solution to it.

The theory that the Brontës wrote in an era of comparative freedom from the restraints of prudery is also shown to be a false one. An examination of the fiction to which the Brontës are likely to have had access shows that these books, written in the period 1750–1825, were far less prudish than the fiction of the 1840s which the Brontës because of poverty and isolation were unable to read. Without contemporary models the Brontës were not typical of the age in which they lived and, as an analysis of contemporary reviews shows, their outspoken views and language met with hostile criticism. Anne is again shown to be the most open to attack; Charlotte is hesitant and appears to have made a not wholly successful attempt to meet her critics; Emily is more bold than Charlotte and less crude than Anne.

Finally it is shown that there is a difficulty in finding factual evidence to relate to the Brontës' views on society, as there is no sociologist to give us a complete and objective picture of nineteenth-century society. Instead we have to look at the partial pictures given by other nineteenth-century novelists. One such writer, Thackeray, is shown to be both a denouncer of social distinctions and a believer in them. Charlotte Brontë is very similar to Thackeray, but she does not seem to know much about the society she describes. Anne falls into the same traps, but lacks the vigour of Charlotte; Emily writes with knowledge, vigour and objectivity about the conflict between the eighteenth-century yeomanry and the nineteenth-century capitalist, although it is a mistake to reduce her novel to a sociological treatise.

This kind of investigation into the Brontës' religion, attitude to literary conventions and social views is not as fragmentary as it looks. There are obvious links between prudery and snobbery, between sex and salvation, and even, without being too fanciful, between a belief in the select aristocracy of birth and a belief in the Elect aristocracy of Grace. It can hardly be coincidental that the reviewer of *Jane Eyre* in *The Mirror* for December 1847, linked all three themes in the following outburst:

> *Religion is stabbed in the dark – our social distinctions attempted to be levelled, and all absurdly moral notions done away with.*

Nor is this kind of investigation unconnected with the earlier investigation into the unreliability of our primary evidence and our secondary authorities. Nineteenth-century religion, social life and literary conventions are both sufficiently like their twentieth-century counterparts for a knowledge of them to be too readily assumed, and sufficiently unlike them for a careful and thorough examination of all available evidence to be necessary. Since we have some of Charlotte Brontë's letters only in a bowdlerised form and there are suspicions about the authorship of some of the juvenilia with their accounts of licentious, irreligious aristocrats, we must be aware that religious unorthodoxy, literary prudery and social snobbery are areas in which we have to be peculiarly sensitive to the fallibility of the primary evidence. Because opinion on all three subjects has changed so radically in the last hundred years, we have also to be on our guard against the personal prejudice of our secondary authorities.

I

Biographers and Critics

MRS GASKELL'S *Life of Charlotte Brontë* is a classic of English biography, and she has immortalised the lives of the three Brontë sisters. Of course her concentration on Charlotte, whom she first met as a famous authoress after her sisters' death, means that we see Emily and Anne through Charlotte's eyes. Of course the restrictions of Victorian decorum meant that Mrs Gaskell had to slur over the love affair with M. Heger. Mr Nicholls and Mr Brontë were alive when Mrs Gaskell wrote, and their relations with Charlotte had to be handled delicately, although Mrs Gaskell's dislike of both men shows itself in an exaggeration of Mr Brontë's eccentricity and Mr Nicholls's lack of romance. For all her delicacy Mrs Gaskell succeeded in falling foul of the Carus Wilson and Robinson family, and we are still uncertain how harsh the regimen was at Cowan Bridge School, or whether Branwell Bronte was more sinned against than sinning at Thorp Green.[1] Finally Mrs Gaskell was not a professional scholar, trained to give an accurate transcription of documents or an objective appraisal of events, but a novelist in her own right; it is not too harsh to blame her for being the prime source of the fatal blurring of fiction and fact which has bedevilled Brontë studies ever since the publication of the first, soon to be hastily revised, edition of *The Life of Charlotte Brontë*.

Mrs Gaskell's successors in the field of Brontë biography, many of them also novelists, have not altogether succeeded in eliminating the faults of subjectivity, inaccuracy, controversy and even prudery,[2] which characterised the first Brontë biography. It seems likely, however, that the merits of all these biographers have done more of a disservice than their faults to the proper study of the Brontës as writers. For the Brontë story

1

is a deeply moving one, set in the same sombre setting and with
the same note of inevitable tragedy as *Wuthering Heights*, and
ever since the publication of *Jane Eyre* it has been all too easy to
assume that the life of the Brontës is another Brontë novel, or
that the Brontë novels are autobiographical fragments. Thus
Thackeray spoke of Charlotte as Jane Eyre, Mrs Gaskell's *Life*
is commonly printed in a uniform edition with the novels, a
lonely farmhouse near Haworth is generally known as Wuthering Heights, and biographers have produced elaborate parallels
between events in the Brontë novels and events in their authors'
lives. The lines between fact and fiction are blurred once again.

Naturally the Brontës with their horizons fairly limited to
Haworth or at any rate to Yorkshire, apart from their brief
sojourn in Brussels, derived inspiration from their background,
although it is possible to exaggerate local influence in their
writing; none of the novels is set in a village like Haworth, and
only *Shirley* has a definitely Yorkshire setting. Naturally too it is
obvious that we must be sensitive to the autobiographical
element in the Brontë novels; this is especially true of Charlotte's
work. But too narrow a focus on Haworth and too great an
interest in biography have had an unhealthy effect on the study
of the Brontës as writers.

In an ideal world literary biography and literary criticism
would be sister sciences, devoted to a common cause, the elucida-
tion and evaluation of great literature. As it is, they have something of the uneasy relationship of sisters-in-law towards each
other, possessing nothing in common but their devotion to
literature, and squabbling over the best way to serve it. This
is particularly true of authors like Byron and the Rossettis,
whose lives have a scandalous interest in their own right, but
nowhere is the gap between biographers and critics more marked
than in the case of the Brontës. When one reads an account in
the *Brontë Society Transactions* of what Charlotte Brontë's
wedding dress looked like,[3] and then turns to an analysis in
Nineteenth Century Fiction of the sexual symbolism of *Wuthering Heights*,[4] it is hard to realise that the same Brontës are being
discussed.

The biographers have mainly been amateurs, making up in

enthusiasm for what they lacked in scholarly training. Their chief fault has been their eagerness for regarding the Brontë novels as case histories of the Brontë lives. This is dangerous, since if they return to consider the novels their argument is liable to be circular, and if they do not return they have debased the value of the novels to that of mere autobiographical novelettes. It is harmless if misguided to study Keats's laundry lists; the harm comes when we start examining *The Ode to a Nightingale* for information about Keats's shirts.

The other main fault of Brontë biographers has been their unwillingness to probe to the solid facts provided by primary documentary evidence; and they have depended all too often on unsatisfactory printed texts. A failure to examine documents properly has resulted in some wild conjectures like the notorious Louis Parensell, but equally distressing has been the conservative reluctance to admit any new evidence.[5]

Opposed to such biographers have been the critics. Relying on the hostility to biography of the New Criticism they have tended to fight shy of any biographical information. This is of course understandable in view of the unscholarly and purely sentimental nature of so many Brontë biographies, but such an attitude ignores the extent to which the Brontë novels are attached to a particular time and locality. Occasionally such critics betray themselves by ludicrous errors; the suggestion that Charlotte was cocking a snook at Victorian conventions by using an overt phallic symbol in the sentence, 'He was as stiff about urging his point as ever you could be'[6] shows little knowledge of Victorian conventions. This example of a preoccupation with sex points to a basic weakness in much of this criticism. Even if we accept the arguments against the Intentional fallacy and acknowledge the value of trying to penetrate behind the conscious purpose of the novelists, we cannot ignore their intentions altogether. In the twentieth century the marriage bed is openly discussed, and the death bed has become taboo; in the nineteenth century these roles were reversed. It is therefore as narrow to ignore the preoccupation of the Brontës with death and the future life as it is to ignore sexual motifs in their novels. The latter are hidden behind a veil of prudery, even though by the standards of their time the Brontës were not at all prudish, but the former are obvious, though to explore them we have to know something about the life and background of the Brontës.

Thus a knowledge of the Brontës' lives can help us to elucidate their works. It can also help us to evaluate them. By relating Charlotte's life to her novels we see how narrowly auto-biograhpical they are, as opposed to the more universal *Wuthering Heights*. By investigating the various topics in which Charlotte was interested we see how she occasionally allowed the preacher to get the better of the novelist; Emily does not preach and her novel is the better for it, although her contemporaries preferred the obvious message and topical, if ephemeral, interest of Charlotte. In the case of Anne, the preacher outweighs the novelist to such an extent that contemporary critics, baffled by Emily and prepared to forgive Charlotte for her faults, made Anne chief whipping boy for her unpalatable doctrines on eternal punishment, sexual morality and the social hierarchy. Some modern critics do not seem aware that the Brontës had something to say on each of these subjects, and therefore cannot direct our attention to the different way in which they are handled by each sister.

There is obviously room for a fresh attempt to see the fiction of the Brontës in the context of the facts of their lives, while severely separating the fact and fiction in order to avoid the faults of so many Brontë biographers. Unfortunately recent Brontë scholarship has largely been directed into the not very profitable fields of Gondal and Angria. The discovery of the Brontës' juvenilia at first sight seemed a boon both to biographers for the light they shone on the Brontës' lonely precocious childhood, and to critics, able to trace the forerunners of Rochester and Heathcliff in Zamorna and A.G.A. But we know already that the Brontës had a lonely precocious child-hood, and it hardly helps our appreciation of either Rochester or Heathcliff to find them translated from their eighteenth- or nineteenth-century background to the less substantial realms of Angria and Gondal. The study of the Brontës' juvenilia pro-vides confirmatory evidence of the sisters' preoccupation with the aristocracy, their emancipation from Victorian prudery, and the attraction of the Byronic hero, beautiful but damned. But too great a devotion to Gondal and Angria betrays a failure to appreciate Matthew Arnold's warning against the historical fallacy. The Brontës' juvenilia are larger in bulk than their adult writings, but this does not mean that we should devote more attention to the juvenilia than to the novels. Still less should we follow the example of Miss Fannie Ratchford who in between the writing of The Brontës' Web of Childhood and Gondal's Queen appears to pass from the view that Angria and Gondal are worth studying as means to an appreciation of the novels to the view that at any rate Gondal is worth studying as an end in itself.[7] Admittedly Emily Brontë did, unlike her sisters, write some impressive poetry, and this poetry, unlike the poetry of her sisters, has been adequately edited.[8] But the debatable question as to whether the whole of Emily's poetry is concerned with Gondal, or whether the whole of the poetry of Gondal is concerned with a single set of characters, with A.G.A. doubling up for Rosina Alcona, hardly seem to merit the attention they have received. On the one hand there is no good way of deciding them, although in both cases Miss Ratchford ignores a great deal of the evidence against her,[9] and on the other our opinion of Emily Brontë's achievement is not altered by whatever decision we eventually take.

With scholarship directed into these unprofitable channels the way is open for a work like Winifred Gerin's Charlotte Brontë: the Evolution of Genius. This book won both popular and scholarly acclaim.[10] Its popularity is a tribute to the wide interest in the Brontës, and to Miss Gerin's skill in evoking the atmosphere appropriate to the Brontë legend. The praise of scholars is a sad tribute to the fact that we do not have any proper standards in Brontë scholarship. The authority on another nineteenth-century figure has declared that one knows by instinct that Miss Gerin had got her facts right;[11] and his statement gives an unconscious indication of Miss Gerin's methods. It is instinct rather than evidence which leads Miss Gerin to regard as certain the hypotheses that Anne Brontë was in love with William Weightman, or that Miss Branwell was responsible for the

Brontës' Calvinistic fears.[12] In literary matters Miss Gerin is
equally at sea; the statement in her index that G. H. Lewes was
the editor of the *Edinburgh Review* may be a slip,[13] but it is a revealing one, and while we can admire the loyalty to her subject
and spirit of Yorkshire chauvinism which enables Miss Gerin to
entitle a chapter 'The Miracle of Shirley', we cannot but deplore
her quoting as evidence of the favourable reputation of *Shirley*
a publisher's extract from the very unfavourable *Times* review.[14]

Miss Gerin's most damaging fault is her reliance on untrustworthy printed evidence. She says in her introduction that,

> To the student in search of facts ... what emerges from this
> ocean of print is that the one reliable source of truth upon
> Charlotte Brontë are the letters of Charlotte herself, collected
> and published under the enthusiastic direction of Clement
> Shorter in the first place (between 1896 and 1908), and of T. J.
> Wise and J. A. Symington in the corrected and more compre-
> hensive texts of the Shakespeare Head Press edition of 1932 –
> a labour not yet complete.[15]

The labour is indeed not complete, and anyone who has anything to do with either of these editions knows that they are unreliable about dates, and that their text is often very different
from the text of the manuscript where this is available. This
basic unreliability does not prevent Miss Gerin from citing
Symington and Wise, and even in some cases the inferior
editions of Shorter, as authorities for her texts and dates.[16] She
does pay lip service to the need to consult manuscripts, and says
she has done this where they are available,[17] but she does not
seem to have looked very far beyond the Brontë Parsonage
Museum, where there is usually agreement between the text of
manuscripts and the text of the Shakespeare Head edition. In the
case of what is alleged to be the first letter to Ellen Nussey there
is a divergence, and Miss Gerin is able to give us a new text,
but unfortunately neither text nor date is correct.[18] This basic
uncertainty in what is likely to be regarded as a definitive and
reliable source of information about the Brontës[19] must lead us
to make a thorough examination of Brontë texts and their
transmission.

2

Texts and Transmission

AN INVESTIGATION of the primary manuscript evidence is an immensely complicated task owing to the activities of T. J. Wise. The extent to which Wise dominates the Brontë scene like a crooked colossus can be best appreciated by an examination of the history of the letters which Charlotte Brontë wrote to Ellen Nussey. These letters have occupied a peculiar position in all Brontë biographies from Mrs Gaskell's time to the present day. On the one hand, biographers have used the correspondence with Ellen Nussey as an indispensable framework for their stories;[1] on the other hand there has been a tendency to dismiss Ellen as a correspondent who elicited uninteresting letters from Charlotte.[2] The peculiar history of these letters however makes it clear that Ellen Nussey cannot be blamed for not provoking more interesting letters, for she destroyed many of the letters likely to prove interesting. It is also clear that we cannot rely on the letters to Ellen Nussey to provide a really reliable framework, because the letters have been edited so badly.

The idea that we have all the letters Charlotte wrote to Ellen Nussey is widely maintained,[3] but easy to refute. In the first place there are strange gaps in the correspondence as it stands in the Shakespeare Head edition. The dating by Symington and Wise is unreliable, and we should not make too much of short gaps, which can sometimes be explained by Charlotte and Ellen's being in the same house or by difficulties in sending letters from places like Brussels.[4] But what are we to make of the fact that from 20 June 1853 to 1 March 1854, Charlotte Brontë apparently wrote only one letter to her oldest friend?[5]

This gap covers the middle of Mr Nicholls's strange courtship, and in it Charlotte is likely to have made some remarks of a personal nature about both Mr Nicholls and Mr Brontë. Since Mr Nicholls disapproved of the correspondence with Ellen, she might have destroyed the really damaging letters when requested to do so by Charlotte in 1854, although any promises on this score appear to have been disregarded fairly freely.[6] Writing to an unnamed correspondent, almost certainly T. J. Wise, on 18 November, 1892,[7] Ellen Nussey said that the request from Mr Brontë for letters to help Mrs Gaskell had caused her to destroy a large number at once. An additional motive for such a destruction would be that at some stage between the summer of 1853 and the spring of 1854 a coolness would appear to have sprung up between Charlotte and Ellen. This coolness would of course mean that fewer letters were written which Ellen would not want to preserve. Both these points are made clear by a letter from Mary Hewitt to Ellen during the period in question, in which Mary says that she is glad that Ellen has heard from Charlotte.[8]

In the letter of 18 November 1892, Ellen says that she had had over 500 letters when Charlotte died. This figure is also used in a letter from M. Heger to Ellen in 1863 referring to a possible edition of 'près de 500 lettres', and in articles in *The Transactions of the Brontë Society*, recording conversations with Ellen Nussey by W. Scruton and Mrs Cortazzo.[9] In both these latter cases Ellen admits to having destroyed some of her correspondence when Mrs Gaskell asked for it, but the mention of nearly 500 letters in 1863, some years after Mrs Gaskell's *Life*, suggests that the amount destroyed at this stage is likely to have been fairly small.

J. Horsfall Turner in the first abortive edition of the letters of Charlotte Brontë to Ellen Nussey[10] printed about 370 letters, and this number was not greatly increased in the subsequent editions of Shorter and Symington and Wise. Even allowing for the fact that printed editions may publish as one letter what is really more than one, a fact which makes exact calculations of numbers almost impossible,[11] there still seems a large gap between the number printed and the number alleged to have survived as late as 1863. However, although Ellen Nussey was extraordinarily sensitive in exercising censorship over the letters Charlotte wrote to her, it seems unlikely that she would have destroyed as many as 120 letters as being liable to cause offence. In this connection it is worth remarking that quite a few letters likely to cause offence have in fact been retained, perhaps largely through accident; there is in Oakwell Hall, Batley, a letter containing some not very complimentary remarks about Mr Nicholls, and the envelope which apparently belongs to this letter has the words 'To destroy' on it in Ellen Nussey's handwriting.[12]

As well as not destroying what she aimed to destroy Ellen Nussey may have been muddled about the figures of letters she once had: 500 is an easy approximation, and we find modern authorities using it for the number of letters to survive in print from Charlotte Brontë to Ellen Nussey.[13] Since we cannot trace all the manuscripts of even those 380 or so letters that have been printed, it seems unlikely that any additional manuscripts are going to turn up, though Ellen Nussey's talk of losing manuscripts,[14] as opposed to destroying them, is an encouraging sign. A more promising area of investigation is a study of the text of the letters which have survived in a printed form.

Mrs Gaskell printed about a hundred of the letters to Ellen Nussey in a fairly complete version, and referred to or printed short extracts from another fifty. She was not aiming at a complete text, and indeed virtually no letter is complete. Ellen Nussey's extraordinary sensitivity about mentioning living persons meant that even of the 380 printed by the Shakespeare Head, some were not made available to Mrs Gaskell,[15] and those that were made available would appear to have had certain names and passages stricken out.[16]

Ellen Nussey did not think that Mrs Gaskell had done full justice to the memory of Charlotte, and shortly after the publication of *The Life of Charlotte Brontë* she began her efforts to produce her own edition of the letters to her. These efforts are recorded in the fourth volume of the Shakespeare Head edition, which points out the main drawback, Mr Nicholls's ownership of the copyright, but by no means gives the full story of Ellen's frustrations.[17]

In 1868, after her previous failure with M. Heger, Ellen Nussey approached George Smith. For him she had made some copies of the letters which were bought at the sale of Ellen Nussey's property by a Mrs Needham of Blackburn and have survived to this day.[18] Once again in these copies Ellen Nussey carried her delicacy about revealing anything about anyone to ridiculous lengths, and by most standards these copies are very bad ones. Unfortunately it would seem that these copies rather than the manuscript are in certain cases the source for the printed versions we now have.

George Smith informed Ellen Nussey of the copyright difficulty and, after delicate enquiries about relations between Mr Nicholls and Miss Nussey, said that permission to print the letters was unlikely to be granted. Ellen Nussey then turned to America, and about a hundred of the letters, with the text derived from the Needham copies, were in 1870 printed in the magazine, *Hours at Home*.[19] In 1876 Macmillan produced three articles by T. Wemyss Reid which were extended into a book in 1877;[20] letters not published by Mrs Gaskell were used extensively here, it being Reid's intention to correct any unfavourable impression created by Mrs Gaskell but, although he printed over a hundred letters and appears to have used the original manuscripts and not the Needham copies, neither Reid's edition nor the printing in *Hours at Home* is important in the history of the text.

After lending her letters to Mr Wilkes, who was accused of losing some of them, and to Sidney Biddell, who thought he had lost some of them, Ellen Nussey turned to J. Horsfall Turner, who in between 1885 and 1889 produced the first complete edition of the letters. This edition had to be destroyed because of the law of copyright, but twelve copies were retained,[21] and this edition was the basis for the future editions of Shorter, Symington and Wise.

At this stage the story takes a more sinister turn. Not all the evidence relating to the disposal of Ellen Nussey's letters from Charlotte Brontë has been made available, but there is sufficient evidence both in the Brontë Parsonage Museum and in the Brotherton Collection, Leeds, to call into question the honesty of Horsfall Turner, C. K. Shorter and T. J. Wise, who successively edited Charlotte Brontë's letters. From the evidence avail-

able Wise is fairly clearly proved guilty of misappropriating
Ellen Nussey's property under false pretences,[22] and such villainy
from such a man is hardly unexpected. The case against Shorter
and Horsfall Turner is not proven, nor perhaps is it worth proving, since we are not at this stage concerned so much with the
honesty of the editors as with the accuracy of their editions.

Horsfall Turner would seem to have used both the Needham
copies and the original manuscripts.[23] We know he had access to
the original manuscripts, because Ellen Nussey accused him of
stealing them and because his edition, though marred by some of
the omissions of proper names and personal remarks in the
Needham copies, in certain cases amplifies the Needham copies
from the original manuscripts.[24] Shorter used the Horsfall Turner
edition as his main source, and we know from a letter of Ellen
Nussey to Wise,[25] written at a time when Ellen was on good
terms with both Shorter and Wise, that he also had most of
the proper names supplied to him by Ellen Nussey. Shorter,
whose achievement in winning over both Ellen Nussey, the
owner of the letters, and Mr Nicholls, the owner of the copyright, should not be minimised, was friendly for a time with
Ellen before she had parted with the manuscripts and with Wise
who had received these manuscripts; he too should have had
access to the original letters.

Nevertheless, neither Shorter's *Charlotte Brontë and her Circle*,
published in 1896, nor the fuller *The Brontës: Life and Letters*,
published in 1908, are at all reliable.[26] The former work was
hampered by a clumsy non-chronological arrangement, by the
copyright of Mrs Gaskell's *Life of Charlotte Brontë* still being in
force, and, one suspects, by some of the reverberations of Ellen
Nussey's dispute with Shorter and Wise. It is interesting that,
though Shorter printed in 1896 for the first time many letters
to correspondents other than Ellen Nussey, the number of letters
to Ellen Nussey in this edition, about one hundred and seventy-
five, does not compare all that favourably with the amount in
previous editions.[27] It is not clear whether Shorter was trying
to please Ellen Nussey by not publishing certain manuscripts, or
trying to please Wise whose manuscripts would be more valuable
if not published.

The 1908 edition is far more complete, and is still used by many as a basis for biographies, being much more accessible than the Shakespeare Head edition which is something of a collector's piece.[28] Shorter was however a journalist rather than a scholar, and it is easy to multiply instances where his edition can be shown to be incorrect by a simple comparison with the Shakespeare Head text. There was certainly a need for a definitive edition of the Brontë letters, and the Shakespeare Head edition was intended to supply the deficiency. Unfortunately one of the editors, J. A. Symington, had quarrelled with the Brontë Society after being Curator to that Society from 1927 to 1930,[29] and his access to manuscripts is likely to have been limited. The other editor selected by Blackwells was by a fine stroke of irony, T. J. Wise, the one man who more than anyone else had made a complete edition impossible.

Under such auspices it was scarcely surprising that the Shakespeare Head edition was not a success. By 1932 the manuscripts were well and truly scattered; those in the Bonnell collection had crossed the Atlantic twice to join those already at Haworth, but even the Brontë Parsonage Museum held less than a sixth of the letters to Ellen Nussey. Symington did make a location index,[30] and could not find many manuscripts except in the obvious places, but in general he copied faithfully those he could find, although it is not clear how far he was able to consult manuscripts in America.[31] Wise, through whose hands so many letters had passed, was not accurate as a copyist at the best of times[32] and does not seem to have made many copies of the letters which he had so rapidly scattered. At all events there were many cases where Symington and Wise had no alternative but to copy the previous version of Shorter.

This edition was, as has been shown, inaccurate, both because Shorter was not interested in accuracy, and because Shorter relied on Horsfall Turner's edition. Horsfall Turner's edition is inaccurate because in certain cases he follows not the original manuscripts, but the Needham copies. So in certain cases we find the Shakespeare Head edition is, via Shorter and Horsfall Turner, copying the Needham copies rather than the originals. In letter 20 of the Shakespeare Head edition all editors follow the text and date of the Needham copies; the manuscript in the Brontë Parsonage Museum gives a different reading. In letter 212 all editors again follow the Needham copies, thus omitting some sarcastic remarks about the 'warm hearted sisterly kindness' of Mrs Henry Nussey which appear in the manuscript at Haworth. In letter 25 all editors again follow the Needham version, though supplying certain names; the correct version may be found in Volume 74 of the *Brontë Society Transactions*, although in this case there is some excuse for the omission of one sentence which has been crossed out in the manuscript, but it still clearly legible.[33] Crossings out of this kind, usually of proper names, presumably go back to the time when Ellen Nussey gave most of the letters to Mrs Gaskell. In most cases however it is possible to supply the omitted name, and such lacunae in the manuscripts are not usually a handicap to a proper understanding of the Brontës, since they are so easily recognisable.[34]

More serious are the hidden lacunae, deriving from the omissions in the Needham copies, reproduced by all subsequent editors. Where the manuscripts are available we can check whether the reading of Symington and Wise is based on manuscript evidence or an untrustworthy printed source but, since most of the manuscripts available to us were easily available to Symington and Wise, this gives an unfairly optimistic picture of the accuracy of the Shakespeare Head edition. In this connection it is unfortunate that Miss Mildred Christian in her *Census of Brontë manuscripts in the U.S.A.* says that she gives only a representative selection of errors in the Shakespeare Head edition[35] and that we do not know whether these errors are due to inaccurate copying of a manuscript or not consulting the manuscript at all.

Where no manuscript is traceable either in England or America there is of course no way of checking the accuracy of Symington and Wise, but the Needham copies make it clear that it is just in these cases that the Shakespeare Head edition is suspect. In the period between 16 June 1853 and 1 April 1854, Charlotte Brontë's attitude to Mr Nicholls changed significantly and she quarrelled with Ellen Nussey. We learn very little about either of these processes from the letters to Ellen Nussey in this period, and almost certainly some letters were destroyed entirely. Of the letters printed by the Shakespeare Head covering this period four are to be found in manuscript form, three at Haworth and one in the Henry Huntington Library, allegedly consulted by Symington and Wise. In all four cases (letters 854, 870, 881 and 883) there are interesting divergences between the Shakespeare Head and manuscript reading on the one hand and the Needham copies on the other.[36] In the case of the other four letters, apart from the addition of names and dates, easily inferred or supplied by Ellen Nussey when friendly to Horsfall Turner or Shorter, the only difference is the omission of an unimportant phrase by the Needham copies in letter 880, a few minor alterations in letter 884, and the omission of a single word by the Shakespeare Head in letter 885.[37] In the case of letter 855 the Shakespeare Head reproduces the dots which Ellen Nussey has used in the Needham copies to indicate an omission, but this is no guarantee that in other cases, where omissions are not marked, such as letter 884, there is nothing left out, as it is evident from even the most cursory glance at the Needham copies that here Ellen Nussey is quite unreliable about indicating omissions.[38]

It might be possible to use this method of comparing the Needham copies with the Shakespeare Head edition in order to establish the extent of the damage done by them. Unfortunately there are too many uncertain factors to make this worth while. The Needham copies do not contain every letter, and in many cases merely give a page reference to the first edition of Mrs Gaskell's *Life*. Some of the Needham letters are copied with few omissions; at the beginning of the first eleven sections into which the copies are divided Ellen Nussey states that she has left out very little, and this seems generally true of the first two and a half sections, from 1832 to 1836, transcribed with double spacing. It is, therefore, unnecessarily gloomy to say that any coincidence between Needham copies and the Shakespeare Head indicates that the latter is following a faulty copy. Sometimes the Shakespeare Head makes errors which are not attributable to the Needham copies.[39] It is, therefore, unnecessarily optimistic to assume that the absence of any coincidence between the

Needham copies and the Shakespeare Head indicates that the latter is following the manuscript. Horsfall Turner and Shorter were friendly for a time with Ellen Nussey, and therefore a letter, which is similar to, but not exactly the same as the Needham version, may be a Needham copy, corrected by Ellen Nussey, or even a conflation between the Needham version and the manuscript.[40]

The period between June 1853 and April 1854 is perhaps an unfair one to select for a detailed examination of the Needham copies, as it is one where Ellen Nussey would be particularly keen to exercise censorship, and where, coming to the end of her task, she seemed to become careless and to suffer apparently from a shortage of paper. But the inference to be drawn from an examination of this period is clear; the Shakespeare Head edition, which is generally reliable when a manuscript is available, is likely to be very unreliable when no manuscript is accessible. We depend for part of the truth about the Brontës on texts which have been bowdlerised, not very intelligently, by Ellen Nussey, and thanks to T. J. Wise it is not going to be easy to find the manuscripts to supply the deficiencies in these texts.

Wise's role in handling the Nussey letters draws attention to the enormous part he played in the Brontë affairs.[41] Fortunately, so far as the text of the Brontë novels is concerned, Wise's activities are negligible; the manuscripts of the novels did not pass through his hands, although the boosting of a text of *Wuthering Heights* with alleged corrections in the hand of Emily Brontë may possibly be his work.[42] With letters to correspondents other than Ellen Nussey, often more interesting for literary matters, although less useful for providing the necessary framework of basic facts and dates, Wise did not exercise anything like the monopoly he held over letters to Ellen Nussey. Where Wise did exercise something of a stranglehold was in securing and editing the Brontë juvenilia. He and Shorter obtained almost all the hitherto unpublished stories and poems of the Brontës from Mr Nicholls, and he and Shorter were responsible for the publication of most of these manuscripts, which are now widely scattered for the same reasons and in the same way that the letters to Ellen Nussey are widely scattered. In certain cases our knowledge of the text of a poem depends upon one of Wise's or Shorter's printed editions; they were slovenly editors at the best of times, and the minute Brontë handwriting cannot have made their task any easier.

This unfortunately is not the only difficulty. Wise was dishonest, and as owner and editor of so many of the Brontë manuscripts he had an unrivalled opportunity for dishonesty. The close similarity in subject matter and handwriting of the stories and poems alleged to have been written by various members of the Brontë family makes it difficult to distinguish the author of the various juvenilia. Sometimes a signature appears to put the matter beyond doubt, but a signature is easy to forge, and there was a good motive for such forgery when Charlotte's manuscripts were so much more valuable than Branwell's.

Wise, who was an expert on Charlotte Brontë's signature, had both motive and opportunity for forging it, and his record of forgeries, albeit of a different kind, is an impressive one. But the evidence needed to convict him of Brontë forgeries is so widely scattered that it is almost impossible to unravel the complicated questions of whether it was Branwell or Charlotte who was responsible for the major part of the Angrian cycle of stories and poems, especially as some degree of collaboration between the two Brontës is generally accepted. Certain of the manuscripts that are available have a signature by Charlotte that looks very suspicious,[43] and other manuscripts on subjective grounds appear to belong to Branwell rather than to Charlotte, to whom they are attributed.[44] Wise's habit of binding together manuscripts before disposal has been acknowledged as an endless source of trouble for Brontë students; what has not been acknowledged is the ease with which Wise could pad out a short piece by Charlotte with Branwell material. Editing the final volume of the Shakespeare Head Brontë after Wise's death, Symington was able to hint that many earlier attributions to Charlotte may have been incorrect, and was able to show his suspicion of the activities of Wise by reproducing facsimiles of various manuscripts in this and the previous volume of the *Miscellaneous and Unpublished Writings of Charlotte and P. B. Brontë*.[45]

In the case of Emily Brontë widespread confusion about the

authorship of certain poems has already been cleared up through the labours of C. W. Hatfield and, though we have the complication of multiple copies of the same poem, the problem is simplified by the absence of any prose narrative and the presence of Gondal as an identifying factor.[46] The same is true of Anne Brontë, and there can have been less incentive to attribute a poem to her when it was written by some other member of the family.[47] There is of course the possibility that some of the Brontë juvenilia were written by no member of the Brontë family. Wise, though he forged first editions and got hold of manuscripts by underhand means, has not yet been convicted of forging manuscripts,[48] and the possibility of this kind of Brontë forgery is therefore a slight one, though it can at any rate be raised.

Wise was engaged in manufacturing bogus first editions at the same time as he was acquiring the Brontë juvenilia, and the forging of manuscripts may have seemed a profitable sideline, easier to perpetrate than the forgery of a first edition, as there was no genuine article with which the forgery could be compared. The small print-like handwriting of most of the juvenilia was a gift to the forger. It is surprising that the vast quantity of the juvenilia was not appreciated for so many years, although the inferior quality of much of this early work makes its neglect by Mrs Gaskell and other early biographers quite understandable. The poor quality of much that is alleged to have been written by Emily and Charlotte is yet another reason why doubts must be raised about the authenticity of some of their early work, and parallels that have been drawn between this early work and the mature novels are as easy for forgers to manufacture as they are for scholars to discover.

However it is probably impertinent to suggest that much of the research into the juvenilia has been in fact research into T. J. Wise in his prime. There can be no doubt that the Brontës wrote a great many stories and poems in their youth, and because of the close collaboration between them at this period of their lives it does not matter a great deal who wrote what. The sheer length of many of the stories is a strong argument against forgery on a massive scale, and the badness of much of this early writing makes it difficult to draw many conclusions from it about the novels. This is indeed fortunate, since the prospect of making a satisfactory edition of the juvenilia would be a daunting one even if no dishonesty had been involved. As it is, by drawing attention to Wise's dishonesty we can help towards diverting some of the research on the Brontës' juvenilia into more profitable fields. There is of course something to be learnt from a general study of the juvenilia, but an individual poem or story is unlikely to repay close study, as it may be something other than it seems.[49]

With the letters the position is rather different. There are no problems of authorship, the manuscripts when available are generally legible, we do not find different versions of the same letter, and there is considerably less material on which to work. There are forgeries extant, both letters which Charlotte could never have written and copies of original manuscripts masquerading as the original.[50] Both are fairly easy to detect, and neither is a serious handicap to a proper study of the Brontës. Nor is there any indication that Wise had anything to do with either kind of forgery. What he was responsible for was a series of incomplete and inaccurate editions of the letters, and for making it virtually impossible to produce a satisfactory edition. We then have to ask how much does this matter, and what should be done about it.

A comparison with some other Victorian authors might suggest that the absence of a complete or reliable edition of the letters of the Brontës is not after all such a serious handicap to a proper study of them. The modern edition of Mrs Gaskell's letters still relies in part on earlier printed versions, including the Shakespeare Head Brontë.[51] In preparing any edition of Matthew Arnold's letters modern scholars have to face the fact that many of the most interesting and personal letters have been destroyed.[52] Ellen Nussey's preservation of her friend's letters, and early intense interest in the biography of the Brontës, mean that we do have a considerable, if not complete, body of evidence on which to work. But the peculiar autobiographical nature of the Brontë novels does make an accurate edition of their letters especially desirable. The fact that we have so little information about Emily and Anne makes every scrap of evidence about them valuable. Finally the essentially contradictory nature which Charlotte shared with her master Thackeray, and which made her at once orthodox and heterodox in religion, prudish and bold in literary taste, snobbish and anti-aristocratic in her social views, makes in necessary for us to have as complete a record as possible, since by placing undue emphasis on one facet of those contradictory standpoints we can distort her attitude.

It is not difficult, even with the limited amount of new manuscript material available, to show ways in which a knowledge of manuscripts can illuminate our understanding of the Brontës. Charlotte Brontë's religion is a sufficiently ill-comprehended subject for it to be vital that we have every piece of evidence about it. And yet her clearest statement of the iniquity of the doctrine of eternal punishment comes in a letter to Mrs Gaskell, unpublished in the Shakespeare Head edition.[53] An interesting statement, involving a rather primitive superstition about the souls of the dead, comes in a part of a letter unpublished by Symington and Wise.[54] Even a word, omitted by the Shakespeare Head editors, can reveal a great deal, as the following illustration will show.

A promising opening for those anxious to find the origin of Charlotte Brontë's Calvinism is to be found in the letter from Roe Head, in which Charlotte talks of '... ghastly Calvinistic doctrines'. Most editors print '...'s ghastly', [55] and various suggestions, including 'Anne' and 'Aunt', have been made to fill the gap.[56] Miss Gerin, although an enthusiastic believer in the theory that Charlotte owed her Calvinism to the influence of her aunt Branwell, does on p. 34, but not on p. 101 of *Charlotte Brontë: the Evolution of Genius*, print '... ghastly'. This reading is correct, since the manuscript in the Brontë Museum contains no trace of the ''s' which is an editorial interpolation. It might seem a reasonable interpolation in view of Ellen Nussey's habit of crossing out proper names. But a closer look at the original manuscript suggests that the word crossed out cannot be a proper name. Ellen Nussey has obliterated the word in such a way that it is not visible to the naked eye, but we can say certain things about it. It is a word of four or five letters with the loop of the first letter appearing below the crossing out, but nothing visible above the not very broad line which Ellen used to score out that which she thought offensive.

The word crossed out cannot therefore be a proper name, since a proper name would begin with a capital letter, and a capital letter would appear above the line. But if Ellen Nussey did not cross out a proper name we are at a loss to explain why she crossed out the word, until we remember her morbid anxiety to avoid any mention of her family or herself. In fact the obvious reading is 'your ghastly Calvinistic doctrines'. 'Your' is one of the very few four- or five-letter words beginning with a descender and having no other ascenders or descenders, and it is the only such word likely to be censored in this context.

It is of course very surprising to find Ellen Nussey associated with Calvinism. From other evidence she would appear a model of Church of England orthodoxy, and from the other letters from Roe Head, unfortunately difficult to date exactly, she would appear to be offering comforting doctrines to Charlotte. But 'your doctrines' may mean the 'doctrines you were mentioning' rather than 'the doctrines you were upholding'. In this case we would be no further forward in our search for the source of Charlotte's Calvinism, since Ellen might have been mentioning almost anyone. But though 'your' might have been crossed out to avoid misunderstanding, there may have been an additional reason for Ellen's sensitivity about the origin of her Calvinistic ideas, and perhaps we need look no further than Henry Nussey to fill the role of the preacher of ghastly Calvinistic doctrines.

Like St John Rivers in *Jane Eyre*, Henry Nussey was an Evangelical, as we know from his diary recording his sitting at the feet of Simeon at Cambridge. His unfortunate diary entries about his successive proposals to Mary Lutwidge and Charlotte Brontë have an air of Calvinistic fatalism about them, as well as being another reminder of St John Rivers.[57] Less well known quotations from Henry Nussey's diary in the British Museum are a straightforward statement of belief in eternal punishment:

But for *thy mercy in Christ Jesus, O Lord, I had now, even*

now, been in hell, without pardon, without peace, without
hope and in torment for ever,

and a slightly baffling reference to Calvinism, which suggests
that Henry Nussey had successfully passed through a period of
Calvinistic doubt. He mentions

> Mrs W *a very kind, nice looking, and truly excellent person
> (?) but imbued with Calvinastic (sic) sentiments, and not to
> her comfort I fear, being a doubting person, partly arising
> from these views; which I know from experience to be very
> distressing, if we do not find inward and outward evidences of
> our call strong and lively.*[58]

It is a mistake to look for parallels between Charlotte's life and
her novels, and certainly there is much in the tediously sancti-
monious diary of Henry Nussey that is very unlike what we
would expect from St John Rivers. But it would not be too fanciful to conjecture that it was from Henry Nussey, who after all
did think of becoming a missionary,[59] that Charlotte derived
her Calvinistic fears in the same way that Jane Eyre heard
Calvinistic doctrines from St John Rivers.

For unpublished evidence about Charlotte's literary activities
the letters to Ellen Nussey, whose library at the time of her
death consisted largely of theological works and the novels of
the Brontës, are hardly a good source. There is one piece of
unpublished evidence which underlines the literary ignorance
of Ellen Nussey, a factor to be borne in mind when considering
the literary background of the Brontës. Writing to Ellen on 26
June 1848, Charlotte Brontë says:

> Your naïveté in gravely inquiring my opinion of the 'last new
> novel' amuses me: we do not subscribe to a circulating library
> at Haworth and consequently 'new novels' rarely indeed come
> in our way, and consequently again we are not qualified to
> give opinions thereon.

On the envelope of this letter Ellen Nussey has written the
words 'Jane Eyre', making it clear that the last new novel, on
which Charlotte disingenuously refuses to comment, is none

other than the novel she herself had written.[60] Ellen Nussey too
is a trifle disingenuous, since her diary for the year 1849 in the
Brontë Parsonage Museum suggests that she did not begin reading *Jane Eyre* until that year, and she is obviously, as in previous letters, merely trying to elicit from her friend a straight
answer to the question whether she had written *Jane Eyre*.[61]
The fact that she calls *Jane Eyre* the last new novel eight months
after publication, and Charlotte's excuse that she did not have
access to a circulating library serve to remind us how isolated
the Brontës were from contemporary literary influences in their
narrow provincial circle. It is small wonder that their novels
were considered original and shocking as they had no experience
of the literary conventions of their day.

In letters to correspondents other than Ellen Nussey there is
more information about literary matters. A valuable letter to
Hartley Coleridge has only just been published in full.[62] There
is one other piece of unpublished evidence which has some
bearing on Charlotte Brontë's honesty and literary taste. In
printing the letter to G. H. Lewis of January 1848 the editors
of the Shakespeare Head Brontë chose to copy the version of the
letter which appears in Mrs Gaskell's *Life* rather than following
the original manuscript which is in the British Museum.[63] Mrs
Gaskell's version is in the main a correct transcript apart from
some erroneous punctuation and the substitution of 'what a
strange lecture comes next' for 'what a strange sentence comes
next', but there are two lengthy omissions. Just before the reference to a strange sentence there is a paragraph devoted to Lewes's
novel *Ranthorpe*. It reads as follows:

> About 'Ranthorpe' I am right. By the last part of that work
> I understand only from Page 271 to the end; the first portion,
> in which I include the episode of the Hawbuckes, is the best.
> You yourself admit it. You say 'the great merit of the book
> lies in its views of literature and the literary life, and in the
> reflections.' So I think, and it is in the first part these views
> are disclosed, and these reflections made. I like them. The
> views are just, the reflections profound: both are instruc-
> tive.

There are further references to *Ranthorpe* and Lewes's other novel, *Rose, Blanche and Violet* in the published letters,[64] and this unpublished passage merely serves as a reminder of the extraordinary amount of praise Charlotte gives both to *Ranthorpe*, which has a certain historical interest as a kind of *New Grub Street* of the 1840s, but otherwise has no literary merit, and to *Rose, Blanche and Violet*, which has the interest of a very bad novel, perhaps partly modelled on *Jane Eyre*.[65] One wonders whether Charlotte would have been quite so fulsome with her praises if Lewes had not been an influential critic who had already praised *Jane Eyre*.

The praise of Lewes's novels could be sincere, but in this case we have to condemn Charlotte's literary judgement. The evidence for Charlotte's isolation might suggest that we would be right to condemn her, and indeed in this same letter to Lewes Charlotte says that without access to a library she will have difficulty in reading all Jane Austen, and on the evidence of *Pride and Prejudice* declares that Jane Austen, being without poetry, cannot be great. But in a previously unpublished passage towards the end of the letter she adds:

> I have something else to say. You mention the authoress of 'Azeth the Egyptian'; you say you think I should sympathize 'with her daring imagination and pictorial fancy'. Permit me to undeceive you: with infinitely more relish I can sympathize with Miss Austen's clear common sense and subtle shrewdness. If you find no inspiration in Miss Austen's page, neither do you find there windy wordiness; to use your words again, she exquisitely adapts her means to her end: both are very subdued, a little contracted, but never absurd. I have not read 'Azeth', but I did read or begin to read a tale in the 'New Monthly' from the same pen, and harsh as the opinion may sound to you, I must candidly avow that I thought it both turgid and feeble; it reminded me of the most inflated and emptiest parts of Bulwer's novels. I found in it neither strength, sense nor originality.

Charlotte dismisses Eliza Lynn, the authoress of *Azeth the Egyptian*, and *Anymone*, the tale in the *New Monthly*, in almost the same terms when writing to W. S. Williams on 22 November 1848.[66] Nor is her preference for Jane Austen over Eliza Lynn surprising. But the unpublished passage serves to remind us again how far removed Charlotte was from the spirit of her age. Too poor to buy or even borrow contemporary works of fiction she turned to the more easily available books of a previous age, and there are a number of indications that she thought she had gained by this choice of books. Thus the low opinion of Jane Austen, expressed in published letters, is in a sense unfair to Charlotte's preference for the literature of an earlier generation, and the unpublished passage draws attention to the view of Charlotte Brontë that the golden age of literature had been replaced by an age of mediocrity.[67]

For Charlotte's social background the letters to Ellen Nussey, if properly edited, could provide a wealth of information. It is true that references to obscure friends of Ellen Nussey, so often excised in the Needham copies and not always restored by subsequent editors, are for the most part tedious. But this background of gossip, not always friendly, is a necessary corrective to the school of biographers who, unable to find out much about the people in Charlotte's life, people it instead with the characters of her novels, and the school of biography which approaches hagiography in its refusal to allow that the Brontës could do anything wrong. In fact both Charlotte's letters and her novels reveal that in spite or perhaps because of her great gifts she felt herself underprivileged, and it is as well to admit the occasional note of rancour which creeps in as a result of this. The Shakespeare Head Brontë reveals very little about Mrs Henry Nussey, a character of little interest apart from the fact that Charlotte might have been Mrs Henry Nussey, but the following hitherto unpublished quotation from a letter, heavily bowdlerised in the Needham copies and in all subsequent editions,[68] shows Charlotte in typically acid vein.

I was much struck with the account you gave me of the warm hearted sisterly kindness, the justice and the gratitude with which you were treated at Hathersage. I see how it is – I could not live with one so cold and narrow though she were

as correct as a mathematical straight line and upright as per-
pendicularity itself – still I think she is just the person for
Henry – she will obtain influence over him and keep it. I had
very much regretted ......[69] *after all to pay for the broken*
window-pane – but when I read that you nearly had to pay
for your washing – my regrets ceased. It is most surprising to
me that she should not have asked you to remain with her and
been even fearful of losing your company. How a woman can
be affectionately devoted to her husband and not feel some
regard for that husband's sister is inexplicable. Depend on it,
Nell, if we knew how much selfishness goes to the composition
of such affection as this, we should be amazed.

Unfortunately it is very rare to find so much information in
so accessible a manuscript and, though it is easy to show that a
complete and reliable edition of Charlotte Brontë's letters is
a necessary preliminary to any scholarly study of the Brontës, it
is much harder to suggest what should be done in the absence of
such an edition.

Professor Christian in her *Census of Brontë Manuscripts* has
already revealed the difficulties in the way of the preliminary
steps towards such an edition. It is hard enough to make a check
list of all available manuscripts because of the presence of forgeries, the frequent changes of ownership, and the wide range of
collections to be consulted. Some manuscripts still seem to be
inaccessible, as can be seen by a consideration of the manuscripts
of letters to Ellen Nussey. Professor Christian lists 180 such
letters, but her location list of manuscripts in the U.S.A., made
in 1947–8, is likely to be out of date. In England the Brontë
Society has about 75 letters to Ellen Nussey, and a few other
letters are to be found in the British Museum (three), the Bodleian Library (a fragment), Oakwell Hall, Batley (one).[70] This
leaves to be traced over 100 manuscripts of letters to Ellen
Nussey, of which the Shakespeare Head printed versions. The
envelopes of these letters, a useful guide for accurate dating, are
also widely scattered.[71] It very much looks as if after berating
the Shakespeare Head for its failings we have to rely on it in
part for its findings.

Where we do this in cases when no manuscript is available we must recognise that there is a strong likelihood that we are relying on an incomplete version, and we must not build too much on the evidence of any such letter in the same way that we must not build too much on any particular poem or juvenile story because of the uncertainty about authorship. Any statement made by Charlotte in letters for which no manuscript is available must be treated with caution, and we must not base our views of Charlotte's views on any partial statement made in such a letter.

And here attention must be drawn to a peculiar feature of existing Brontë biographies. There has always been a feeling that we only have a part of the Brontë story, and biographers have rushed in to provide keys and clues to fill in the missing parts. Sometimes, as with the discovery of the Heger letters in 1913 and the juvenilia, missing evidence has turned up, although this evidence has not been quite as interesting as its novelty value has indicated. Sometimes the more fanciful biographers have tried to fill in the gaps with mythical Irish Brontë ancestors, a real life Heathcliff, Louis Parensell, a lesbian Emily and various authors for *Wuthering Heights*.[72]

On the other hand we have biographers who seem to hold the view that all the Brontës said or did is to be found in the Shakespeare Head Brontë.[73] It is of course better to repeat an old story based on tainted evidence than to invent a new story based on no evidence at all, but it is about time that we recognised both that some evidence is missing and that new evidence is hardly likely to turn up at this stage. The pessimistic conclusion that biographical certainty about the Brontës is necessarily impossible is disappointing only for the prospective biographer. For the student of literature it serves as a warning against getting too closely involved in the quest for absolute truth. For though there is a relationship between the life of an author and the books he writes, it is not a relationship of which it is possible to speak with any certainty. We can only draw probable conclusions about an author's books from an author's letters and, if our evidence for the text of these letters is incomplete, then our conclusions are just a little less probable. What is important is that we should avoid the false certainty of many biographer critics who build their theories on uncertain evidence, while at the same time avoiding the complete pessimism of many pure critics who keep clear of the biography altogether.[74]

For although the text of the letters is in places suspect, and the text of the juvenilia generally unreliable, our knowledge of the text of the Brontë novels is relatively certain,[75] and it is as novelists rather than as letter writers or eccentrically precocious children that they must primarily be considered. Much can be learnt from a combination of a close examination of the text of the novels and a balanced weighing of all available evidence outside the novels. It is an attempt to supply this combination that the following chapters have been written.

3

Heaven and Hell

THE INFLUENCE of religion on the Brontës is both obvious and
obscure. It is obvious that much of what the Brontës saw, heard
and read was concerned with religion. It is not obvious how
their original minds reacted to the variety of religious beliefs
which they encountered. It is therefore not unduly surprising
that discussions of the Brontës' religion have been few and unsatisfactory. General studies of the Brontës have tended to minimise the part played by religion in their lives, or to portray it in
too crude colours, ignoring the variety of religious sects in nineteenth-century England, and ignoring the ability of the Brontës
to react against or reject some of the religious teaching they had
to endure.[1]

Specialist studies on the religion of the Brontës are few and
far between, and they suffer from the fault of similar specialist
studies, namely an excess of eagerness to fit all the facts about the
Brontës into a chosen pattern. Thus Grace E. Harrison's *The
Clue to the Brontës*[2] provides some useful information about
Methodism and performs a valuable service by drawing attention to the links between the Brontës and the Methodist movement, but she overstates her case. Some of the parallels between
the poetry of the Brontës and the hymns of the Wesleys are over-
strained, and it seems fanciful to derive the names Shirley and
Huntingdon from the Brontës' knowledge of the family of Whitfield's patron. In addition this book is marred by a reliance on
secondary sources, an excessive hostility to Mr Brontë, and a
reluctance to distinguish closely between the Brontës' adoption
of Methodist ideas and their reaction against them.

Rather similar is the short article by Miss Eanne Oram, 'Emily
Brontë and F. D. Maurice'.[3] This article is again useful in that it

draws attention to Emily's dislike, shared by Maurice, of the doctrine of eternal punishment. But in suggesting a direct link between Maurice and Emily Brontë Miss Oram undoubtedly goes too far. The primary evidence connecting the two is extremely fragile,[4] and many of the parallels drawn between the writing of Maurice and Emily are over-subtle. Finally, as Miss Oram admits, some of these parallels must be coincidental, as she draws on works published by Maurice well after Emily's death;[5] if some must be coincidental, all may be, and it is certainly dangerous to suggest that two writers holding the same views on the same subject must have been in contact with each other.

Miss Oram's other contribution to the study of the Brontës' religion is her article 'A Brief for Miss Branwell'.[6] Although this article is slightly sentimental and hardly exhausts the material, it does show how extremely tenuous is the evidence adduced to condemn Miss Branwell for being the source of the Brontës' Calvinism. Unfortunately, since two well-known books on the Brontës repeated the charge against Miss Branwell after the appearance of Miss Oram's article, it would appear that Miss Oram has been unable to halt the tendency, all too prevalent in Brontë studies, for conjecture to become fact.

The main fault of L. and E. Hanson's *The Four Brontës* and Miss Gerin's books on the Brontës[7] is that they seem unable to unravel the complexities of Victorian religious sects. Thus the Hansons talk blithely of Wesleyan doctrines of predestination,[8] as if Wesley had never quarrelled with Whitfield, and Miss Gerin quotes as evidence for the Calvinist views of the Arminian *Methodist Magazine* a passage from a refutation of Calvinism.[9] Both writers seem to make the error of equating the peculiarly Calvinist belief in predestination with a belief in eternal punishment, common in the nineteenth century to most sects outside and inside the Church of England.

Nor is this their only error. By following Mrs Gaskell uncritically Miss Gerin is led to say in the middle of a discussion of Miss Branwell's religious position and Charlotte's attitude to it:

Looking back in wonder, after she was grown up, at her early infatuation with the Methodist literature, she wrote of the 'mad Methodist Magazines, full of miracles and apparitions, of preternatural warnings, ominous dreams and frenzied fanaticism . . .'[10]

The Hansons quote the same passage in a discussion of the influence of Miss Branwell on the religion of the Brontës,[11] adding that the statement is in 'Charlotte's own words', but Charlotte's own words in *Shirley*[12] are something very different from Charlotte's own words in her letters, and Caroline Helstone's aunt is somebody very different from Charlotte's aunt, although the Hansons explicitly and Miss Gerin implicitly confuse the two. This confusion between fact and fiction in well-established secondary sources makes it hard to discover the true facts of the Brontës' religion.

It so happens that others of our secondary sources are for a variety of reasons equally unreliable. Mrs Gaskell, steering a difficult course between the Scylla of Mr Brontë and Mr Nicholls and the Charybdis of public opinion, would naturally be inclined to omit anything that smacked of religious controversy in *The Life of Charlotte Brontë*. Ellen Nussey was dissatisfied with Mrs Gaskell's account of Charlotte's religion[13] and, as we have shown, edited Charlotte's letters in order to minimise any element of religious unorthodoxy; we can therefore expect insufficient weight to be given to this unorthodox element in the editions of Shorter and Symington and Wise which drew so heavily on Ellen's correspondence. The discovery of the juvenilia was a godsend to those who wished to supplement the account of Mrs Gaskell; since there is little religion in the juvenilia, religion is given less attention than it deserves in biographies which draw heavily on the juvenilia.[14] Such biographies are an improvement on critical works which pay no attention to religion.[15] Thus we find an article, entitled 'The Incest Theme in Wuthering Heights', which begins optimistically

One need not follow the dark Freudian lines of the Emily– Branwell relationship – which have been fully explored by the author's biographers – to prove Emily Brontë's familiarity with the concept of incestuous connections.[16]

This is typical of an attitude which puts forward an interpretation which is both eccentric and unoriginal, while ignoring what is both obvious and not yet fully explored.

The obvious must therefore first be stated. Of the books known to have been owned as opposed to borrowed by the Brontës, the majority were theological.[17] There was an impressive theological section in the library at Ponden House and in the Keighley Mechanics' Institute.[18] Even more impressive evidence of the influence of religion on the lives of the Brontës is provided by the library of the Robinsons of Thorp Green, almost exclusively theological, and by the catalogue of books owned by Ellen Nussey, largely consisting of the Brontë novels and works of devotion.[19]

Nor did the Brontës derive their inspiration merely from books, but also from sermons and presumably from such conversations and arguments as those that took place between their father and aunt. Outside Haworth Parsonage the influence was still persistent. From the severely religious Cowan Bridge Charlotte Brontë passed to the school of Miss Wooler, the sister-in-law of a clergyman, who moved her school to a clergyman's house. It was Miss Wooler's brother-in-law, the Rev. Edward Carter, who found Charlotte her first post with the Sidgwicks, whose nephew was to be Archbishop of Canterbury. Even the move to Brussels was taken under the guidance of the British Chaplain at Brussels. Two of Ellen Nussey's brothers were clergymen, as were three of the four men to propose marriage to Charlotte. Whether the Rev. William Weightman was in love with Anne Brontë, or she with him, he too must be reckoned as an influence in the lives of all three sisters.

Clergymen play a large and obvious part in *Jane Eyre, Shirley* and *Agnes Grey,* although significantly only in *Agnes Grey* is the hero of a Brontë novel a clergyman. But the Brontës did more than translate their clerical acquaintances into their novels. The equation of Jabez Branderham with Jabez Bunting, the controversial Methodist leader, and of St John Rivers with Henry Martyn, the Evangelical missionary, if true, shows that the Brontës were prepared to write about clergymen they had never met.[20] Mary Taylor was amazed at Charlotte's knowledge of heresies outside the Church of England, and both Ellen Nussey and M. Heger were impressed with her knowledge of the Bible.[21] The poetry of the Brontës in vocabulary, sentiment and outlook is reminiscent of the hymnal and prayer book.[22]

In any case the country as a whole was vitally concerned with religion. The 1840s in particular were years of religious controversy and religious novels.[23] Two words, to quote Heathcliff rather inappropriately, hell and death, acted as focal points. Death, as is well known, was a constant visitor in the Brontë household; as is less well known, it was an even more constant visitor in Haworth village, where the churchyard tells its own sombre story and where between 1838 and 1849 41.6 per cent of the population died before reaching the age of six.[24]

Death was both frequent and obvious; the question 'Who is saved?' could therefore be made both relevant and urgent. It was indeed, metaphorically as well as literally, one of the burning issues of the day, perhaps more burning than political issues, since the gospel of reform fought a difficult battle against the doctrine that the next world was far more important than this world. Thus religious enthusiasm could act as a kind of safety valve for political passions,[25] but at the same time it is easy to trace a connection between religious and political views. On the one hand we have High Churchmen and High Tories like Mr Hatfield in *Agnes Grey*, who believed that the poor should be kept in their place in this world and the next, and on the other we have in *Shirley* Mike Hartley, the crazed Antinomian weaver, also a Jacobin and a leveller, convinced of his own salvation and of Robert Moore's perdition, but equally convinced of the necessity of destroying the power of the millowners on this earth. The Brontës were hostile both to people like Mr Hatfield and to people like Mike Hartley, and we can therefore trace a connection between their hatred of religious exclusiveness and their hatred of social exclusiveness, although, as we shall see, perhaps because they were more interested in religion than in politics, their religious doctrines are more convincing and coherent than their social teaching.

A similar parallel can be drawn between views on hell and views on sex. The facts of life are obviously akin to the facts of death, both attracting the same mixture of reverence, amusement and disgust. Because different elements in this mixture have predominated at different times, it is hard for us in the middle of the twentieth century to grasp the nature of the connection in the middle of the nineteenth century. We now talk openly of sex, although occasionally paying lip service to former taboos by getting worried about four-letter words; the problems of life after death and even the very presence of death are kept firmly out of sight. The Victorians talked openly of hell and damnation, though occasionally, as Charlotte mentioned in her preface to *Wuthering Heights*, preferring to substitute decorous dashes for these words.[26] In view of this reversal, we can say that religion channelled off sexual feeling in the same way that it channelled off political passion; this is particularly noticeable in Charlotte's letters to Ellen Nussey during her period of religious doubt when teaching at Miss Wooler's. We can also say that there is a connection between the religious unorthodoxy of the Brontës and their independent attitude to the problems of sex which so shocked their contemporaries.

The equally shocking views of the Brontës on eternal punishment become clear when we consider that in the 1840's most influential parties inside and outside the Church of England were convinced that some were saved and some were damned, although the qualifications for salvation and the quantity of those saved varied from sect to sect. Newman saw a belief in the eternity of future punishment as common ground between the Church of England and the Church of Rome.[27] Although the Wesleys were comparatively restrained in preaching hellfire, their Arminian successors were not; though disagreeing with Calvinists about the possibility of saving oneself through one's own efforts, they agreed with them in condemning many to perdition for ever.[28] It is difficult to be schematic about the various sects, especially as with regard to eternal punishment the distinction between the Anglican Church and Dissenters is not important. Calvinists, like Gorham in fact and St John Rivers in fiction, were clergymen of the Church of England, and the dividing line between the doctrine of Methodists and that of Low Church Evangelicals on personal salvation is very hard to

draw. The most important division for the Brontës was probably
that between moderates, who did not lay down strict rules for
salvation, and extremists, who said that only the few who
followed their own particular path were worthy of heaven.
Extreme Low Churchmen and Nonconformists are usually
thought to be on the opposite end of the scale from extreme
High Churchmen and Roman Catholics. They are in some
respects,[29] but Charlotte Brontë saw that they both set up an
arbitrary standard for salvation and condemned them for it.

It is less easy to find religious sects who did not believe in
the eternity of hellfire. Atheists who believed in neither God,
Heaven or Hell were common in the pious tales which described
their sticky ends, but in real life they rarely had the courage or
opportunity to state their views, and Charlotte Brontë said that
Harriet Martineau was the first such atheist she had met.[30] In the
seventeenth century men like Cambridge Platonists had preached
against the eternity of hell, and in the eighteenth century hell
was preached principally for its deterrent value in ensuring
good conduct on earth,[31] but such tepid defenders of the faith
did not last long in the enthusiastic nineteenth century. The
nearest approach to such a preacher in the novels of the Brontës
is Mr Hatfield, but he is an odd mixture since, though he gabbles
through the service and is full of worldly thoughts in the best
Jane Austen manner, he also has a Puseyite love of ritual.[32] The
Unitarian or Socinian view that the righteous went to heaven,
while the wicked were annihilated, appears to have attracted
Branwell. Charlotte, a friend of the Unitarian Mrs Gaskell,
knew about Socinianism, Anne could have read about Socinianism in Mr Robinson's library,[33] but none of the three sisters
preached Socinian views in their novels. The Roman Catholic
doctrine of Purgatory, whereby some sinners could reach Heaven
after a period of trial and testing, seems a more promising
source for the Brontës' philosophy of divine punishment, but
Charlotte at any rate shared the hostility to Roman Catholicism
that was a feature of her age, and though using purgatorial
imagery in *Jane Eyre* expressly condemns the doctrine of purgatory in *Villette*.[34] In the last years of her life, when she was
famous, Charlotte did move in circles where Broad Church views

would be common, and we find her reading Dr Arnold and listening to Maurice with approval.[35] There are also slight pieces of evidence linking Emily and Anne Brontë with Broad Church teaching against hell. Emily's first biographer, as already noted, said that she called herself a disciple of F. D. Maurice, and there is a record of Anne's being in correspondence with the Rev. David Thom, the leader of a small sect known as the Beroean Universalists, who believed in salvation for all.[36] They may have been in correspondence about Anne's poem, 'A Word to the Elect', which appeared in *The Universalist*.[37] On the other hand *The Universalist*, in which articles by and about Thom are frequent, is devoted to problems like the meaning of αἰώνιος or the deterrent powers of hellfire, in which we know Anne to have been interested.[38] *The Universalist* is also useful for showing the rarity of believers in universal salvation for all, although the fact of its publication and many of the articles in it do suggest some interest in the subject around the year 1850.

Voices doubting eternal punishment were few and far between when compared to those taking eternal punishment for granted and waxing eloquent on its terrors. Of these voices the most obvious for the Brontës was that of the Rev. Patrick Brontë. Recent biographers of the Brontës have tended to represent Mr Brontë as a comparatively moderate preacher, and have looked elsewhere, notably to the Rev. Carus Wilson and Miss Branwell, for the really sinister influences on the Brontës.[39] With his dislike of Calvinists and Puseyite priests, and his wish to avoid the excesses of personal election on the one hand and baptismal regeneration on the other, Mr Brontë did occupy a fairly central position with regard to church discipline, upholding the good old plan of the Church of England.[40] But it is a mistake to regard Mr Brontë as a Laodicean. He was after all at the receiving end of the two great streams, closely connected with one another, which had revitalised religion in Great Britain, Methodism and the Evangelical movement. In Ireland he came under the influence of Thomas Tighe, the friend of John Wesley, while as an undergraduate at Cambridge he imbibed the Evangelical notions fashionable at the time from people like Charles

Simeon and Henry Martyn.[41] As the incumbent of Haworth Mr Brontë could hardly escape the influence of a former incumbent, the Rev. William Grimshaw, who, although like Wesley in the Church of England all his life, may be taken as the typical representative of Yorkshire Methodism.[42] On the whole the Methodists, especially in the left-wing breakaway movements, were more concerned with salvation through faith, and the Evangelicals with salvation through works. Both were however concerned with saving souls, and both were at pains to stress the sacrifice of Christ as the means of salvation. For those who were not saved there was little to offer but weeping and gnashing of teeth.

It depended upon the personality of the preacher and the nature of his audience, rather than on any division inside or outside the Church of England, whether it was salvation or damnation that was stressed. Mr Brontë appears to have preferred damnation. In writing to his former sweetheart Miss Burder he says,

> The world with all its pains, pleasures, fears, and hopes will soon have an end; but an eternity of unutterable happiness or misery is the grand characteristick of the next world.[43]

Nor does Mr Brontë appear to have modified this conventional division into sheep and goats during the course of his long life.[44]

At times he does in his poems and stories seem to be preaching the comforting doctrine, later taken up by his daughters, that suffering on earth brings salvation in heaven.

> With horrible din,
> Afflictions may swell,—
> They cleanse me from sin,
> They save me from hell:
> They're all but the rod
> Of Jesus, in love,
> They lead me to God,
> And blessings, above.[45]

And there are further references to this theme in *The Cottage in the* Wood.[46] There are also a few mentions of redemption through Christ's blood.[47] But more often Mr Brontë strives to terrify rather than to encourage.

> Both rich and poor, who serve not God,
> But live in sin, averse to good,
> Rejecting Christ's atoning blood,
> Midst hellish shoals,
> Shall welter in that fiery flood,
> Which hissing rolls.[48]

There is an abundance of references to the stock themes of the terrors of the last judgement, unquenchable fire, never-ending woe, ever-living worm, opening hell, and deathbed thoughts of demons.[49]

The few sermons of Mr Brontë to survive are equally distressing. The eruption of a bog is a forewarning of the last judgement, a warning apparently ignored by those who on their return home in 'all the giddy frivolity of youth, talked and acted as if they dreamed not either of heaven or hell, death or judgment'.[50] In his sermon on Willie Weightman's death, in spite of his curate's optimistic teaching on the love of God rather than the fear of hell, Mr Brontë seized the opportunity to refer to sin as giving death 'a goad, a poisoned dagger, fatal and tormenting, and capable of destroying both body and soul in hell for ever'.[51]

Mr Brontë had a Bible in several volumes of which only the books from Jeremiah to Malachi survive, but he contrived to insert two New Testament texts on damnation into this volume.[52]

Mr Brontë must not be blamed for all the terrors that disturbed his children. His decriptions of hell by reason of their conventional nature lose something of their horror, and we can free him from any responsibility for the most frightening Calvinistic doctrines. Proceeding logically from the idea that all thoughts and actions spring from an all-powerful God, Calvinists then argue that those whose thoughts and actions are bad enough to merit eternal punishment must have been preordained by God to damnation. In that case anyone with evil thoughts might be tempted to go and sin all the more, and Branwell Brontë seems to have adopted this philosophy, to counter which Calvinists fall back on the well-worn arguments that some mysteries are too deep for man's understanding, and that what the Bible says is always true.[53] These counter-arguments in favour of predestination to damnation would not seem fatuous to children who were taught to revere the Bible, and to whom much of life was a mystery. When in addition those listening to the Calvinist arguments, as well as undergoing the usual stresses of adolescence, were blessed, or perhaps cursed, with enquiring minds and unusually vivid imaginations which sought an outlet in depicting heroes and heroines of Byronic villainy, it can be easily imagined what a terrifying effect would have been produced by a doctrine which said that evil thoughts and doubts were signs of impending damnation.[54] In particular the notion that unchaste thoughts were equivalent to adultery appears to have wrought havoc with Charlotte's life when teaching at Roe Head and Dewsbury Moor. Both she and Anne nearly broke under the strain in this period, and the person responsible for their terror must bear a heavy burden of blame.

The villain is usually held to be Miss Branwell, but the evidence for this, as has been shown, is very slight. She was a Methodist, but of the Arminian variety, a believer in hell, but not in predestination. Helen Huntingdon's aunt, in *The Tenant of Wildfell Hall*, preaches grim doctrines of damnation, but not of predestination to it,[55] and in any case it is too easy to equate aunts in fiction with aunts in fact. Nobody has thought of equating the governess, allegedly the daughter of a clergyman, who becomes the mistress of Arthur Huntingdon, with that other governess, Miss Anne Brontë. With her reading of *The Lady's Magazine*[56] Miss Branwell appears to have been sprightly in her youth, and her arguments with Mr Brontë need not necessarily have been about Calvinism; indeed he is hardly likely to have allowed in his house someone preaching doctrines that directly contradicted his own.

A more likely villain is the Rev. Carus Wilson, but neither in real life as the editor of *The Children's Friend*, nor as Mr Brocklehurst in *Jane Eyre*, does he produce doctrines that are specifically Calvinist. Such lines as,

> Tis dangerous to provoke a God
> Whose power and vengence none can tell;
> One stroke of his almighty rod
> Can send a sinner straight to Hell . . .[57]

although unattractive, do not suggest that God has used his
almighty rod before the young sinners were born. Anne and
Branwell Brontë, perhaps the two worst sufferers from Calvinist
preaching, did not attend the school at Cowan Bridge. There is
secondary evidence attributing Calvinist views to Carus Wilson,
but the reliability of this evidence is uncertain. Carus Wilson's
grandson says that the Bishop of Chester refused to ordain his
grandfather as priest on account of his Calvinist opinions, but
then adds, 'this was simply a contemptuous way of designating
Evangelical views'.[58]

Confusion between Calvinists and Evangelicals was common
among their opponents who tended to lump together all enthusiastic seekers after salvation as Methodists.[59] There were of
course Evangelicals like Thomas Scott who were definitely Calvinists, and many Evangelicals were themselves confused between the rival claims of the possibility of universal salvation
for all and the certainty of future damnation for some, Grimshaw in fact claiming both to be true.[60] The insistence on punish-
ing childish peccadilloes is a reflection of a Calvinist attitude that
sees childhood acts as the first sure signs of God's grace or the
lack of it, and in this case Carus Wilson must be reckoned as a
partial Calvinist.[61] But Broad Churchmen like Dr Arnold and
High Churchwomen like Charlotte M. Yonge were both enthusiastic denouncers of sin among the young, and the primary
evidence still does not support the view that Carus Wilson
claimed that God had determined men's fate before they were
born. There are indeed some signs of encouragement in *The
Children's Friend*. God is said to be of very tender mercy, there is
praise of Moravians, a little boy though cast out of Sunday
School is not cast off from us, and there are plenty of references
to heaven, which does seem fairly easy to obtain by virtue.[62]

Virtue can also help us to avoid hell, as the following quotation shows: 'What would he not give for a few more days on earth, if such a thing could be, that he might secure the salvation of his immortal soul.'[63] The story in *The Children's Friend* about punishment hurting the punisher is copied from Wesley's pious Arminian friend, Mrs Fletcher. Mrs Fletcher's influence may be seen in the rules for such items as dress at Cowan Bridge, and she can also be used to defend Miss Branwell from the charge of being a Calvinist, since she was the godmother of John Fennell, uncle to the Misses Branwell.[64]

Two possible sources for the Brontës' Calvinism are two clergymen of the Church of England, who have hitherto not been allotted anything but a rather undignified role in the Brontë story. As has been shown, the Rev. Henry Nussey can be associated with Calvinism because of the evidence of his diary, the new reading of Charlotte's letter to Ellen Nussey about ghastly Calvinistic fears, and the idea that the portrait of St John Rivers owes something to him. But his Calvinistic views are neither a certain nor a direct influence on the Brontës. The same is true of the Rev. Edward Robinson. It is probably impossible to discover the exact nature of the Robinson household; there is not only the difficulty of disentangling the real Robinsons from the fictional Murrays of *Agnes Grey*, but also the problem of how much to believe of Branwell Brontë's account of the years he spent as tutor at Thorp Green. Certainly there is evidence, apart from *Agnes Grey*, to suggest that there was a worldly streak about the Robinsons.[65] And yet there is no getting round the evidence of Mr Robinson's library with its impressive array of Evangelical sermons;[66] since much of what Anne and Branwell wrote reflecting and rejecting Calvinistic views was written during or immediately after their stay at Thorp Green, there does seem a good case for attributing this interest in Calvinism to Mr Robinson's library.

The theological library is not confined to Evangelical works, ranging indeed from Jeremy Taylor to Dr Arnold, although it is fair to say that Evangelicals are predominant. It is hard to cite any specifically Calvinistic works, since we do not know whether the rather general title, Scott, *Sermons* included that on Romans,

II, 6–9, published in *Sermons on Select Subjects* with its stark conclusion,

> No exceptions, however, are intimated: the saints, even those that believe, will alone stand accepted; and all else will be 'punished with everlasting destruction from his presence'...,[67]

or *The Doctrines of Election and Final Perseverence, Stated from Scripture*, with its grim note of predestination,

> Others left to themselves, and to their own lusts, and to Satan's temptations, meet with those things in the righteous providence of God, which harden them more and more to their destruction.[68]

Scott, though a Calvinist, did not emphasise hell all that much; for a straightforward account of hell, not specifically Calvinist, we do not have to look very far in Mr Robinson's library, since *Death Bed Scenes* by Warton contains the following stirring passage:

> Is it this to which your mind is made up? Then it is made up to dwell with everlasting burnings in lakes of fire and brimstone which will never be quenched; with gnawing worms, with stinging scorpions, with furious devils, exulting in the torments which they will inflict upon you.[69]

It seems a little harsh, however, to blame Mr Robinson for his taste in theological literature, and in any case it is less important to affix blame than to see how the Brontës reacted to the horrible doctrines they heard or read. Branwell, as is well known, thought that he was damned, and, as well as behaving as if he was damned, wrote stories and poems lamenting his damnation. Charlotte after her early Calvinistic agony showed distinct hostility to those who condemned to hell anyone unwilling to obey their rules; Mr Brocklehurst and the Catholic in *Villette* who said 'Quand vous serez morte-vous brûlerez tout de suite dans l'enfer'[70] are obviously mocked. But in her novels she seems reluctant to deny explicitly eternal punishment. Anne and Emily Brontë are more definite in their denial, although it must be admitted that the evidence for Anne and Emily's religious beliefs, coming as it does from their novels, and poems, is rather different from the evidence for Charlotte's religion. It is dangerous to assume that characters in fiction exactly reproduce the views of their authors, and it is difficult to establish the date or even the authorship of the Brontë poems. On the other hand, in view of the unreliability of the text of Charlotte Brontë's letters, and the possibility of shocking or unorthodox opinions being censored we cannot be confident that we have the full record of Charlotte's views, although we obviously have more information about her than about her sisters.

The writing of the three sisters is usually and rightly considered separately, but we do have evidence of their close collaboration,[71] and it is impossible not to get the impression that at any rate with regard to religion they are very much in sympathy with each other. Thus Anne's doubts about her salvation coincide roughly with Charlotte's at Roe Head and Dewsbury Moor, and, more importantly, the three major works condemning eternal punishment, Wuthering Heights, The Tenant of Wildfell Hall and Jane Eyre, were all written at about the same time. Wuthering Heights was of course written first, and a good case can be made out for Emily Brontë, by all accounts the strongest personality of the three, being responsible for the doctrine that salvation could be won by all.

Branwell does not show this sympathy; although there are traces at the end of his life of a slightly more optimistic view which may be due to his sisters' teaching, it seems more likely that his decline and fall caused his sisters to review their position on the punishment of sinners. An examination of Branwell's writings would suggest that he suffered mainly through his own fault, though Calvinism is partly to blame. The comparison of childhood innocence, presided over by his dead sister, Maria, with the disappointment and degeneracy of his adult life drove his over-active brain to despair. His sisters too had faced the fall of innocence, and for Emily at any rate the return of a childhood paradise was a golden prospect, but unlike his sisters Branwell did not face up to this fall, but fell still further.

The juvenile prose stories are an unpromising source for information about the Brontës' religion. Quite apart from the difficulty of distinguishing Charlotte's contributions from Branwell's we are faced with a remarkable reluctance to handle religious themes.[72] The particular theme of punishment after death is especially remote in view of the reluctance of Charlotte and Branwell to kill off any of their characters. We can say that Branwell is obviously interested in the diabolical with the creation of such characters as Quashia Quamina and in the problem of deep-dyed sinners with the creation of Byronic souls like Henry Hastings and Alexander Earl of Northangerland. For a deeper investigation of what happened to these damned souls we have to look at Branwell's poetry.

The creation of Henry Hastings as a Satanic figure coincides with the *Misery I* and *Misery II*[73] poems and with Branwell's first major disappointment in London. The year 1836 is of course near the period when Anne and Charlotte were suffering. Branwell in December 1835 could hope that his guardian star (Maria) could save him. In March 1836 he is gloomier, talks of eternal night, and thinks that either he is condemned to separation from Maria in hell, or both are destined for Socinian annihilation.

> *If there's no God, no Heaven, no Hell*
> *Thou within thy grave must dwell –*
> *I left black'ning in the storm –*
> *Both a banquet for the worm.*
> *If there is a heaven above,*
> *Thou in bliss art shining there . . .*
> *Angel bright and angel fair . . .*
> *While I staid where . . .*
> *Hell's dread night must close my day!*[74]

The Socinian heresy is not much comfort. In 1837 Branwell writes:

> *Eternity – oh, were there none! –*
> *Could I believe what some believe,*
> *Soon might my spirit cease to grieve*
> *At the cold grave and churchyard stone*

> But – God! – To appear, before Thy face
> In all a sinner's nakedness.[75]

Branwell was not of course ruined by 1837. We see sparks of
hope both in his life and in his poetry. It is difficult to be certain about his position, since there is a suspicion both that in his
description of his gloomy prospects he is romanticising, and that
in his doubts about orthodox teaching on damnation he is trying
to comfort himself against the fear that this teaching may be
true. The letters and drawings in which Branwell's gloomy position is outlined are so full of the misery of this world that it is
hard to know what he thought about the next world, and we
are not helped by his frequent shifts from jocular bravado to
the depths of despair.[76] The complaints about the hypocrisy of
the clergy[77] and the really bitter denunciation of the meeting at
Sanctification Chapel in *And the Weary are at Rest*, when Calvinists and Wesleyans argue about salvation which obviously
none of them deserve,[78] may suggest that Branwell had utterly
abandoned his faith in the teaching of the church. This impression
is supported by an examination of Branwell's later poems. In
1838 we find Branwell pondering in the poem *Azrael* on the
difficulty of reconciling God's goodness with his punitive powers,
and doubting the existence of God.[79] In an undated sonnet
Peaceful death and painful life Branwell seems to take the view
that the hell of the Unbeliever is a mixture of hell on earth and
the *poena damni*, of deprivation from heaven.

> Who finds no Heaven beyond Life's gloomy skies,
> Who sees no Hope to brighten up that gloom,
> 'Tis He who feels the worm that never dies –
> The REAL death and darkness of the tomb.[80]

An equally illuminating poem is *Real Rest*, written in the year
between 1845 and 1846, where the contrast is between hell on
earth and Socinian annihilation.[81] Branwell was not optimistic
enough to hope for heaven, but seemed to have some hopes that
he might have escaped the pains of hell.

Charlotte was more optimistic, saying that after Branwell's

death, she felt, 'as I had never felt before, that there was peace
and forgiveness for him in Heaven'.[82] From the context it would
seem that Charlotte's feelings were a result of Branwell's repentance rather than any change in her views about the existence
of hell. As has been shown there is not a great deal of evidence
in the juvenilia about Charlotte's religious views, but what
there is suggests orthodoxy. One of her early poems contains
references to a stock hell,

> Where the wicked ceaseless cry
> And where the pangs of torture never die.[83]

We also find,

> But doubt not that his Spirit groans
> In Hell's eternity.[84]

Assertions of Socinian annihilation and God's mercy are more
tentative.[85] Perhaps the most orthodox feature of Charlotte's
poems is the constant declaration of the joys of heaven, although
the hackneyed imagery of these descriptions hardly gives the
impression of any deeply held feelings.

> But think of Beulah's bowers, the home
> That waits thee when the path is trod,
> Lying all free from clouds and gloom,
> Celestial in the smile of God.[86]

Problems of authorship as well as scarcity of material in the
prose juvenilia prevent a satisfactory discussion of Charlotte's
religious position in them. The story in *Julia*[87] about the Verdo-
politan Methodist preachers is orthodox in that like passages
in Charlotte's novels it is hostile to Methodism, but in its attack
on the hypocrisy of those preaching awful instances of God's
judgement on the wicked it approaches blasphemy. Unfortunately we do not know whether this portion of *Julia* is by
Charlotte; in style and subject matter it is very similar to *And
the Weary are at Rest*. In an earlier story, where there seems
less reason to doubt Charlotte's authorship, we find a note of
conventional orthodoxy.

'Hell will help you', returned Warner quite coolly; 'and I fear,
my lord, God will veil his face from you for ever. Remember
men may so tempt the Holy Spirit that it will finally leave us.
I do not expostulate; I know you are decided; but I fear a man
reprobate and d—d in this life is my Sovereign.'[88]

Conventional orthodoxy is at first sight the key to Charlotte's
religion. With her love for the Establishment with all its faults,[89]
her hatred of any 'isms' inconsistent with Church of England-
ism[90] and her attacks on Roman Catholics and Dissenters in
Shirley and Villette, she might appear to be following very
much in the footsteps of her father. It must be remembered that
most of Charlotte's letters were to Ellen Nussey, that Ellen censored these letters and that a motive in publishing the letters
was a wish to defend Charlotte against the charge of unorthodoxy. Because Ellen Nussey was orthodox she would not elicit
letters like that to W. S. Williams, in which Charlotte is sympathetic about his difficulty in finding any creed which he can
conclusively adopt as his, although she says he is wrong in
thinking men can do without creeds and forms in religion.[91]
Because Ellen Nussey censored the letters to her it is likely that
we miss remarks such as the one that appears in the letter to Mrs
Gaskell; after denouncing the dismissal of F. D. Maurice from
King's College, London, Charlotte asks 'Who that seriously
anticipates an Eternity of Torment for half his race – can keep
sane?'[92] Admittedly the only example of the suppression of an
unorthodox belief in the letters to Ellen Nussey is the passage in
an early letter involving a childish superstition about the souls
of the dead,[93] but the very triviality of this censored passage
suggests the possibility of large-scale suppressions.

Thus we do not have all the evidence, and the evidence we
do have is unfairly weighted in favour of orthodoxy. Even so a
good case can be made out for showing Charlotte's unorthodoxy
in religion; at any rate she shifts her position fairly rapidly.
Church of England clergymen come in for some fairly heavy
satire in Shirley, the message of which would seem to be, 'God
save the Church of England, God also reform it.'[94] In Charlotte's
letters she both attacks the Anglican clergy in general and holds

up individual clergymen to scorn.[95] The strong upholder of the Church of England found no difficulty in forming friendships with the atheist Harriet Martineau and the Unitarian Mrs Gaskell. The mocker of Puseyite curates eventually married Mr Nicholls and once married seems to have accepted his authority fairly tamely.[96] The ambivalent attitude to Calvinism in Charlotte's youth is matched by a later fascination with Catholicism, of which the visit to the confessional in *Villette* and in real life is an appropriate symbol.

Today's orthodoxy is yesterday's heresy. Because we do not now believe in eternal damnation, we find it hard to believe that anyone could be criticised for doubting such a doctrine. The Brontës' religious position has been obscured by contemporary biographers unwilling to concede that the Brontës could have revolted against established dogmas, and by modern biographers unable to see that the doctrines which the Brontës rejected were so well established. Both sets of biographers have done a disservice to the Brontës' originality; a careful examination of the Brontë novels will show that they were prepared in perhaps too didactic a fashion to put forward an original religious position.

4

The Brontës' Religion

AN IMPORTANT element in Charlotte Brontë's religious philosophy, consistent with attachment to the Church of England, but not necessarily indicating any marked degree of orthodoxy, was her hatred of hypocrisy. We know that hypocrisy was one of Charlotte's aversions. In writing to Ellen Nussey she asks if someone is 'a knave, a humbug, a hypocrite, a ninny, a noodle',[1] and a scoundrel is said to be insincere as Lucifer in *Shirley*.[2] The Methodist minister in *Shirley*, the Rev. Moses Barraclough, is expressly called a hypocrite on two occasions:[3] he preaches Christianity, but in fact stirs up trouble, and drinks too much. So does the Puseyite Mr Malone, said to be modelled on Mr Brontë's curate, Mr Smith; another curate, Mr Collins, also drank, and we cannot confine accusations of hypocrisy to sects outside the Church of England.[4] But Dissenters and Roman Catholics do come in for some particularly heavy abuse on this score, being twice significantly linked. Cardinal Wiseman's hypocrisy is compared to that of a canting Methodist preacher, and a canting Catholic book in *Villette* reminds Lucy Snowe of some Wesleyan tracts she had read in her youth.[5] *Shirley* and *The Professor* are both novels dedicated to realism, and both expose the faults of hypocritical sects. *Shirley* is mainly concerned with Dissenters and Puseyites, but contains the sentence, 'The Romish religion especially teaches renunciation of self, submission to others, and nowhere are found so many grasping tyrants as in the ranks of the Romish priesthood',[6] while *The Professor*, mainly devoted to exposing the wickedness of Roman Catholicism, contains the gratuitous insult to Methodism, 'he was "a joined Methodist" which did not (be it understood) prevent him from being at the same time an ingrained rascal'.[7]

A possible explanation for Charlotte's hostility to Roman Catholicism is her dislike of the elaborate ritual mingled with a secret hankering after it. A dislike for the theatrical, combined with a certain fascination, is of course shown in her descriptions of visits to see Rachel in fact and Vashti in fiction. Methodists could also be theatrical, but there is no hostile description of a Methodist service as there is in Branwell's *And the Weary are at Rest*. This can be partly explained by Charlotte's links through her father with the Evangelical Low Church; after all *Shirley* for all its hostility to Dissenters is almost as contemptuous of those who dislike Dissenters. It can be explained by the fact that both the ritual and the doctrine of most Dissenters appeared to have a greater connection with moral conduct than did those of the Roman Catholics. An exception of course must be made of extreme Antinomians who relied on faith to save them and who receive short shrift in *Shirley*. But the average Methodist service was a sober exhortation to decent living with the prospect of a heavenly reward for such conduct. In contrast, the services of Catholics appeared to have nothing to do with virtuous conduct, the practice of the confessional seemed to militate against it, and the doctrine whereby one good act could be reckoned as expiation for a multitude of sins is said to encourage conduct like that of the unregenerate Rochester.[8] *The Professor*, the least overtly religious of Charlotte's novels, attacks the confessional and the lack of solemnity in Catholic prayers, and says that Catholicism is responsible for the deficiency in sound principle of Zoraide Reuter and her pupils,[9] while *Villette* has a passage which expressly condemns the irrelevance of Catholic worship to the problems of the world.

When I thought of sin and sorrow, of earthly corruption, mortal depravity, weighty temporal woe – I could not care for chanting priests or mumming officials; that when the pain of existence and the terrors of dissolution pressed before me – when the mighty hope and measureless doubt of the future arose in view – then even the scientific strain, or prayer in a language learned and dead, harassed with hindrance a heart which only longed to cry – 'God be merciful to me a sinner!'[10]

There are thus two strands in Charlotte's position which are vital. She has a strong attachment to virtue which results in a wish to see the wicked suffer and the righteous prosper, but fighting against this feeling she has a strong reluctance to lay down strict rules for salvation and feels hostile to those who do. We shall find a similar dichotomy in Charlotte's social philosophy; she does not believe in existing rigid class divisions, but does believe that good birth is important. Roman Catholicism lays down strict rules for salvation, but these rules appear to have no connection with morality; for this reason, although Charlotte is not prepared to dismiss all Roman Catholics as bad, she says that Roman Catholicism beats Methodism, Dissenterism, Quakerism, and the extremes of High Churchism for folly.[11] Puseyites are not themselves wicked, but their attachment to the offices of the church is not exactly an incentive to virtuous living, and they can be condemned for their petty dislike of those who disagree with them. Eliza Reed's activity produces few tangible results except ill temper with her sister, and the curates in *Shirley* when they meet to settle the Dissenters discuss theology occasionally but piety never.[12] Low Churchmen and moderate Methodists are sometimes equally intolerant,[13] though usually virtuous, while the reliance on faith rather than works of extreme Methodists breeds people who are not themselves virtuous, but are prepared to condemn virtuous people to perdition, as the Antinomian Mike Hartley condemned Robert Moore in *Shirley*.[14] It is best to be like Charlotte Brontë, virtuous enough to obtain salvation but vague on the question of how it is to be obtained. Her remarks in the preface to the second edition of *Jane Eyre*, 'Conventionality is not morality, Self-righteousness is not religion'[15] are applicable both to the narrow question of literary decorum and more fundamental religious issues.

In trying to find rewards for the righteous while reducing punishment for sinners Charlotte faced a difficult problem. She faced another problem in deciding where the righteous should be rewarded. The Old Testament suggests in the face of much evidence to the contrary that it is God's plan that the virtuous should prosper on earth, and it is left to the New Testament to introduce the next world as a place where recompense will be

made for their sufferings. The Church has never really been able
to make up its mind about the fate of the virtuous on earth, and
in the nineteenth century the same people who were enthusiastic
about preparing oneself for the next world were also insistent
that a work of fiction was only proper if virtue and vice met
with their due reward in this world.[16] Of course believers in
heaven could represent the conventional happy ending as sym-
bolic of the joys of heaven, and in this sense the rather contrived
happy ending of *Jane Eyre* is a satisfactory one. But Rochester
with his strongly delineated physical passion is a somewhat
unlikely symbol of heaven, and perhaps this is one reason why
Jane Eyre ends not with the happy married life of the Rochesters,
but with St John Rivers's impending death, leading presumably
to the heavenly crown. Thus *Jane Eyre* is not exactly clear in
which world the happy ending is to be. *Villette* is clear on this,
since Lucy Snowe and Paul Emanuel are not reunited after their
separation,[17] and the novel ends with the prosperity of Madame
Beck, Père Silas and Madame Walravens, the evil agents of their
separation. On the other hand the despair about this world
leads to uncertainty about the next; it is never said that Lucy
Snowe's sufferings will be rewarded in another sphere, and in
the midst of such gloom it is hard to believe that they ever will
be.

Jane Eyre is far less pessimistic about the fate not only of the
virtuous but also of the wicked. It looks as if Charlotte was at
this time working her way to a compromise between her love of
virtue and her reluctance to penalise the vicious. Two passages
from letters written in 1847 are instructive. Talking of Ellen
Nussey's brother Joseph she says, 'I trust and even believe that
his long sufferings on earth will be taken as sufficient expiation
for his errors',[18] and shortly afterwards she writes,

> The right path is that which necessitates the greatest sacrifice
> of self-interest, – which implies the greatest good to others;
> and this path, steadily followed, will lead, I believe, in time to
> prosperity and to happiness.[19]

Against this philosophy it could be argued that the wicked do
not always expiate their sins by suffering, and that self-sacrifice

with prosperity and happiness as its eventual goal is only a refined form of selfishness. Against this, in return Charlotte could
argue that, if the wicked are not saved by their own suffering,
they can be saved by the sufferings of the virtuous, who are
good not to save their own skins, but to save the souls of others.
She does not say this categorically in *Jane Eyre*, and in fact works
out the doctrine much less clearly than her sisters do, but *Jane
Eyre* does preach a doctrine of universal salvation, and good
people like Helen Burns and St John Rivers do seem to suffer.
Rochester and Jane Eyre are partly good and partly bad; they
suffer enough on earth to gain their happiness there. Mrs Reed
is almost totally depraved, although her salvation is helped by
her deathbed repentance and suffering, but the words of Helen
Burns which Jane recalls at the deathbed of her aunt[20] suggest
salvation even for people like Mrs Reed. Helen's creed, 'which
no one ever taught me, and which I seldom mention; but in
which I delight and to which I cling: for it extends hope to all:
it makes Eternity a rest a mighty home, not a terror and an
abyss'[21] is obviously meant to be taken seriously, since Charlotte later refers to it in a letter.

> I am not sorry the Clergy do not like the doctrine of Universal
> Salvation; I think it is a great pity for their sakes, but surely
> they are not so unreasonable as to expect me to deny or sup-
> press what I believe the truth.[22]

Bertha Mason is a harder case for salvation; perhaps being
more or less an animal, she hardly counts, perhaps her long
years of suffering and terrible death are reckoned sufficient expiation, although we are not told of this. We are principally aware
of her, not as a candidate for salvation, but as an agent in
Rochester's salvation, since she forces him to endure an earthly
hell. On two occasions her fiendish role is made explicit. When
Rochester takes Jane to see Grace Poole and her charge after the
abortive wedding he talks of her as 'this young girl, who stands
so grave and quiet at the mouth of hell, looking collectedly at
the gambols of a demon', and when he is thinking of suicide in
the West Indies with his wife two rooms away he says, 'this life
is hell! This is the air – those are the sounds of the bottomless

pit ... of the fanatic's burning eternity I have no fear; there is not a future state worse than this present one – let me break away, and go home to God.'[23] The blood-red moon in this scene reminds us of Jane's morbid fantasies in the Red room, and there can be little doubt that Charlotte Brontë had her doctrine of the earthly hell well worked out.

Pitted against this we have the conventional hell of Mr Brocklehurst and St John Rivers, to which Rochester pays passing reference when he says that for bigamy, as his pastor would tell him, he deserves even 'the quenchless fire and deathless worm', and to which Miss Abbot thinks Jane Eyre will go if she is naughty.[24] With his frightening stories of little children snatched away to eternal punishment after childish peccadilloes Mr Brocklehurst is almost a comic figure. Obviously meant to be a villain because of his connection with the villainous Reeds, he is the victim of some very broad satire against his hypocrisy in denouncing smart clothes and elaborate hair styles when his own family are conspicuous for their finery. Mr Brocklehurst is modelled on a real person,[25] and the satire against him is presumably meant to be serious, but his terrifying stories seem almost as ridiculous as his account of the small boy who says that he prefers a psalm to learn rather than a gingerbread nut to eat, and is rewarded with two gingernuts for his pains.[26]

Unlike this small boy and Mr Brocklehurst, St John Rivers is no hypocrite. He does not spare himself the pains he inflicts on others, and his statement of his own faith is sincere. Though St John Rivers is like Mr Brocklehurst in preaching gloomy doctrines, made even gloomier by Calvinism, and like him too in being compared to a pillar,[27] it takes Jane Eyre longer to find that he is not on the right track. Though she calls his preaching sad, springing from disappointment, she is impressed by his insistence on being a missionary and his claim to be the servant of an infallible master.[28] Even when on her refusal to be his wife he begins to show his Calvinist teeth by talking of her as a brand which might be saved from the burning, but was otherwise not one of the chosen but a castaway,[29] Jane is still tempted to obey him, and it requires the almost supernatural intervention of Rochester's voice to prevent her. Thackeray found St

John Rivers a failure,[30] Mary Taylor did not believe in him,[31] and modern readers can scarcely comprehend him, but Jane Eyre calls him a good and great man,[32] and Charlotte Brontë ends her novel with his heroism.

Moreover the philosophy of St John Rivers is supported in *Shirley* and *Villette*. His gloom and his Calvinism, but not his confidence, affect these books, which do not contain the un-orthodox doctrine of salvation outlined in *Jane Eyre*. Shirley herself, though she can put the curates in their place and is allowed unorthodox views on the place of women, does not pronounce any unorthodox theological views except perhaps in Eva's dream. She is said to be modelled on Emily Brontë, but is not allowed to state her creed very authoritatively. There is in fact little positive preaching in *Shirley*; most of Charlotte's reli-gious message is confined to the negative task of showing the folly of Dissenters and Puseyites. There is also little joy except in the knockabout satire of the first volume. The decline and death of her sisters obviously affected Charlotte deeply, and there are indications in the latter half of *Shirley* of a less con-fident attitude to divine justice. Even in *Jane Eyre* there are times when the heroine seems uncertain on this score, as when her mind makes its first earnest effort to comprehend what had been infused into it concerning heaven and hell and recoils baffled from the unfathomable gulfs of the past and future, or again when banished from her false elysium of married bliss with Rochester at Thornfield she feels the future, 'an awful blank; something like the world when the deluge was gone by'[33] But Jane Eyre wins her way to something like salvation; in spite of the unsatisfactory happy ending in *Shirley* we cannot feel so confident of the salvation of the Moores and their wives, and in any case the doubts beforehand are more pronounced.

In describing Caroline Helstone's temptation to become a Calvinist Charlotte appears to be reverting to the pessimism of the years at Roe Head; a person who was gloomy and melancholy must be a person from whom God has turned his face, one destined for the doom of reprobation. Charlotte then turns from the particular case to general encouragement. 'Yet let whoever grieves still cling fast to love and faith in God: God will never deceive, never finally desert him', and she is again encouraged when thinking of Miss Ainley's life.[34] A little later Charlotte appears to be pondering on Determinism when she makes Caroline say, 'Fate has written it down in to-day's page of her eternal book, that I am not to have the pleasure I long for', and there is a similar discussion of the future which 'sometimes seems to sob a low warning of the events it is bringing us . . . at other times . . . bursts suddenly.'[35] What the future is bringing is Caroline's illness; she recovers after her mother has prayed for her, but Charlotte acknowledges that, 'not always do those who dare such divine conflict prevail'. Sometimes, 'the watcher . . . knows that it is God's will his idol shall be broken, and bends his head, and subdues his soul to the sentence he cannot avert, and scarce can bear.'[36]

In *Jane Eyre* the idol, Mr Rochester, is broken, but only that greater happiness may result. In *Shirley* the happiness of being married to the Moores does not seem very great, and it is not made at all clear that it follows from the suffering experienced by either Caroline or Shirley. In *Villette* there is plenty of suffering, but almost no happiness except for John Bretton and Polly Home, and their happiness is almost made a reproach against them in the same way that the prosperity outlined for Madame Beck and Père Silas confirms their villainy. As Charlotte says in her letters,[37] she had become increasingly aware that suffering does not bring salvation on this earth; it usually brings death. Why then did she not state more vigorously that suffering and self-sacrifice brought salvation in the next world?

The answer must be that she had become increasingly less confident of such salvation as she saw the folly of sects which promised heaven for those who followed a particular rule. The attack on the Roman Catholic church is more definite and more vehement than in *The Professor*, though the vehemence is tempered by enthusiasm for individual Catholics like Paul Emanuel and even, in places, Père Silas. But the church is compared to Moloch and Lucifer,[38] and in addition to the usual charges of falsehood and spying resulting from the confessional and undue formalism in worship, the church is accused of breeding ignorance, abasement and bigotry.[39] Lucy Snowe practises the opposite virtues, trying to find out and tell the truth, refusing to allow circumstances to overcome her and visiting broadmindedly the churches of all three Protestant denominations. But where does this virtue get her? There is no hint of any happy destiny for her, although we do not believe like one of her Catholic pupils that she is destined as a Protestant for *l'enfer*. The only trace of any consistent doctrine of recompense for suffering comes in an ambiguous and negative form.

> In winding up Mistress Fanshawe's memoirs, the reader will no doubt expect to hear that she comes finally to bitter expiation of her youthful levities. Of course, a large share of suffering lies in reserve for her future.[40]

Is this her future life on earth or her future life after death? Lucy Snowe's account of Ginevra's later difficulties, resulting from her unsatisfactory husband, ends with the words, 'and so she got on – fighting the battle of life by proxy and, on the whole, suffering as little as any human being I have ever known'.[41] Thus Ginevra Fanshawe's sufferings would appear to be reserved until after death, but it may be that the sentence about a large share of suffering is a piece of sarcasm like the previous sentence at the reader's expense.

Charlotte thus ends her life with some uncertainty about salvation. Her unwillingness to die, for which the evidence is admittedly not very trustworthy,[42] is very different from the calmness, even eagerness, with which Anne and Emily are usually thought to have met their deaths.[43] Yet Anne at any rate had experienced doubts. The first trace of these is to be found, as with Charlotte, at Roe Head. While Charlotte poured out her worries in letters to Ellen Nussey, Anne took refuge in consultations with a Moravian minister, the Rev. James la Trobe.[44] For the daughter of an Anglican minister to summon help from a dissenter was a remarkable step, the more so as there were plenty of Anglican ministers at hand. Perhaps, like Mr Hatfield in *Agnes Grey*, these were not comforting enough, for Anne sought solace from a sect which laid emphasis on salvation by faith rather than by works. Charlotte, probably because of this reliance on faith, is oddly contemptuous of the

Moravians,[45] whom we know both in general and on this occasion to have treated children kindly.

The Moravian doctrines saw Anne through to her next crisis, and fortified her for it. The history of this crisis is recorded in the key poems, written between 1841 and 1845, *Despondency, to Cowper, A Word to the Elect, Music on Christmas Morn, A Prayer, If This be all* and *Vanitas Vanitatum Omnia Vanitas.*[46] In these years Anne possibly fell in love with Willie Weightman, who,[47] like Miss Branwell, died in 1842; she also endured an unhappy time at Thorp Green where she saw obvious evidence of Branwell's degeneration and had an ample library pointing out in graphic terms the fate of the degenerate. A lonely unhappy existence in this world is a good preparation for meditation about the next world, and the death of a relative and a friend, perhaps a lover, is an added stimulus. It looks however as if it was the disgrace of Branwell, by orthodox standards a candidate for hellfire, which really caused Anne to adopt an unorthodox attitude to salvation. Until 1845 all the poems seem to be saying is that souls are not predestined to be saved or damned, and in the poems of 1841 and 1842 she is as at Roe Head still worried about her salvation. Anne does not seem to have advanced a great deal beyond the position of Cowper, whose vision of himself as a castaway appears to have had a considerable, but not a comforting, influence on all the Brontës.[48]

Willie Weightman may have been both the cause and the cure of Anne's doubts. If she did feel some love for him and was sorry at his death, then by strict Calvinist standards she was doing wrong in listening to the promptings of the flesh and questioning God's purpose. On the other hand the teaching of Willie Weightman in fact and Mr Weston in fiction is strongly opposed to Calvinism, and this may explain the defiant note struck in *A Word to the Elect,* written in May 1843, where it is said that all shall be saved after a requisite period of purgation.

> That even the wicked shall at last
> Be fitted for the skies;
> And when their dreadful doom is past,
> To light and life arise.[49]

In October 1844, Anne is full of doubt again.

> *Unless Thou hasten to relieve,*
> *Thy suppliant is a castaway.*[50]

Possibly by this time Anne was aware of Branwell's degradation at Thorp Green. She was certainly aware of this by the time she wrote her birthday note in 1845 when she says she had, 'had some very unpleasant and undreamt-of experiences of human nature.'[51] Branwell did not leave the Robinsons until July 1845, but in poems of May and June Anne is grieving to look on vice and sin and oppressed with sin and woe.[52] But in the latter poem at any rate she will not despair, and in an undated poem about this period Anne can write,

> *A sinless God, for sinful men,*
> *Descends to suffer and to bleed;*
> *Hell must renounce its empire then;*
> *The price is paid, the world is freed,*
> *And Satan's self must now confess*
> *That Christ has earned a right to bless.*[53]

We see thus in the poems a gradual change in mood between the anxiety of 1841 and the confidence of 1845 on the subject of salvation. Originally Anne had her doubts about her own salvation; soon she began to feel that other far greater sinners might be saved. A similar change can be seen in *Agnes Grey*, if we assume, as seems possible, that this was written over a period of some years.[54] In the early part of the novel there is a straightforward statement by Agnes Grey herself about the place where wicked people go when they die;[55] in the part written later Mr Weston is more hopeful about people who may enter in at the strait gate, and Mr Hatfield's views are by implication condemned.[56] *Agnes Grey* is however surprisingly free from religion in view of the fact that the narrator is the daughter of a clergyman who marries a clergyman; apart from the rather naïve message that good girls like Agnes Grey prosper while bad girls like Rosalie Murray do not, there is little of a specifically religious nature except in the chapters, 'The Church' and 'The Cottagers',

and here, as we have shown, the confused account of Mr Hatfield's religious proclivities does not enable us to form any clear
picture of what Anne is trying to attack.

This is far from being the case in *The Tenant of Wildfell Hall*,
although here apart from slight portraits of the gluttonous Mr
Millward and the studious Richard Wilson there are no clergymen to discuss. References to salvation are, however, numerous,
and Anne's unorthodox views attracted unfavourable comment
in *Sharpes' London Magazine*.[57] The most important passage
occurs in the conversation between Helen and her aunt, where
there are embarrassingly direct references to thirty Biblical
passages which suggest universal salvation and to the meaning
of the Greek word αἰώνιος for which 'long-enduring' is suggested
as an alternative translation in place of 'eternal'. Moreover there
is a hint, reminiscent of Helen Burns, that the deterrent power of
hell is still valuable in the words, 'As for the danger of the belief,
I would not publish it abroad if I thought any poor wretch would
be likely to presume upon it to his own destruction, but it is a
glorious thought to cherish in one's own heart.'[58] The whole
passage is more like a page from a tract than a novel, though
perhaps Anne is fortunate that she is writing a novel; this saves
her from quoting chapter and verse for her thirty Bible references
or Liddell and Scott for her Greek scholarship, since she would
have a difficult case to prove.[59] In any case the whole force of
Helen's theological argument against her aunt is weakened by
the fact that when it comes to an estimate of Arthur Huntingdon's character her aunt is obviously in the right.

The next series of references to perdition come in Huntingdon's description of Lord Lowborough's attempts to save himself
from ruin. Perhaps we should not make too much of this; jovial
references to 'hell broth'[60] are part of Anne's not very convincing attempts to portray a masculine world of oaths and
brutality. The most important passage comes when Lord Lowborough imagines he has found salvation in marriage with
Arabella Wilmot. 'Huntingdon,' he exclaims, 'I am not a castaway.'[61] But, as we know, his wife is an artful minx, who is
later destined to lead Lord Lowborough to the pit of hell.[62]

After Helen has discovered Lady Lowborough's affair with

her husband she is sorely tempted by Mr Hargrave who says that it cannot be offensive to God 'to raise a devoted heart from purgatorial torments to a state of heavenly bliss',[63] and a few pages and years later says that it cannot be the will of God to refrain from doing this. When first appealed to, Helen curtly replies, 'Mr Hargrave, do you mean to insult me?', but after suffering increased neglect she counters with theology rather than standing on her dignity. 'There is another life for you and me. If it be the will of God that we should sow in tears now, it is only that we may reap in joy hereafter.'[64] It is with similar thoughts of God's eventual mercy that Helen comforts herself immediately after she has discovered her husband's adultery. 'In spite of earth and hell I should have strength for all my trials, and win a glorious rest at last.'[65]

When Helen returns to her husband after rejecting Gilbert Markham with the comforting thought that they would meet in heaven, she finds him worried by thoughts of death, and tries to bring him to a proper realisation of the danger of his position. Asking again, rather awkwardly after her conversation with Gilbert, 'Are you determined, Arthur, that I shall not meet you in heaven?' she receives the reply, 'Humph! What should I do there, I should like to know?', and shortly afterwards Huntingdon dismisses hell as a fable.[66] But at the time of Huntingdon's death the positions are reversed. Huntingdon is tormented by thoughts of judgement, and his wife returns to the optimistic position she had earlier adopted in arguing with her aunt.

> Thank God, I have hope – not only from a vague dependence on the possibility that penitence and pardon might have reached him at the last, but from the blessed confidence that, through whatever purging fires the erring spirit may be doomed to pass – whatever fate awaits it – still it is not lost, and God who hateth nothing that He hath made, will bless it in the end![67]

The force of this passage, combined with the original argument about the Biblical evidence for hell, would seem to render invalid the numerous passages in the book which suggest that the good, after various trials, go to heaven, while the wicked go to hell.

'I'm sorry papa's wicked', says little Arthur Huntingdon, 'for I don't want him to go to hell.'[68] Anne may not have realised the apparent contradiction between this point of view and her strenuous plea for universal salvation, or she may have thought that she had covered herself by the references to purging fires in the passages denying eternal punishment. But a belief in purging fires as a fitting punishment is almost as bad as a contradiction, since if Anne really believed that we go through a vale of tears now in order to avoid the torments of purgatory hereafter, she believed a doctrine that makes the virtuous seem selfish and gives the vicious an incentive to sin. As in any doctrine where a heavenly crown may be worn by virtuous self-restraint, there is a temptation to regard those aspiring to a heavenly crown as practising a form of selfishness only slightly more refined than that practised by those who restrain their lusts on earth for a little time in order to enjoy them more fully later. If one is like Huntingdon and does not restrain oneself, then one may be punished later but, as this punishment is not eternal and only hypothetical, it may seem worth the risk.

To escape from this danger we can imagine somebody working out a doctrine like that suggested in *Jane Eyre*, whereby men are virtuous, not to save their own souls but to save the souls of the wicked. This theory deals with the objection of selfishness, and keeps the deterrent power of purgatory, since the wicked will be released from their torture only if enough people are virtuous. It also removes the injustice of condemning people to hell who are only marginally more wicked than those who get to heaven, since the mildly wicked will be saved by the mildly virtuous, while the very wicked will have to wait longer for the very virtuous to save them. In addition the doctrine is a natural extension of the doctrine of Redemption, much favoured by Mr Brontë, and it provides some rationale for the Last Judgement, normally it would seem an unnecessary refinement on the part of the Almighty, who has already judged most people on their deathbeds. If we follow this doctrine however the Last Judgement does serve a purpose, since it refers to the time when sufficient virtue had been accumulated to make further judgement unnecessary.

In the light of this doctrine the apparent contradictions in
The Tenant of Wildfell Hall disappear. The sufferings of Helen
Huntingdon, of Lord Lowborough, sufferings made worse by his
apparent salvation, and even of Mr Hargrave, are all necessary
to save Huntingdon's soul. Huntingdon himself suffers, but not
sufficiently to earn salvation straightaway. The conventional
happy ending with wedding bells for Helen Huntingdon and
Gilbert Markham and, for that matter, for Frederick Lawrence
and Esther Hargrave, is not important in itself; indeed it would
be a weakness of the novel if it were so, since it appears to be
largely a matter of chance that the novel does not end with
Helen still tied to her husband while her lover is in gaol for the
murder of her brother. The happy ending is important in that
it reflects the heavenly crown that the good characters were soon
to enjoy and that by their privations they had won even for the
bad. Additional confirmation for this interpretation of *The
Tenant of Wildfell Hall* is to be found in the close connection
between Emily and Anne Brontë. Almost all the first-hand
biographical information we have about them shows them working together.[69] Acton and Ellis Bell were naturally confused, and
perhaps in reaction to this some have been at pains to stress the
differences between *The Tenant of Wildfell Hall* and *Wuthering
Heights*. But there are also obvious resemblances, such as the
similarity in initials of the houses and the main characters, the
arrival of a new tenant at the beginning of each book, the
gambling, drinking and swearing so surprising in books written
by a clergyman's daughters, and perhaps the most important
resemblance from the formal point of view, the double switch
of narrators. These similarities, far greater than any suggested
by a comparison of *Jane Eyre* and *Wuthering Heights*, have been
noted,[70] but less attention has been paid to the close resemblance
of theme, which is also similar to that of *Jane Eyre*. The violence
of language and behaviour in the centre of both novels is perhaps a little overdone, but it reflects the unhappiness of the
characters, as they work their way to the quiet elegiac ending of
Wuthering Heights and the joyful conclusion of *The Tenant of
Wildfell Hall*. In both novels there are frequent references to
heaven and hell to act as pointers to the theme that through

suffering hell on this earth we remove hell's power over the world.

The clearest statement of this theme comes in an essay written by Emily Brontë for M. Heger on *The Butterfly*.

> *God is the God of justice and mercy; then, assuredly, each pain that he inflicts on his creatures, be they human or animal, rational or irrational, each suffering of our unhappy nature is only a seed for that divine harvest which will be gathered when sin having spent its last drop of poison, death having thrown its last dart, both will expire on the funeral pyre of a universe in flame, and will leave their former victims to an eternal realm of happiness and glory.*[71]

For other evidence of Emily's religious position apart from *Wuthering Heights* there are only the poems to consult, since the one piece of biographical information on this subject is singularly unhelpful. In the words of Charlotte,

> *One time I mentioned that someone had asked me what religion I was of (with a view to getting me for a partisan), and that I had said that was between God and me. Emily (who was lying on the hearthrug) exclaimed, 'That's right'.*[72] *This was all I ever heard Emily say on religious subjects.*

Even the poems have been discounted as evidence by the thesis of Miss Ratchford that they are all part of an immense Gondal Saga. This thesis is difficult to uphold since so many of the poems cannot be fitted into the saga, and there are also inconsistent pieces of evidence such as Emily's annoyance at the discovery of her poems and her division of her poems into two notebooks, only one of which was entitled *Gondal poems*.[73] In any case we could not ignore the subjective element in the poems, even if they were all part of an immense Gondal saga.

In fact the Gondal element can be used to explain contradictions that do appear in the poems, since it is obvious that not all characters will hold the same theological views. The poems are also written over a period of ten years,[74] during which it would be only natural for the author to modify her views. In spite of these two reservations there is in the poems a considerable body of evidence to support the view that Emily held the following consistent and connecting set of axioms: (1) Hell exists only on earth, and no souls suffer torment after death. (2) A soul that has suffered sufficiently on earth attains its heaven. (3) A soul that has not suffered is in limbo for a time, but is redeemed by others' sufferings if not by its own, after enduring the *poena damni*, deprivation of the desired heaven.

In poems written before 1840 there are plenty of references to stoical suffering,[75] a childhood heaven similar to that described in *Wuthering Heights*,[76] and a general sympathy with sinners.

> *Do I despise the timid deer*
> *Because his limbs are fleet with fear?*
> *Or would I mock the wolf's death-howl*
> *Because his form is gaunt and foul?*
> *Or hear with joy the leveret's cry*
> *Because it cannot bravely die?*[77]

There are also traces of a rather Wagnerian doctrine of redemption, not through suffering, but through love. Such a doctrine does draw attention to a difficulty of orthodox believers in hell. If one was virtuous and loved someone who was not, then after death, not only did the wicked suffer the hell, but the righteous suffered in heaven deprived of the presence of the loved one and tortured by thoughts of his torture. The problem may seem an artificial one, relying as it does on a rather literal view of the after-life. But it was not thought artificial in the nineteenth century, finding expression in poems like *Festus* and *The Blessed Damozel*.[78] Emily Brontë saw the problem and was to find a solution to it, although not perhaps in this early period, in which the poems contain plenty of references to heaven and hell but no very convincing exposition of the three axioms and some contradictions of them.

> *Shut from his Maker's smile*
> *The accursed man shall be:*
> *Compasion reigns a little while,*
> *Revenge eternally.*[79]

In the next four years Emily wrote poems that did much to clear

away the cobwebs of a conventional heaven and hell. Eternal
punishment is clearly rejected,

> No that I *feel can never be;*
> *A God of hate could hardly bear*
> *To watch through all eternity*
> *His own creation's dread despair!* . . . ,[80]

and suffering brings salvation,

> *If I have sinned, long, long ago*
> *That sin was purified by woe.*[81]

The first two axioms are also supported in other poems,[82] but
the third is only hinted at in the idea of atonement,

> *There let thy bleeding branch atone*
> *For every torturing tear* . . .[83]

and the idea that the souls of the wicked do have some hope
from the help of the good,

> *And in all space, and in all time,*
> *And through Eternity,*
> *To aid a Spirit lost in crime,*
> *I have no hope but thee.*[84]

On the other hand the latter passage comes from a poem which
contains lines like,

> *The guiltless blood upon my hands*
> *Will shut me out from Heaven* . . . ,[85]

which appear to re-assert the orthodox beliefs, and it is very
difficult to formulate a coherent philosophy from poems of
which the interpretation is so obscure.

In the last period of her life from 1844 onwards, Emily
Brontë worked her way towards a clear picture of how heaven
was won and what it was like, as she herself worked her own
grim way to salvation. It is harder to find contradiction of the
axioms, and there is an abundance of references to support

them. The lines,

> No promised Heaven, these wild Desires
> Could all or half fulfil;
> No threatened Hell, with quenchless fires,
> Subdue this quenchless will! . . .,[86]

suggest a rejection of the conventional heaven and hell; indeed conventional religion is condemned in,

> Vain are the thousand creeds
> That move men's hearts, unutterably vain
> Worthless as withered weeds,
> Or idlest froth amid the boundless main.[87]

It is also satisfying to find the sinful A.G.A. apparently winning a quiet grave. The intensely moving lines,

> I would lose no sting, would wish no torture less;
> The more that anguish racks the earlier it will bless;
> And robed in fires of Hell, or bright with heavenly shine,
> If it but herald Death, the vision is divine . . .,[88]

contain a clear statement of the second axiom.

What is less certain is the third axiom. This is a pity, because without it the doctrine is sinisterly masochistic. The more we suffer in this world, the quicker we get what we want in the next, Emily may have reflected as she tottered down to feed the animals on the day of her death, but such an attitude is selfish and short-sighted if it leads, as it did in Heathcliff's case, to the misery of others. There are traces of asceticism in Emily's life and lines like,

> So stood I, in Heaven's glorious sun
> And in the glare of Hell
> My spirit drank a mingled tone
> Of seraph's song and demon's moan . . .,[89]

and the doctrine, found in the essay on *The Butterfly*, that we do not and should not suffer for our own salvation but for the sake of others, sometimes finds it hard to make its way against this *Schadenfreude*. The doctrine is best suggested in the lines,

> Yet thou a future peace shall win
> Because thy soul is clear;
> And I who had the heart to sin
> Will find a heart to bear.
> Till far beyond earth's frenzied strife
> That makes destruction joy,
> Thy perished faith shall spring to life
> And my remorse shall die.[90]

The words,

> Strike it down, that other boughs may flourish
> Where that perished sapling used to be . . . ,[91]

give the necessary idea of sacrifice, though much of the sacrifice and despair of the poems seems purposeless, just as much of the grimness and the brutality of Wuthering Heights seem to have no message of hope.

The composition of Wuthering Heights is usually dated to the last period of Emily's life, although this is not certain.[92] The novel gives a fairly definite, though cryptic, account of salvation won by suffering; there are references to more orthodox heavens and hells, but these are by implication criticised. The only satisfactory guide to Emily's beliefs in Wuthering Heights is an analysis of all references to heaven and hell; we can eliminate merely the conventional uses of heaven as a synonym for God, hell for death, and both heaven and hell in oaths. Even these conventional uses are perhaps indicative of the way in which Emily Brontë's mind was concerned with salvation.

Of greater significance than these conventional uses are the passages where Emily Brontë uses these words and their synonyms as images to refer to earthly joy and discontent. Thus Lockwood greets with delight 'a perfect misanthropist's heaven', Hindley sits with Frances in his 'paradise on the hearth', while Joseph finds his elysium sitting 'alone, beside a roaring fire; a quart of ale on the table near him, bristling with large pieces of toasted oatcake; and his black short pipe in his mouth'.[93] Emily does not pass moral judgement on her characters, being usually reckoned to be above morality, but it is difficult to escape the conclusion that she thought, as we think, Lockwood, Hindley and Joseph characters of extraordinary selfishness, especially on the occasions in which their elysium is being described. It looks as if by enjoying the pleasures of this world they are missing the full joys of heaven which they would have obtained had they been prepared to endure a little suffering. There is more to heaven than toasted oatcakes.

That heaven can be different for different people is made abundantly clear in the passage where Linton and Cathy compare their differing ideas of the pleasantest way of spending a hot July day.

> He wanted all to lie in an ecstasy of peace; I wanted all to sparkle and dance in a glorious jubilee. I said his heaven would be only half alive; and he said mine would be drunk: I said I should fall asleep in his; and he said he could not breathe in mine.[94]

This discussion is used principally to show that Linton and Cathy are unsuited to each other in this world, but it does raise interesting questions about Linton's future fate. Lacking the heroic qualities of his father without any redeeming conventional virtues,[95] Linton might seem an unlikely candidate for salvation; yet this passage suggests he has a vision and a hope of heaven. On the other hand it is a heaven which Cathy is right to call half alive, and since it involves lying on a bank of heath with the larks singing high up overhead it does look suspiciously like Socinian annihilation.

A third passage where heaven is used principally as an image of earthly happiness, but with undertones of real heaven, comes when Heathcliff and Catherine see Isabella and Edgar quarrelling over a dog, alone in Thrushcross Grange, and say that they would have thought themselves in heaven in such a situation.[96] This passage is indicative of Catherine's and Heathcliff's idea of an earthly heaven, the paradise of childhood innocence, to which there are many references in the poems. But it is Catherine rather than Heathcliff who says that she imagines the pampered existence in Thrushcross Grange to be heavenly, and this warns us of Catherine's future marriage to Edgar Linton, a marriage which is as wrong for Catherine as the heaven of which she dreamt and which did not seem to be her home. This reference to heaven and others made by Catherine and Heathcliff must be reserved for later discussion, as they are not to be taken as images, but taken literally as referring to a better world beyond this one.

With hell the distinction between the image use and the literal use is less easy to make, as if we do believe that Emily thought hell was on earth, any reference to earthly suffering as hellish can be taken literally. Perhaps we could say that Heathcliff was not really in hell until Catherine's death. When he says that he will be in hell until Nelly has carried his message to Catherine[97] he is speaking figuratively, as he is also when he says that Catherine is in hell isolated from him.[98] These passages are different from the one where he says, 'Two words would comprehend my future – *death* and *hell*: existence after losing her would be hell.'[99] Or again a key passage for showing the earthly hell of Heathcliff and the purgatory suffered by Catherine as a ghost is this:

> 'Is it not sufficient for your infernal selfishness that while you are at peace I shall writhe in the torments of hell?' 'I shall not be at peace,' moaned Catherine ... 'I'm not wishing you greater torment than I have, Heathcliff. I only wish us never to be parted: and should a word of mine distress you hereafter, think I feel the same distress underground, and for my own sake, forgive me.'[100]

Catherine suffers as she would suffer in an orthodox hell or purgatory, but, since her life was so clearly connected with Heathcliff's, she would have suffered just as much in an orthodox heaven. In fact Catherine appears to suffer in a kind of ghostly limbo from which she tries to gain access through Lockwood's window to the real world. Ghosts seem to have no very clear defined place in an orthodox theological framework, their sufferings being neither substantial nor severe enough for hell, and their restlessness not making them very good candidates for heaven. But Catherine's ghost shows the way in which salvation is won by suffering. Catherine is not the only person to suffer. Heathcliff prays that Catherine may wake in torment to haunt him as long as he is living. His prayer is granted. 'She showed herself, as she often was in life, a devil to me. And, since then, sometimes more and sometimes less, I've been the sport of that intolerable torture!'[101] This is the earthly hell in which Emily Brontë believes, but it leads to heaven. 'Last night I was on the threshold of hell. To-day, I am within sight of my heaven.'[102]

Before coming on to the mystical heaven of Catherine and Heathcliff it is necessary to eliminate the views on heaven and hell of Joseph and Nelly Dean. We need not quote extensively to show the views of Joseph who condemns even Nelly Dean to perdition for her attempts to show a little life. Joseph is a Calvinist, although his belief in predestination is not important, and indeed is only once mentioned by him. 'All warks togither for gooid to them as is chozzen, and piked out fro'th' rubbidge.'[103] The important thing for Joseph is that many were damned and few were saved. Such a view is explicitly condemned in the poems, and Nelly Dean criticises Joseph for his pharisaical outlook. And yet, though she rejected eternal damnation, we feel a certain affinity between Emily and Joseph; both seem to believe that gloom is good for the soul, and there are traces of determinism in Emily's outlook.

Indeed it is a feature of Emily Brontë's art and her morality that she extends the net of her sympathy so widely. In concentrating on the heroic struggles of Heathcliff we should not lose sight of the more elegiac pathos of Edgar or the robust common sense of Nelly Dean. Nelly Dean, however, though more of an amiable character than Joseph, does not, as far as theology is concerned, have as much affinity with Emily Brontë. She may be held to represent the orthodox Anglican attitude in the same way that Joseph represents the outlook of the extreme Dissenter.[104] We learn a great deal about her conventional morality, but not a great deal about her theology. She urges Heathcliff to read a Bible before his death, and says that it is God's job to punish sinners, but we do not obtain any information about her idea of hell. Conventional Christians are rarely clear on this point, especially if they belong to the school of thought which emphasises the tranquillity of heaven.

I don't know if it be a peculiarity in me, but I am seldom otherwise than happy while watching in the chamber of death, should no frenzied or despairing mourner share the duty with me. I see a repose that neither earth nor hell can break, and I feel an assurance of the endless and shadowless hereafter — the Eternity they have entered — where life is boundless in its duration, and love in its sympathy, and joy in its fulness.[105]

Nelly shares Emily's views about the importance of heaven, but is wrong in thinking Catherine has attained it. Her conventional morality is shown throughout the book to be a series of half truths, although in this particular passage she seems more full of doubt than usual. She is interesting in making frequent comparisons between Heathcliff and the devil. Sometimes the references to Heathcliff's diabolical nature and fiendish appearance are merely figurative but, as we have seen before in the case of hell, it is difficult to distinguish image from reality. Sometimes, moreover, Nelly expressly drops the image, as when she says, 'and, truly, it appeared as if the lad *were* possessed of something diabolical at that period'.[106] Other characters apart from Heathcliff are described as being possessed by a devil, but it is Heathcliff who is generally compared with the devil. Cathy makes the most appropriate comparison when she says, 'You *are* miserable, are you not? Lonely, like the devil, and envious like him? *Nobody* loves you – *nobody* will cry for you when you die! I wouldn't be you!'[107] Orthodox Christians have often been worried by the exact status of the devil. Is he an independent monarch, God's viceroy in hell, or a prisoner suffering the most damnable tortures, merely consoling himself by finding fellow-sufferers? Like Marlowe's Mephistophilis, Emily Brontë seems to favour the devil's being the chief prisoner and like Marlowe too she places hell on earth.

> *Within the bowels of these elements,*
> *Where we are tortured and remain for ever.*
> *Hell hath no limits, nor is circumscribed*
> *In one self place, but where we are is hell,*
> *And where hell is, there must we ever be:*

And to be short, when all the world dissolves
And every creature shall be purified,
All places shall be hell that are not heaven.[108]

And so to heaven, to which the references in Wuthering Heights
are few but important. Firstly we have the passage where Nelly
Dean comments on the behaviour of Heathcliff and Catherine
after Mr Earnshaw's death.

> The little souls were comforting each other with better
> thoughts than I could have hit on: no parson in the world
> ever pictured heaven so beautifully as they did, in their inno-
> cent talk; and while I sobbed and listened, I could not help
> wishing we were all there safe together.[109]

This is further evidence, if we need it, of Nelly's conventional
piety, but it also suggests a childhood heaven to which we find
other references in the poems. The asexual nature of Heathcliff's
and Catherine's love is another link with the childhood heaven.[110]
A more revealing passage comes when Catherine dreams that
she has been in heaven and disliked it.

> I was only going to say that heaven did not seem to be my
> home; and I broke my heart with weeping to come back to
> earth; and the angels were so angry that they flung me out in
> the middle of the heath on the top of Wuthering Heights;
> where I woke sobbing for joy ... I've no more business to
> marry Edgar Linton than I have to be in heaven.[111]

Catherine neither desires nor deserves heaven, and, if we take
the reference to her ghost literally, she does not obtain it for
some time. Does she obtain it with Heathcliff in the end? This is
not clearly stated. We get what in Lockwood's eyes are contradictory thoughts on the subject, the notion that Catherine and
Heathcliff are to be seen walking, and his own view that no one
could imagine unquiet slumbers in that quiet earth.[112] Lockwood's conventional ideas of contradiction are not to be taken
seriously. For Catherine and Heathcliff to be united would be
heaven, even if were not a tranquil heaven.

There is one further negative piece of evidence to support the thesis that suffering brings salvation. Suicide is twice mentioned in the book. Catherine, with typical selfishness, talks of killing herself to spite Edgar,[113] and Heathcliff, when he comes back after his absence, says that he intended to kill himself after killing Hindley and catching a glimpse of Catherine.[114] After the death of Catherine, Heathcliff does not raise the subject; it could be argued that Heathcliff does, like Emily Brontë, virtually kill himself through neglect, but he does not do this for some time. If heaven was to be with Catherine, why did he not make haste to join her? Pride may have detained him, zeal for revenge may have added strength to his resolve, but he had achieved his revenge and soothed his pride before the book begins, and yet lives on. Heaven was not so easy for him to gain, either for himself or for Catherine.

It so happens that in *Wuthering Heights* we begin with Cathy and Hareton in the depths of misery and end with them living in comparative happiness; in between we have the story of Heathcliff's protracted agony. Their happiness, however, is only a pale shadow of the happiness in heaven of Heathcliff and Catherine, the main characters of the book. In *Jane Eyre* and *The Tenant of Wildfell Hall* it is the main characters who win earthly happiness after much suffering, and thus the message that earthly tribulation brings heavenly salvation for others as well as for oneself is blurred, although Arthur Huntingdon and St John Rivers in their different ways suggest the message. There are other differences between the three books. Anne and Charlotte still have hankerings after the conventional heaven and hell, in which characters like Helen Huntingdon's aunt and St John Rivers, who are not all that wrong-headed, believe. Against this we have the theology of Joseph who believes that all songs are the signs of the devil, of Nelly Dean who believes that Edgar Linton is an ideal specimen of manhood, and of Mr Lockwood who thinks that young Cathy is married to Heathcliff and that a pile of dead rabbits constitute her pets. In *The Tenant of Wildfell Hall* and *Jane Eyre* it is easy to make a conventional division of good and bad characters; this is impossible in *Wuthering Heights*, as can be seen from an examination of the articles making heroes and villains out of the most unlikely people;[115] *Wuthering Heights* has the sincerity of original thought, while *The Tenant of Wildfell Hall* and to a lesser extent *Jane Eyre* are derivative. Anne's and Charlotte's theological teaching is not integrated into the body of the novel, and the shift from the novelist to the preacher is obvious; with Emily there is no such shift, and, though the whole novel seems full of the doctrine of salvation through suffering, the existence of this doctrine has escaped many readers.

We shall find these same differences between the three sisters in spheres other than the theological. In the case of Anne Brontë it is easy to extract the theological, sexual and social doctrines, and to comment on them separately; contemporary reviewers did this, and though we may not agree with the unfavourable comments on the unorthodoxy of the doctrines, it is not unfair to consider her novels in this way, because they have so little else to offer. Charlottes views are a little more difficult to disentangle because she appears to have made some effort to modify them in the light of contemporary opinion which she was so much more successful than her sisters in satisfying. Nor is it wholly fair to Charlotte Brontë to consider her novels merely by an objective appraisal of the views expressed in them. To do so is to leave out of account the force of what Matthew Arnold, a perceptive though hostile critic, has called the 'hunger, rebellion and rage',[116] which raises Charlotte Brontë out of the ruck of English novelists. Yet we can ascribe definite views to Charlotte and comment on the coherence and confidence with which these views are expressed. But, although we have shown Emily Brontë to be more bold and more consistent than her sisters in her theological teaching, it still seems almost insulting to her novel to dissect it in such a way that we only consider it from one point of view. As Matthew Arnold, an early admirer of Emily,[117] said of Shakespeare, 'Others abide our question; thou art free.'[118] Or again, as Virginia Woolf fittingly, if despairingly, summed up *Wuthering Heights*,

That gigantic ambition is to be felt throughout the novel – a struggle half thwarted but of superb conviction, to say some-

thing through the mouths of her characters which is not
merely 'I love' or 'I hate', but 'we, the whole human race'
and 'you, the eternal powers...' the sentence remains
unfinished.[119]

5

Prudes and Prudery

A MID-TWENTIETH-CENTURY critic translated into a mid-nineteenth-century discussion of hell would find himself baffled by what he would regard as the unreality of the discussion and angered by the cruelty of some of the sentiments expressed. But his feelings would be as nothing when compared to the reactions of a nineteenth-century critic to the treatment of sex in the twentieth-century novel. There is thus an even more marked lack of sympathy between the two centuries on the subject of sex than on the subject of hell. Most Brontë biographers have been dimly aware that the Brontës' treatment of sexual matters was considered unusual at the time they wrote but, unwilling to find fault with their heroines and unable to find any reason for faulting them on this score, they have contented themselves by listing a few hostile reviews of the novels, such as the famous review by Miss Rigby in the *Quarterly*, and expressing their disapproval of such criticisms.

The subject of prudery is a complex one, partly because prudes are confused people; public opinion changes rapidly in the space of a few years, and one's public voice rarely expresses one's private opinion. In view of these complexities, one could scarcely expect a satisfactory account of the subject from the average Brontë biographer or critic, but it so happens that we have in *Novels of the 1840s* by Professor Kathleen Tillotson what appears to be the definitive verdict on prudery and the Brontës.[1] She argues that the decade in which all the Brontë novels apart from *Villette* were written was more free than either the twenties or the sixties from the restrictions of what is misleadingly called Victorian prudery. Professor Tillotson per-

forms a valuable service both in drawing attention to the existence of prudery in the time of the Regency,[2] and in destroying
the popular idea that the force of prudery remained unchanged
throughout Victoria's reign.[3] But in citing the Brontës as
examples of the unprudish '40s Professor Tillotson is wrong;
they were not typical of their decade, but as a result of their isolation from contemporary influences should be regarded as a kind
of throwback to an earlier and freer generation. Nor was the
reception of their works as favourable as is sometimes made out;
Miss Rigby was very far from being the exception that proves
the rule. Befor considering the isolation of the Brontës and the
reaction of their critics it is necessary to examine some of the
confusions that have prevented a satisfactory analysis of this
important factor in Victorian literature.[4]

It is of course inevitable that we should make generalisations
from particular instances of prudery at work. Books that became
causes célèbres like Byron's *Don Juan* or Mrs Gaskell's *Ruth* or
Swinburne's *Poems and Ballads* are bound to loom large in the
history of prudery, and because the '40s lack such a *cause célèbre*
it might appear that they were free from prudery. In fact the
outcry against French novels, dubbed by the *Quarterly Review* in
1836 as 'that mass of profligacy', and by Brimley in 1855 as
'the literature of prostitution',[5] is evidence that prudery was
permanently active during this period but, because French novels
exist only on the periphery of English literature, this evidence is
regarded as less important than the more transitory hostility to
a single book.[6]

More impressive than generalisations from isolated cases of
prudery are generalisations from references which indicate a
definite trend in the increase or decrease of prudery. Professor
Tillotson draws support from the statement in 1860 of Trollope
to Thackeray that novelists of previous decades had failed to live
up to the standard Thackeray was setting in rejecting *Mrs
General Talboys*. But we must allow for some element of special
pleading before conceding that Trollope was noting a change in
manners rather than defending his story. There is a record of a
a change in manners in the opposite direction to be found in an
article on 'Recent Novels' in *Blackwood's* for September 1867.

The article says that from the days of Sir Walter Scott the English novelist had kept prose fiction 'pure from all noxious topics', but since Jane Eyre had made her protest 'against the conventionalities in which the world clothes itself' the novel had been in a seriously tainted condition. This writer is Mrs Oliphant,[7] and it is some support for Professor Tillotson that she seems more prudish than Charlotte Brontë, but in every other way this article contradicts the thesis that prudery was more active in 1867 than 1847.

Finally Professor Tillotson makes great play with the remarks of Thackeray and Dickens in the '40s and later. Here again it can be shown that the statements and actions of almost every Victorian novelist are so inconsistent with each other that it is almost impossible to trace any pattern in them. Thackeray's record as a denouncer of prudery is particularly unconvincing, since quite apart from his later activities as editor of *The Cornhill* we find him in *The Paris Sketch Book* (1840) and various essays in *Punch* (1849) adopting a frankly Podsnappish attitude to French morality.[8] With other writers there may seem a tendency to record or take a more prudish attitude in the latter half of the century, but there are three factors, only incidentally connected with chronology, to explain this. In the first place we naturally associate prudery with middle age or old age, and an attack on prudery with youth. Thus Matthew Arnold, the young admirer of George Sand, could turn into the denouncer of the great goddess Aselgeia.[9] Secondly authors, although they may have fought against Mrs Grundy when writing their own books, were less sympathetic to the struggles of others when called upon to do this as editors or advisers to editors. Thus Mrs Gaskell's *Ruth* met with an outraged reception, but she herself saw nothing wrong with it; she did however find serious errors in the coarseness of what is seemingly a more innocent novel, *The Professor*.[10] George Meredith's difficulties with Mudies and Geraldine Jewsbury's experiences with her first novel *Zoe*, in which the heroine was insufficiently clothed, did not prevent them from making harsh comments on the novels of Rhoda Broughton, Mrs Henry Wood and Ouida.[11] Finally, the growth of serial publication in periodicals led to an increasing worry about the cheek of the young person, since periodicals were more easy to obtain than books, and less easy to lock away.

So much for generalisations from actual examples of prudery. Even more dangerous are generalisations from the absence of such examples. The fact that the *Quarterly Review* reviewed no novels between *Jane Eyre* in 1848 and *The Newcomes* in 1855 should make us cautious about leaping to conclusions after noting the absence of reviews hostile to coarseness.[12] The novel was only gradually attaining respectability in the 1840s,[13] and some novels were still beneath contempt. Secondly the absence of prudish reviewers and publishers in the '40s would suggest, not that the age was an outspoken one, but that it was a cautious one. Prudery and pruriency have always gone hand in hand, with the Restoration producing Jeremy Collier and our own permissive age boasting Mrs Whitehouse; the absence of any comparable figure in the 1840s would seem to indicate that it was an age in which people were not prepared to say shocking things rather than an age in which people were not easily shocked. A third form of confusion arises from a failure to compare like with like. Works like Theodore Hook's *Fathers and Sons* may seem good evidence for the broadmindedness of the 1840s, compared with the prudery of the earlier era in which Bowdler and the even more ridiculous Reverend James Plumptre flourished, or the later era in which Hardy was forced to introduce a wheelbarrow in order that Angel Clare might carry the milkmaids with propriety. But it is evident that neither Bowdler nor Plumptre are representative figures of the age of Byron and the Prince Regent, as Professor Tillotson perhaps admits when she says that Theodore Hook was a survival from the coarser period of the Regency. She also acknowledges that Froude's *Shadows of the Clouds* was too difficult a book for light reading, and it is a little unfair to compare either it or the masculine *Fathers and Sons* with the books likely to be read by the young persons whose blushes the Podsnaps of the '60s were so anxious to spare. When it comes to light novels of the '40s involving risky situations, Professor Tillotson is obliged to admit that Geraldine Jewsbury and Eliza Lynn met with difficulties.

Shadows of the Clouds consists of two stories, of which the

first and longer, *The Spirit's Trials*, is a story of exemplary
propriety about a man meeting a former love, now married to
another, on his deathbed. The narrator thinks the situation
fraught with danger, but all is well, since with his dying breath
the hero joins husband and wife together with a moving speech,
beginning 'Emma, if your heart has ever lingered upon me with
a thought which should have been his'. The second story, *The
Lieutenant's Daughter*, is more sensational in that it does describe a girl's ruin fairly graphically. On the other hand it is hard
to get excited about a story which opens, 'I have often been
haunted by Hooker's definition of time', and continues with
thirteen pages of philosophical disquisition. If we are looking for
late survivals of the masculine Regency coarseness Surtees,
whose *Mr Sponge's Sporting Tour*, published in 1851, contains
a joke about strumpets, is perhaps the best example. On the
whole a comic treatment of sex was rare in Victoria's reign. A
joke like that in *Nicholas Nickleby* about a maternal aunt being
really a maternal parent is not to be found in Dickens's later
works.

Similarly we must avoid confusion between fact and fiction.
The sixty-page *Westminster Review* article on prostitution in
1850 was too weighty for family reading, and might be excused.
It would seem in fact that there were more such articles after
1850 than before[14] but, provided that they do not reach unpalatable conclusions,[15] factual accounts of sexual matters have always
been treated more sympathetically by prudes than fictional
accounts. This is understandable; factual accounts are less attractive, especially to the young and ill-educated, and there is more
excuse for stating unsavoury truths than inventing unsavoury
situations. It is perhaps not wholly frivolous to note that the
brother of Miss Rigby, who attacked the Brontës for their coarseness, wrote several textbooks on obstetrics.

The Brontës' novels might seem to be better candidates for the
role of risky novels which passed unscathed. They did of course
meet with hostile criticism, and in the case of Anne and Emily
Brontë there was little favourable criticism to balance this, but
Professor Tillotson points out that the criticism in the *Quarterly*
against *Jane Eyre* was directed against its unchristian jacobinical

sentiments, and that accusations of coarse language referred to
the bluntness of Yorkshire speech rather than improper expressions. Here we touch upon another source of confusion. All
prudes have difficulty in expressing the nature of that which
they find distasteful. The *Quarterly Review's* article on French
novels in 1836 expresses doubt about how it can manage 'even
the most cautious sketch of such a mass of impurities so as to
render it tolerable to an English eye'.[16] There seems some doubt
in this review whether it is atheism, jacobinism, sensationalism
or sexual immorality that is the main enemy. To accuse a work
of using coarse language may mean that it uses oaths, refers to
scenes of low life, calls a spade a spade, or even, as in the first
chapter of *Shirley* which so disgusted Charles Kingsley, uses
Biblical language out of context. This ambiguity weakens the
case for saying that the 1840s were free from prudery. The
reviews hostile to the Brontës may refer to other faults than
sexual impropriety, but they can always be interpreted as hinting at this vice. Likewise some later examples of prudery, which
might appear to have a purely sexual meaning, could have a
wider reference, and cannot be used as evidence of excessive delicacy in sexual matters. Mr Podsnap and Mrs General in
particular would seem to be more concerned with disasters in
general than sexual misdemeanours.

Even in a purely sexual sphere there is an ambiguity.
Byron's *Don Juan* was attacked not because of its language which
is always decorous, but because it treated Juan's escapades as
objects of affectionate amusement rather than shocked reproach.
Vizetelly's translation of Zola's *La Terre*, which describes with
appropriate anatomical detail the mating of a cow and a bull,
was condemned not because of its morals, but because of its improper language. These two cases are clear cut but, since prudery
can extend improper morals to cover any description of sexual
irregularity that does not include an explicit condemnation of
this irregularity and, since it can extend improper language to
include any circumlocution that even hints at the naked truth,
it is not always clear whether it is language or morality that is
being attacked. There are two good examples in the '30s of this
exaggerated prudery. Dickens was attacked by the *Quarterly*

Review for approaching the French novelists in *Oliver Twist*; one of his crimes was to portray Nancy without an appropriate denunciation of her state.[17] Leigh Hunt was not allowed to publish a poem with the seemingly innocent title of *The Three Knights and the Smock*.[18] In the circumstances it is scarcely surprising that *Jane Eyre* met with some opposition; it is not however altogether clear whether Rochester's frankness about his mistresses or the sympathy he provokes in spite of his mistresses is the main object of attack.

One final source of confusion is to be found in the different standards allowed to men and women both as characters in fiction and as authors. We tend to remember Anne and Charlotte Brontë vigorously asserting that it did not matter whether Acton and Currer Bell were men or women, and to forget their critics who said that the Brontë novels were disgraceful if written by a woman.[19] But such criticisms show that it is clearly unwise to compare the reputation of a book when the sex of the author was unknown with its reputation when it was known to be by a woman. And yet this is what we do if we build a case for showing that the 1840s were not prudish on the difference between the contemporary reaction to *Jane Eyre* and *Mary Barton* and later shocked reactions. As G. H. Lewes said to Blackwood in connection with the preservation of George Eliot's pseudonym, Jane Eyre had suffered when it was known she was a woman.[20]

Nor of course should the Brontë sisters be compared to the country parson's daughters of whom Leslie Stephen told Thomas Hardy to beware when writing *The Hand of Ethelberta*.[21] The Brontë sisters cannot be regarded as typical representatives of a parsonage upbringing in the middle of the nineteenth century and we cannot regard their reading habits as typical of their age. Trollope, born one year before Charlotte Brontë, said that unrestricted reading was exceptional in his childhood, though common by the time he wrote his autobiography in the seventies.[22] Trollope's upbringing was so extraordinary and so lonely that we cannot regard him as a very good authority on the reading habits of the first part of the century, but he does serve to draw attention to the exceptional nature of the Brontës' reading habits. Had the Brontës been typical representatives of their generation their story would have seemed less remarkable and their stories would have seemed less shocking. Unlike their contemporaries however they read widely, but through poverty and isolation their reading of recent novels was restricted, and they derived more inspiration from the fiction of the previous generation, of which contemporary taste disapproved.

6

The Brontës and their Books

A CONSIDERABLE amount of work has gone into tracing literary influences on the Brontës.[1] Inevitably much of this work is conjectural; a fancied parallel between some aspect of the Brontës' work and some other work of English literature may be coincidental or indirect. The Brontës could use the same image as Shakespeare and the same episode as Scott without conscious or unconscious plagiarism, and, if they could draw on the work of previous generations, so could other less well-known authors who may have been the direct source of the Brontës' inspiration.

Of course Scott and Shakespeare, together with the Bible, are the most obvious sources for the Brontës to draw upon. Not only does the multiplicity of allusions and borrowings make coincidence impossible in every case, but we also have direct evidence for the Brontës' deriving inspiration from these authors.[2] It is when we come to less tangible pieces of evidence that conjecture must be distinguished from certainty. We cannot assume that because Jane Eyre says 'you had given the world for love, and considered it well lost' that Charlotte Brontë had read Dryden's play, *All for Love, or The World Well Lost.*[3] References in Charlotte's letters to works she had read are obviously useful, although, as so many of her letters were to the unliterary Ellen Nussey, these letters do not give a very complete picture of the Brontës' reading. The letters to Williams and Lewes are more valuable, especially when they provide information about books that Charlotte had not read.

Neither the Brontës' letters nor their novels can give us a satisfactory account of how the Brontës came by their books. On account of their poverty they would not have been able to buy many new books; books known to have been owned by the

84

Brontës have been shown to be largely theological, and Mrs Gaskell confirms that it was only after Charlotte became famous that new books began to enter the house.[4] Mrs Gaskell through her daughter Marianne also asked Ellen Nussey where Charlotte had got the books she had recommended to Ellen, adding rather puzzlingly that she knew Charlotte could get novels from Keighley, and Ellen would seem to have said that she got them from a circulating library, since Mrs Gaskell, duly followed by many modern authorities, says that a circulating library was the main source of books for the Brontës.[5]

Mrs Gaskell may be referring misleadingly to the library of the Keighley Mechanics' Institute. This had an ample supply of books, but was comparatively weak on fiction, and certainly had no new novels, whereas the ordinary circulating library would be where the writer of contemporary fiction would hope to achieve the bulk of his sales. We know that the Brontës did not have access to such a library, because Charlotte rather tartly says so when Ellen Nussey asked her whether she had read the latest new novel.[6] It has even been suggested that the Brontës did not use the Keighley Mechanics' Institute library, although here we have definite evidence that Mr Brontë was a subscriber, and the similarities between the books in the library and books known to have been read by the Brontës are impressive.[7]

Another library which the Brontës may have used is that at Ponden House. Links between the Heatons of Ponden House and the Brontës are fairly tenuous, but Miss Gerin has made out a good case for showing that there is internal evidence in the Brontës' early manuscripts for their use of this library which certainly contained many volumes that the Brontës in their youth could otherwise hardly have seen.[8] Of course access to a few books is not the same as access to the whole library, and we do not know how free the Brontës were to browse around in the libraries to which they did have access.

References to Agnes Gray being encouraged to spend time in the Ashbys' library and to Jane Eyre being surprised, though content for the present, that only one bookcase in the library at Thornfield was open, would suggest some degree of familiarity with old libraries.[9] If we make the dangerous assumption that

Jane Eyre and *Agnes Grey* are autobiographical, the reference in the former to one bookcase, full mainly of light literature, being thought sufficient for the governess, would suggest that Charlotte was less fortunate in her employers than Anne, whose heroine enjoys more freedom. Certainly the Robinsons appear to have been the only household in which a sister established a reasonably friendly relationship. Similarly the Robinson girls were the only Brontë pupils old enough and friendly enough to lend their own books, although Anne Brontë may have been reluctant to borrow contemporary novels from her charges. In this connection it is interesting, but at the same time disappointing, that the Robinson library should contain no fiction.

Once it has been established that the task of tracking down particular literary influences is a difficult one, and that we must distinguish between the various claims of internal and external evidence in deciding whether the Brontës certainly, probably, or possibly read a particular book, we can begin to build up a general picture of the Brontës' reading. We can do this by taking fiction of different types and different periods and seeing which period and type is likely to have had the most influence on the Brontës. This method has the additional advantage of enabling us to see how the English novel became more or less prudish at different stages of its development.

Although there are references to *Pamela* and *Rasselas* in *Jane Eyre*, to *Sir Charles Grandison* and *The Vicar of Wakefield* in *The Professor*, to *The Italian* in *Shirley*, and *The Vicar of Wakefield* again in *Villette*,[10] there is not a great deal of evidence to connect the Brontës with the more outspoken eighteenth-century novels. The Ponden House catalogue, as well as being rich in unrestrained Elizabethan and Jacobean dramatists, also includes such tempting eighteenth-century titles as *Fashionable Folly*, *History of a Parisian Family*, *Indiscretions of Youth*, *Trials for Adultery or History of Divorces*, and *Maxims of Gallantry*,[11] but there is no evidence that the Brontës read these books, or that they were formative influences in the writing of their novels. *Humphrey Clinker* and *Roderick Random* were in the Keighley library, Charlotte compares Fielding unfavourably with Thackeray, and Branwell, who had access to a circulating library at Luddenden Foot containing *Tom Jones* and *Roderick Random*, complains of the emasculation of the English novel since the days of Smollett and Fielding.[12] Most eighteenth-century novels in the nineteenth century had a poor reputation, and William Hale White in *The Autobiography of Mark Rutherford* shows us that even *The Vicar of Wakefield*, obviously used as a text-book in Belgium, was not thought proper in some English circles in the middle of the century.[13]

Richardson occupies a somewhat ambiguous position in the debate on prudery. On the one hand many Evangelicals specifi-cally exempted him from their prescriptions on fiction; on the other Lockhart with more acumen complained about the obscen-ity of 'pious Richardson's pious Pamela'.[14] It is not difficult to trace parallels between Richardson and the Brontës, and there is definite proof of Charlotte's study of him in the newly dis-covered letter to Hartley Coleridge.[15] Admittedly Charlotte's main interest seems to be in *Sir Charles Grandison* rather than in the sexually more provocative *Pamela* and *Clarissa Harlowe*, but Charlotte also comments that Richardson can write like an old woman. Without making too much of this remark, made in the context of a discussion whether the sex of an author could be determined from a study of his writing, we can say that this is a possible indication that Charlotte had, like Lockhart, pene-trated to the passion repressed beneath Richardson's surface respectability, and was deploring the appearance of respectability.

In the same letter to Hartley Coleridge we have the full text of Charlotte's views on the *Lady's Magazine*. From the pre-viously published draft of this letter we already knew of Miss Branwell's preference, shared by Charlotte, for the *Lady's Maga-zine* over the trash of modern literature. The new text gives us examples of some tales in the *Lady's Magazine*, and provides the additional information that Charlotte had read them in her very early youth, and that Mr Brontë had burnt them because they contained foolish love stories. This is the only instance of Mr Brontë acting as a censor, and if *Ethelinda*, one of the stories mentioned by Charlotte, is *Ethelinde* by Charlotte Smith, an extract from which appeared in numerous eighteenth-century periodicals, then Mr Brontë's censorship is not surprising, as

Caroline Montgomery, the heroine of the extract, not only like Jane Eyre falls in love with a man chained to an imbecile wife, but also bears him two children. *Derwent Priory* by A. Kendall appeared in the *Lady's Magazine* from January 1796 to September 1797, and in the same year we find a tale entitled *Grassville Abbey*, which may be *The Abbey*, the third tale cited by Charlotte. *Derwent Priory*, an epistolary novel of high life, is a much watered down *Clarissa*, but in 1796 we find in the *Lady's Magazine* a summary of Mrs Inchbald's *Nature and Art* which makes Mr Brontë's censorship understandable.[16]

There is no very wide gap however between the fiction of the late eighteenth century and the fiction of the early nineteenth century which the Brontës without parental disapproval could have borrowed from the Keighley library or read in periodicals like *Blackwood's*. The early nineteenth century was not as prudish as it is sometimes represented to be. It is difficult to date the beginnings of Victorian prudery. It was after all in the eighteenth century that the Proclamation Society was founded, Codpiece Row was renamed Coppice Row, Mrs Grundy was invented, and a reviewer criticised a lady for using the simile of a bather in a poem.[17] The latter part of the eighteenth century is usually thought to have been more permissive than the first quarter of the nineteenth century on the evidence of Scott's great-aunt, who was horrified by a re-reading of the works of Aphra Behn, although she had read them with a clear conscience in her youth.[18] It is possible however that too much has been read into this one anecdote, gathered at second hand from a not very reliable source. In spite of the existence of Bowdler and the hostility to Byron there are several indications that the early years of the nineteenth century were not as prudish as might appear at first sight.

Bowdler was an Evangelical. At this stage the Evangelicals, though more of a vital source of religion than later in the century, were numerically less strong, and it is impossible to equate Evangelical tastes with the tastes of the country as a whole. This is especially true of their views on the novel, since many Evangelicals regarded the reading of novels as a terrible crime.[19] Among the opponents of the Evangelicals were the great periodicals, the *Edinburgh Review* and the *Quarterly Review*. This is important, since later in the century it was contributors to those two reviews who were to join religious periodicals in finding coarseness in the most unexpected places. We can see the difference between the two periodicals if we compare Sidney Smith's attacks on the Evangelicals in the *Edinburgh Review* for 1808 and 1809, including the improper *reductio ad absurdum* of the Evangelical philosophy of dress, with the attack on French novels in the *Edinburgh Review* for 1855. Lady Eastlake as well as denouncing *Jane Eyre* in 1848 made some scathing comments on Evangelical novels in the *Quarterly Review* for May 1843. The *Anti-Jacobin Review*, inspired by the same Tory philosophy as the *Quarterly*, was full of attacks on Evangelicals and also full of coarse language. Thus the Evangelical attitude cannot be regarded as a typical one in the early nineteenth century.

A more representative figure of the first quarter of the nineteenth century is Sir Walter Scott. Since Scott's novels with the exception of the censored incident in *St Ronan's Well* were so free from any possible taint of indecency that he succeeded in making the novel respectable to all but the most hardened Evangelical, he may seem an unlikely figure to quote in support of the view that his age was a relatively broadminded one. But we only have to look at his sane and restrained comments on the indecencies of such writers as Swift, Sterne and Smollett[20] to realise how much more prudish is Thackeray, who may be regarded as a representative figure of the 1840s.

Nor did Scott have to go back to the past to find indecent novels. In 1822 there appeared a novel entitled *Some Passages in the Life of Mr Adam Blair*. It was admittedly published anonymously and attracted some unfavourable comment, although the *Edinburgh Review* allowed it to pass comparatively unscathed.[21] Adam Blair is a widowed minister who commits adultery; after a due period of contrition he is allowed to resume his parochial duties. Mrs Campbell, the heroine of the novel, is less sympathetically treated and is allowed to expiate her sins with death; on the other hand she is presented as a foolish rather than a wicked woman in spite of the fact that there is a digression early in the book to explain how she divorced her first husband before marrying Captain Campbell. Not only are the sentiments of the novel daring, but the language is also surprisingly outspoken. Mrs Campbell is twice allowed to appear dishevelled in décolleté, Adam Blair leaps naked from his sickbed, and the scene where an old Highland crone surprises her mistress 'asleep in the arms of a man – and a stranger' is indeed daring, especially as it is the Sabbath-bell which eventually arouses Adam Blair.

The author of this sensational tale was John Gibson Lockhart. His other novels are less sensational, although in *The History of Matthew Wald*, which the reviewer in the *Atlas* found similar to *Wuthering Heights*, there are two illegitimate births, that of the hero's wife being rendered legitimate by a common-law marriage. Lockhart's criticism in the early part of the century follows the same sensible pattern as that of his father-in-law. Thus he defends *Don Juan* in *Blackwood's* for September 1823 at the same time that he complains about the obscenity in *Pamela*. Later however as editor of the *Quarterly*, he allowed articles of which Lady Eastlake's on *Jane Eyre* is a typical specimen.[22] Lockhart himself admired *Jane Eyre*, but thought her rather a brazen Miss.[23]

Another author to retreat from early outspokenness was De Quincey, whose 1856 version of *The Confessions of an English Opium-eater* was both more reticent and more apologetic than the shorter 1822 version about the author's association with the prostitute Ann.[24] De Quincey was one of the authors to whom the Brontës sent a copy of their poems in 1847, and in doing so they acknowledged the 'pleasure and profit we have often and long derived from your works'.[25] Frederick Harrison noted a resemblance between *Villette* and *The Confessions*,[26] and De Quincey was a regular contributor to *Blackwood's*, staple reading in the Brontë household. Branwell's addiction to opium may have been a less fortunate inheritance from De Quincey.

Lockhart was also sent a copy of the Brontës' poems[27] and he too was a frequent contributor to the periodicals read by the Brontës. In addition Charlotte praised his *Life of Burns*, resemblances have been traced between the last sentence of *Wuthering Heights* and a passage in the *Life of Scott*, and Scott, Lockhart and Johnny Lockhart are Emily's three characters in the 1827

Play of the Islanders.[28] It is perhaps not totally without significance that the maiden name of the heroine of *Adam Blair* is
Charlotte Bell.

Closely associated with Scott, Lockhart and *Blackwood's
Magazine* was James Hogg, the Ettrick Shepherd. In this case
the connection with the Brontës is more tenuous, depending on
one letter from Branwell to Blackwood in 1835 suggesting that
he should take Hogg's place as a contributor.[29] There is thus no
certain evidence that the Brontës read *The Confessions of a
Justified Sinner* which certainly fails to live up to the standards
of prudery expected in the middle of the century. The book
opens with a wedding night and passes rapidly to a fairly explicit account of adultery and illegitimacy. Words like 'strumpet'
and 'bagnio' (meaning brothel) are used quite openly, and what
is even more shocking, whereas the villain of the book commits
practically every crime except sexual indulgence, loose living is
almost the only fault of his brother who is presented as an
admirable character. In both language and sentiments *The Confessions of a Justified Sinner* would seem to be a most immoral
work, and not surprisingly it was revised in 1837 after Hogg's
death. Offensive expressions like 'bagnio' were removed in this
bowlerised version.[30]

In the same Scottish circle we find John Wilson, editor and
contributor to *Blackwood's* and a favourite in the Brontë household.[31] The Brontës could have read *The Trials of Margaret Lindsay* in the Keighley Mechanics' Institute library. Although the
morality of this novel, published in 1823, hardly seems in doubt
owing to the unflinching purity of its heroine, it could be
argued that the author shows an almost prurient interest in the
temptations which face Margaret Lindsay. Deaths are frequent
in this novel, but so are fates worse than death. The desertion by
Margaret's father of her mother in favour of a paramour, the
attempts of Margaret's first suitor to lure her into a false marriage, the unnecessary episode of Margaret's friend Mary
Mitchell, who is unsympathetic because she has lost her virtue,
all prepare us for the main episode of the book, the marriage of
Margaret to Ludovic Oswald, who unfortunately has a previous
wife living. This wife, Hannah Blantyre, conveniently dies,

Ludovic after a due period of penance marries Margaret again, and the proprieties are preserved in the end. It might be argued that too much favour is shown to Oswald; unlike Bertha Rochester his wife is not mad, and she has a child. Unlike Charles Reade in *Griffith Gaunt* forty years later Wilson does not apologise for making his heroine technically, though unwittingly, a fallen woman; indeed this aspect of Oswald's wickedness is not emphasised, although the presence in the background of a virtuous suitor, slightly resembling St John Rivers, adds to Margaret's trials. Nor is Wilson exactly cautious about his language; thus Oswald is said to have treated Hannah Blantyre like a prostitute.[32]

It is worth examining the other titles in the Keighley library. No prude could fault Hofland's moral tales, although these may have influenced Charlotte Brontë.[33] Jane Porter's *Thaddeus of Warsaw* (1803) and Lady Morgan's *O'Donnel, a National Tale* (1814) are equally blameless, although the former, containing a tutor who is a count, and the latter, containing a governess who becomes a duchess, may have provided some inspiration for the Brontës in their time as teachers. *The Hungarian Brothers* (1807) by Anna Maria Porter does contain some sensational material in that the younger brother, Demetrius, nearly compromises himself with a married woman and is only rescued by his brother, the painfully virtuous Charles. It may be an indication of growing prudery that in revising this book in 1831 for inclusion in the *Bentley's Standard Novels* series the authoress felt bound to make some of her characters more discreet and to introduce more religion into her work.[34]

Presumably the Brontës read these works in the cheap editions of the '30s, and thus in considering the library at Keighley we are really considering the fiction of the '30s. S. Warren's *Passages from the Diary of a Late Physician*, which first appeared in *Blackwood's* from 1830 to 1837, is not without interest for students of the Brontës and students of prudery, especially as Warren's connection with the Brontës is not a tenuous one.[35] There are veiled but definite references to prostitution and seduction in the chapters, *The Magdalen* and *The Destroyer*, and the account of *The Man About Town* may well be the source of the scenes of debauchery in *The Tenant of Wildfell Hall*. There are close verbal parallels between Warren's account of the death of St John Effingstone and the deathbed of Arthur Huntingdon. In particular we may note the scenes when the sufferer thinks the crisis is over, but the doctor knows that mortification has begun.[36] It is again interesting to note that *The Man About Town*, though like *The Tenant of Wildfell Hall* an admirably moral tale in that it showed a sinner duly punished, was considered by some to be an immoral book, because it had described both the sinning and the punishment in too graphic a fashion. In including *The Man About Town* in his book Warren added that, though he had taken scrupulous care and had drawn a veil over the more ghastly features of the case, angry complaints and 'insulting, nay beastly insinuations' had been made against it.[37] Anne Brontë's work met with more complaints, although it is less outspoken than *The Diary of a Late Physician*.

Deaths are frequent in Warren's book with consumption the main killer. More violent deaths are a feature of three more masculine books in the Keighley library, Maxwell's *Stories of Waterloo*, *The Cruise of the Midge* and *Tom Cringle's Log*, both by Michael Scott. *Stories of Waterloo* does contain one seduction and one woman who gives birth four months after her wedding, but is otherwise blameless. Both Michael Scott's books first appeared in *Blackwood's* and in *Tom Cringle's Log* (1829–34) we find quite apart from rapes and executions, lovingly lingered over a preoccupation with what is not always so euphemistically described as 'what part of your honour's body touches your chair'.[38] *The Cruise of the Midge* (1834–5) is less outspoken.

Also less outspoken is Captain Marryat, whose *Peter Simple* (1834) and *Newton Foster* (1832) both appear in the Keighley catalogue. Marryat's picture of a midshipman's existence as good clean fun with the occasional villain put in his place by such idealised worthies as Terence O'Brien seems a bowdlerised version of the harsh realities of naval life, and there is also rather an unpleasant moralising strain in his books. Nevertheless Peter Simple's early adventures, when in his innocence he has to be rescued from a prostitute, and the drunken Mrs Trotter climbs into his bed, might well bring a blush to a maiden's cheek. There is also in *Peter Simple* a passage mocking prudes represented by a lady who is shocked at the mention of 'breast of turkey' and suggests 'bosom' instead.[39] *Newton Foster* too has people climbing into the wrong bed, and it hardly helps the situation to discover that the two parties turn out to be married after all. We would expect Marryat's book to appeal more to Branwell than to his sisters, and there is indeed a close parallel between *Peter Simple* and *And the Weary are at Rest*.[40] Possibly the West Indian scenes in *Jane Eyre* may owe something to Marryat and Michael Scott.

It would be impossible to conclude this survey of the Brontës' reading of fiction without some reference to the periodicals which on account of their poverty were likely to be their main source for fiction. In taking *Fraser's* and *Blackwood's* the Brontës allied themselves to those hostile to the prudery of the new annuals,[41] although the example of the poem by Lamb which *Blackwood's* accepted in 1828 after it had been rejected by *The Gem* hardly suggests that *Blackwood's* were being unduly permissive, as the poem with its mild suggestion of breast feeding is a singularly innocent one.[42] In the Keighley Mechanics' Institute the periodicals were mainly the harmless ones one would expect in an institution designed to prevent the passions of the working class from being inflamed. Thus Limbird's *Mirror of Literature* met with great approbation among the clergy and respectable classes, while Chambers' *Edinburgh Journal* and Knight's *Penny Magazine* were intended to provide cheap wholesome literature.[43] The Ponden House library contained periodicals from an earlier age, but the two periodicals best represented in this collection, *The Monthly Review* and *The Critical Review*, only contained selections from novels which they reviewed in a fairly decorous manner, while there were only a few volumes of more racy periodicals containing fiction, like the *London Magazine* and the *Town and Country Magazine*.[44] The rather contemptuous reference in *Shirley* to Methodist Magazines and faded Lady's magazines in the library of Caroline Helstone's aunt[45] would suggest that Charlotte outgrew her taste for fiction in periodicals, but for financial reasons periodicals are likely to have played a considerable part in the Brontës' early reading.

It would be wrong to confine an account of the literary influences behind the Brontës to works of fiction alone. Indeed a
notable feature of the libraries at Ponden House and at Keighley
was the scarcity of fiction, and we must not forget the Brontës'
links with the fiction-hating Evangelical movement, or Charlotte
Brontë's remarks in a letter to Ellen Nussey of 1834 that all
fiction after Scott was worthless.[46] In the same letter she has
some warm praise for Byron apart from *Don Juan* and *Cain*, and
she might seem to have read even these works at least once. A
copy of Byron's poems was in the possession of Mr Brontë who
in his own poetry did not beat about the bush in denouncing
prostitution.[47] There is further evidence for Mr Brontë's broadmindedness,[48] and although we do find him censoring the foolish
love stories in the *Lady's Magazine*, he does not seem to have
exercised much control over his daughters' reading. He shared
their enthusiasm for newspapers, which with the excuse that
the public has a right to know the truth have always been able
to impart otherwise unpalatable facts. Thus the *Leeds Mercury*,
taken by the Brontës, had on 4 January 1840 a horrifying
account of brothels in Leeds.[49]
There is, however, an important difference between fiction
and non-fiction when it comes to tracing literary influences on
novels. The Bible, Shakespeare and Byron are obvious influences
on the novels of the Brontës, but they could hardly be regarded
as models for aspiring novel-writers. In examining the literary
standards which the Brontës were trying to follow we must confine ourselves to the other novels they read. Most novelists,
whether consciously or unconsciously, are influenced by other
novels they read, which are likely to be contemporary novels,
and they are especially likely to be influenced if, like the
Brontës, they are aspiring novelists anxious for their first book
to be published. Where the Brontës were exceptional is that they
were remarkably ignorant of contemporary novelists. We need
not take too literally the remark to Ellen Nussey, 'For fiction
read Scott alone; all novels after his are worthless.' This was
written in 1834 before the advent of Thackeray and Dickens.
but is perhaps more interesting for its attitude to other novelists
rather than for its praise of Scott which is reinforced by other

letters.[50] The attitude of the Brontës to contemporary novelists
was influenced by two factors. The first was their Evangelical
upbringing which left them with the feeling that fiction was
frivolous if not actually wrong. Thus the flirtatious Miss
Murray in *Agnes Grey*, the vain Georgiana Reed in *Jane Eyre*
and the adulterous Lady Lowborough in *The Tenant of Wildfell
Hall* are all novel-readers.[51] The second reason was economic.
The Brontës did not have access to a circulating library, the
libraries they probably did use were not strong in contemporary
fiction, and they were too poor to buy books.[52] Of course when
Charlotte became famous she was sent books by W. S. Williams
and others, but this sending and a number of references in the
correspondence involved in the dispatch of the books make it
clear how starved the Brontës had been. Thus Charlotte said that
she had never read a word by Mrs Marsh and in the same letter
that she had read 'comparatively few novels.'[53] Eliza Lynn's first
two novels were read only in periodicals.[54] In thanking G. H.
Lewes for *Ranthorpe*[55] Charlotte said that she had read 'a new
book – not a reprint – not a reflection on any other book, but a
new book'. There is a passage in *Jane Eyre* when St John Rivers
gives Jane a copy of *Marmion*, in which Charlotte Brontë turns
aside from her story to compare the golden age of literature
(Scott's) with the present era which is less favoured.[56] *Shirley*
and *Villette* may owe something to other novels of the age, but
with the other five novels we would do better to look to the
influence of a previous generation.

This conclusion, and the previous conclusion that the treatment of sex in this previous generation was more cautious, might
seem to be brought into doubt if we emerge from a consideration of the minor fiction of these two periods to have a look at
the major figures of Jane Austen, Dickens and Thackeray. In
the first place, it could be argued that Jane Austen sheds no
light on the lurid world of Nancy and Becky Sharp. In the
second place, whereas Charlotte was both ignorant and contemptuous of Jane Austen's achievement, her admiration for
Thackeray was pronounced, and the similarities between Dotheboys Hall and Lowood make it easy to posit some debt to Dickens
as well.

It is of course, because of her sex, hard to compare Jane Austen with Dickens and Thackeray when we are considering the issue of prudery. Jane Austen does not stray from the respectable circles of the gentry to consider the more licentious aristocracy and lower classes, and she restricts herself still more by not reporting the conversations of her male characters with each other. Within this narrow range however Jane Austen's treatment of sexual matters is straightforwardly frank, and compares favourably with the strange mixture of fascination, repulsion and reticence which is a characteristic of Dickens and even more of Thackeray.[57]

So far as the reading of the Brontës is concerned, the unpublished portion of the letter to Lewes, quoted in the second chapter, makes it clear that, though Charlotte Brontë condemned Jane Austen's limited range, she preferred her to contemporary female authors. As for Dickens and Thackeray, though there are many favourable references to the latter and a few to the former after the publication of *Jane Eyre*, before this publication the only mention of either novelist in the letters in the Shakespeare Head edition is a reference to Dickens's *The Chimes*, which Charlotte says she has not read.[58] Thackeray did of course influence Charlotte Brontë by his contributions in *Fraser's*, and there are indications that Charlotte had read Dickens in the letter to Hartley Coleridge, in a reference to Mr Squeers in the juvenilia, as well as in the easily drawn parallels between *Jane Eyre* and *Nicholas Nickleby*.[59] But there is nothing to suggest that these were the authors from whom the Brontës adopted standards of sexual decorum.

It so happens that the Brontës were open to some contemporary influences which also encouraged outspokenness. The first was the reading of French novels. In a letter to Ellen Nussey of 1840[60] Charlotte says that she has

> got another bale of French books from Gomersal – containing
> upwards of 40 volumes – I have read about half – they are like
> the rest clever wicked sophisticated and immoral – the best of
> it is they give one a thorough idea of France and Paris – and
> are the best substitute for French Conversation I have met with.

This may seem slightly reminiscent of the *Punch* cartoon[61] showing a small boy being berated by his mother for not following his father's example and reading Zola to improve his French, but it does show a surprisingly wide knowledge of French novels even before the visit to Brussels. In Belgium the Brontës had both an incentive to keep up their French and the opportunity and leisure to do so.[62] After leaving Brussels the tie with M. Heger may have encouraged Charlotte to read other French works apart from the newspapers of which we hear a good deal.[63]

It would be interesting to know what French novels were read by the Brontës. Writing to Hartley Coleridge Charlotte mentions Rouseau, but since she says that he, like Richardson, often writes like an old woman, he is hardly likely to have been considered by Charlotte as very immoral. The library of Hunsden in *The Professor*, consisting of Thiers, Villemain, Paul de Kock, George Sand and Eugene Sue, may indicate the contents of the batch from Gomersal, as Hunsden is modelled on Mr Taylor. Writing to G. H. Lewes in early 1848 Charlotte shows some knowledge of George Sand, and in 1850 Lewes sent her some books by George Sand; this suggests that George Sand was one of the authors read as early as 1840, and that Charlotte had asked Lewes to refresh her memory. In the letter thanking Lewes for his books in 1850[64] Charlotte says that Balzac was quite a new author to her and that she had pleasure in making his acquaintance. On 7 February 1853[65] however she denied in a letter to George Smith any acquaintance with Balzac and, though it is hard to accuse Charlotte of more than forgetfulness, we lose confidence in the earlier statement to Lewes. The only other French novelist known to have been read by Charlotte is Eugene Sue; in a recently published letter to K.T.[66] of 9 November 1850 she expresses surprise that the author of *Mathilde* should stoop to plagiarism. The *Wandering Jew* was in the Keighley Mechanic's Library. M. Heger's admiration for Victor Hugo makes him a likely author to be read by both Charlotte and Emily. All these authors were denounced by the *Quarterly Review* in 1836.

Closely associated with French fiction were the cheap periodicals, produced by people like Reynolds and Lloyd, which the serious reviews tended to lump together with French fiction as equally deplorable.[67] One hesitates to ascribe to such an unworthy source any influence on the Brontës, and indeed both their Evangelical upbringing and reading of such periodicals as *Blackwood's* would militate against such an influence. On the other hand the Brontës' voracious reading, their poverty and the frankly fustian nature of some of the juvenilia might suggest such a source. The lowest depths, as represented by Lloyd's penny dreadfuls and the Holywell Square school of fiction, were perhaps too disgraceful to pass muster in the Brontë household. But if the Brontës read Eugene Sue with approval, they could hardly despise Reynolds, whose periodicals contain both translations and imitations of Sue.[68]

The higher range of popular fiction, as represented by such authors as G. P. R. James, of whose voluminous output Charlotte seemed aware,[69] was too expensive for the Brontës, it not being until 1847 that the cheap parlour edition of popular novels came out. Another prolific author of the '40s was Mrs Trollope, to one of whose novels Charlotte makes one slighting allusion.[70] She need not have of course have read either James or Mrs Trollope, and although it is hard to complain of the morality of James's boring romances, it is odd that Mrs Trollope should have been as unlucky as her son in attracting accusations of coarseness. The *New Spirit of the Age* said of Mrs Trollope:[71]

> She owes everything to that audacious contempt of public opinion which is the distinguishing mark of persons who are said to stick at nothing. . . . Her constitutional coarseness is the natural element of a low popularity which is sure to pass for cleverness, shrewdness and strength, where cultivated judgement and chaste inspiration would be thrown away. . . . She takes a strange delight in the hideous and revolting and dwells with gusto upon the sins of vulgarity.

Another author to be denounced by the periodicals was Bulwer Lytton. His crime was sympathy with criminals in general rather than outspokenness on sexual issues,[72] although we do find prudery involved in these attacks and in Bulwer's retaliations. He was one of the authors in the Keighley Mechanics' Institute library, and an early birthday fragment of Anne Brontë's describes Branwell reading *Eugene Aram* aloud to Charlotte.[73] He is mentioned in the same terms as Cooper, Warren and Dickens in the letter to Hartley Coleridge; in a letter to W. S. Williams of 8 May 1849 Charlotte brackets Bulwer with Scott, Dickens and Thackeray as examples of the male novelists whose giant strides Currer Bell could not hope to emulate; and there is a similar allusion in a letter a year earlier to Bulwer and Byron heroes and heroines being suitable for portraits, unlike Charlotte's characters.[74] But other references are less polite. In particular the description of Eliza Lynn as a Bulwer in petticoats is not very complimentary to either party.[75] In the same letter Charlotte praises the *North American Review* for its harsh remarks on Bulwer, although this review had been hostile to *Jane Eyre* and *Wuthering Heights*. Finally, in praising a novel by G. H. Lewes to W. S. Williams on 26 April 1848, Charlotte says that the book deserves a cordial reception far beyond anything due to a Bulwer or D'Israeli production.[76]

This novel is *Rose, Blanche and Violet*, bracketed by Lewes in 1850 with *Jane Eyre* as a naughty novel, much to Charlotte's indignation.[77] Charlotte's attitude to this work, favourable at first but, following some harsh criticism by Williams hostile with some cordial reservations about a Branwell-like character,[78] indicates her ignorance of the contemporary novel. Not only is *Rose, Blanche and Violet* an extraordinarily bad novel, but it would seem to derive some of its inspiration from other novels. Written in 1848 and published by Smith Elder and Company, the book would appear to owe its title to George Sand's *Rose et Blanche*[79] and its account of a school where the rich girls are treated differently from the poor girls to *Vanity Fair*. Among the rich girls there is a Miss Pinkerton, and by a similar process of taking a name from another novel and giving it to a different character in that novel we arrive at an ugly masterful hero called St John to whom Rose is married after a long separation.

This resemblance might seem coincidental or trivial, but in view of his interest in *Jane Eyre* as a model for charting the success of George Eliot's novels,[80] and his remark about the naughty books, there would seem a good case for making *Rose*,

Blanche and Violet the first of the outspoken imitators of *Jane Eyre* of whom Mrs Oliphant talks. For there can be no doubt that it is outspoken. Even Charlotte, who was ignorant of literary conventions and was in any case disposed to be lenient to Lewes because of his kindly review of *Jane Eyre* in *Fraser's*, admitted that he took a French pen in his hand.[81]

We begin quite mildly with Rose mocking at her school mistress for her prudery in avoiding the word belly and not mentioning sparrows as they had a libertine reputation.[82] This is good evidence of the existence of excessive prudery in the '40s although, as Rose accuses Miss Smith of reading *Don Juan* on the sly, the prudery is hardly portrayed as being sincere or treated sympathetically. Nor is there any sympathy for the Puritans who disapprove of a Mrs Langely Turner for giving entertainments on Sunday evenings and inviting dubious characters to them, whereas Mrs Langley Turner, who 'had the un-Britannic audacity of thinking for herself without reference to the opinions of Mrs Grundy',[83] is kindly handled.

Rose's sister Blanche is less forward in mocking her school-mistress, but towards the end of the first volume finds herself in an awkward predicament. Her lover, Cecil Chamberlayne, thwarted from being her suitor in an orthodox way because he has not listened to her father's views on Horace's metres, has climbed on to the balcony of her room by means of a ladder which his rival Captain Heath removes. One would have thought that the easiest thing for Cecil to do was to walk through the house, but he does not do this until early morning, when Captain Heath sees him and assumes Blanche has lost her virginity. She nearly had, as Cecil for no obvious reason tries, in the words of Blanche, 'to outrage the memory of that night hitherto so sacred',[84] but 'his wild instincts and gross passions'[85] are calmed by Blanche falling into a timely faint. The lovers elope and with the help of Captain Heath, now determined to salvage what he can of Blanche's reputation, they marry.

Meanwhile an entirely new, and for the story of the the three sisters, Rose, Blanche and Violet, almost entirely irrelevant, character is introduced in the shape of the local poetess, Hester Mason. She scandalises Walton society by first carrying on and then running away with an elderly admirer, Sir Chetsom Chetsom. The curate's wife and surgeon's wife discuss the scandal in a way that reflects little credit on them, especially as they are prepared to listen to risqué *doubles entendres* about Hester's interest in the rapid development of humanity.[86] In comparison Hester's character is fairly kindly treated, although her poetry and stout legs are mocked. After running away with Sir Chetsom she sets up a salon in London, attended by some frightening literary ladies and by Cecil Chamberlayne, with whom she discusses the iniquity of marriage and, rather surprisingly, the double standard whereby women must be pure and men need not be.[87] Later she persuades Sir Chetsom to marry her, but he dies before the marriage can be effected, and after failing to make a success as a woman of letters she returns home. Here the women raise up their hands in horror, while the men think she is an easy conquest; in despair she returns to London and becomes a prostitute, meeting Cecil Chamberlayne just before his suicide.

In spite of her ghastly end both Hester's career and her ideas are handled without contempt. Charlotte Brontë, who thought that the portrait of Hester Mason excusable if drawn from life, but in bad taste if it was the invention of Lewes's fancy,[88] exaggerates the grimness of the portrait. The young poetess, trying to make a living out of literature and disbelieving in the institution of marriage while upholding broad humanistic ideals, reminds us, if only faintly, of George Eliot, absurd though it is to imagine the latter on the streets. Certainly Hester Mason comes out well in contrast with the villainess of the book, Mrs Meredith Vyner, the stepmother of Rose, Blanche and Violet. This lady had sworn undying love in youth to Marmaduke Ashley, a prosperous Brazilian, later the husband of Violet, but had jilted him in favour of the pedantic Mr Vyner. After her marriage she encourages Marmaduke to make love to her rather than to Violet whom she hates. In doing this Mrs Vyner preserves technically her honour, as is made clear by several pointed references to Platonic love, but her wickedness in simultaneously torturing her husband, Marmaduke and Violet is shown to be a far greater crime than mere adultery.[89] Eventually Marmaduke, whose wish to commit adultery is not held up as reprehensible, becomes disillusioned after Mrs Vyner has tried to get him to confess that he would murder Mr Vyner. In the third volume she encourages two new lovers, George Maxwell and Lord ——. When her husband remonstrates with her, she denies that she has overstepped the limits to which 'even English rigidity confines a young woman',[90] but shortly afterwards she runs away with George Maxwell. Her eventual fate is an unhappy one, and in this respect Lewes follows the convention that the fallen woman should not be allowed to prosper. What is unconventional about the portrayal of Mrs Vyner is that she is shown to be much more wicked before her fall than after it, when she receives some sympathy.[91]

Rose, Blanche and Violet is not entirely concerned with these indelicate incidents or characters. Cecil Chamberlayne, whom Charlotte rightly praised as a well-drawn character, behaves disgracefully but, after the attempted rape of Blanche, never indelicately, although his gambling causes Blanche such distress that when she puts her child to her breast 'the life-giving fountains dry up'.[92]

The three heroines after whom the book is named are blameless if boring, and the novel is padded out with tedious moralising and learned quotations, some of which, from authors such as Wycherley, might themselves be considered indelicate. It is certainly odd to find Lewes linking his novel with *Jane Eyre* as a naughty one, as Charlotte Brontë is neither so sympathetic to sexual impropriety nor so outspoken about the nature of this impropriety. There would also seem to be the important difference between the two novels, that Lewes deliberately flouts conventions by including improper characters and incidents which are not necessary to his story, while Charlotte Brontë is innocent of any wish to exploit sexual matters for their own sake.[93]

This criterion, involving the author's intention, might seem to be an invaluable one in any age for distinguishing between true realism and sensational pornography. But critics cannot know what an author's intention is. Nor can the author be sure of his or her intention. The innocence of Charlotte Brontë's nature might seem apparent from a study of her letters. These

were of course censored by Ellen Nussey before publication, and
the censored or bowdlerised passages are a curious indication of
Ellen's excessive prudery. Thus 'varmint' is substituted for
'bitch', 'deuce' for 'devil' and the incautious word 'chemises' is
replaced by 'things'.[94] It is not certain how much a complete text
of all the letters would have revealed, although we get such an
impression of stilted decorum in connection with the absorbing
subject of husband-hunting from the letters of which we do have
the full text that it does not seem likely that Charlotte could
have expressed herself in a very startling fashion. On the other
hand Mrs Gaskell's statement that Charlotte Brontë put all her
naughtiness into her books, thus working off a great deal that is
morbid out of her life,[95] would support the view that the self-
conscious letters are a much less sure guide to the Brontës' feelings than the novels and, better still, the early outpourings of
the juvenilia.

The world of Angria has been described by the chief expert
on it as a completely amoral one.[96] Before extending this judgement to imply that by the standards of the time the stories of
Angria, if they had been published, would have seemed completely immoral, it is as well to state a few cautions. Though
the life and loves of Zamorna may seem the most identifiable and
the most interesting theme of the confused Angrian cycle, it
should be borne in mind that these love affairs only tend to
become illicit ones in the stories written after 1836; although
Harriet Martineau could have found fault with both the degree
and the kind of love displayed in the earlier stories, they did
not as a rule involve adultery.[97] In the period between 1836 and
1839, a period in which, as we have seen, Charlotte went
through some kind of adolescent religious crisis, both Zamorna
and his father-in-law Northangerland do commit adultery. The
very nature of the Angrian stories, whereby each tale is loosely
attached to the central framework, makes it hard to keep track
of either hero's legal or illegal unions, especially when a dead
wife can be revived.[98] But there can be no getting round such
facts as the sympathetic treatment of Mina Laury, undoubtedly
the mistress of Zamorna, in the story named after her, the situation in *Caroline Vernon*, where Zamorna is pursued by his ward,

the illegitimate daughter of Northangerland, the proposal by Sir William Percy to make Elizabeth Hastings his mistress in *Henry Hastings*, the strange account of debauchery which opens the rather disconnected tales in the *Duke of Zamorna* and the jealous exchanges between Louisa Vernon and Mary Percy in *The Return of Zamorna*.

We can of course suggest that Branwell, who is definitely not prudish in some of the stories assigned to him,[99] may be the author of some of these pieces. The manuscripts of *Henry Hastings*, *Caroline Vernon* and *Julia*, another tale of passion belonging to this period, are accepted as being Charlotte's by both Professor Mildred Christian and Miss Fannie Ratchford, and there seems no real reason to doubt their authority. We could raise some doubt by pointing out that *Henry Hastings* is apparently only signed by Charles Townshend, *Caroline Vernon* is not signed at all, and *Julia*, which Wise sold to Wrenn remarkably cheaply, has a signature by Charlotte attached to a poem at the end of the manuscript.[100] The kind of forgery whereby a short piece by Charlotte could be attached to a manuscript by Branwell is quite probable in the very disconnected *Duke of Zamorna*, of which the manuscript was in the Law Collection as was *The Return of Zamorna*, which contains incidents that are strikingly at variance with stories written at about the same date.[101]

If Charlotte did write all the stories ascribed to her, we can still defend her against the charge of licentious writing. Though the sentiments of these late juvenilia are surprisingly bold, the language used in them is fairly restrained. Though Mina Laury has won the author's respect in spite of her disregard for the marriage tie, it is taken for granted that she is not regarded as a respectable woman. Zamorna may not be blamed for his infidelities, but he is allowed to feel occasional remorse, as in his entanglement with Caroline Vernon. Finally the essential nature of Angria is that it is a world of fantasy, where normal moral and social rules do not operate. This is why we must not take Angria too seriously when considering what were Charlotte Brontë's views on sexual morality and the expression of sex in literature.

The same is true of Emily and Anne Brontë, although in their case we know so little about Gondal that it is difficult to say whether any unusual boldness is to be seen in it. Certainly there is nothing bold about the language; indeed, unlike Charlotte, whose descriptions of passion become more restrained when she wrote novels for publication, Anne Brontë would seem to have gained in boldness in passing from her tepid Gondal lyrics[102] to the description of debauchery in *The Tenant of Wildfell Hall.* Emily's lyrics are not tepid, and yet she too would seem to have gained in boldness, not of language but of sentiments, in passing from Gondal to *Wuthering Heights,* if we take the conventional view of *Wuthering Heights* as an amoral work and accept Miss Ratchford's view that in Gondal Emily adhered undeviatingly to eternal principles of morality and human psychology.[103] Against this it must be said that the amoral nature of *Wuthering Heights* cannot be taken for granted,[104] and that so far as matrimonial morality is concerned it is difficult to pin down guilt in Gondal with quite the certainty of Miss Ratchford. Not only does the loose cycle of stories make it difficult in Gondal, as in Angria, to determine whether a character is committing adultery or not; we cannot even be certain whether a character with more than one spouse is not really more than one character.[105]

It is a relief to pass from these uncertainties to the solid ground of the published novels. But when we turn from the unpublished juvenilia to the published novels, we are at once faced with a difficulty in trying to prove the thesis that the Brontës were exceptional in their emancipation from the influences and re-straints of contemporary prudery, and in trying to disprove Professor Tillotson's argument that the Brontës' emancipation is a sign that the 1840s were less prudish than other decades in the nineteenth century. For at first sight both theses seem to founder against the objection that there is nothing very shock-ing in the novels after all. Post-Freudian generations can of course find hidden sexual symbols in the Brontë novels but, especially after the heady waters of the juvenilia, it is hard to find much evidence of the daring views or outspoken language that both theses seem to require.

Agnes Grey is too slight a work for there to be much opportunity for daring views or outspoken language, although there is a hint of both in Rosalie Murray's complaint of her unhappiness with Sir Thomas Ashby.

> *And then he must needs have me down in the country, to lead the life of a nun, lest I should dishonour him or bring him to ruin; as if he had not been ten times worse every way, with his betting-book, and his gaming-table, and his opera-girls and his Lady This and Mrs That.*[106]

In *Shirley* there seems little likely to cause offence, except that the two heroines do not consult their families before falling in love and marrying. In *Villette*, when Ginevra Fanshawe does this, she meets with disapproval, the courtship of Lucy Snowe and Paul Emanuel is conducted with such propriety that we hardly know it is happening, and Paul Emanuel's habit of bowdlerising his pupils' reading[107] is a trait as full of Victorian propriety as Guy Mannering's disapproval of Byron.[108]

The Professor is in a slightly different category. The text has been censored by Mr Nicholls,[109] although not as much as Mrs Gaskell wished.[110] We can discover the gist of some of the censored passages, and these are hardly sensational.[111] Mrs Gaskell was presumably worried about reminders of the Heger story as well as straightforward coarseness, but there does not seem a great deal of the latter in the text as we have it. Monsieur Pelet's Parisian 'notions about matrimony and women'[112] are mentioned and deplored, and Crimsworth leaves him for fear that 'a practical modern French novel would be in full process of concoction under the roof of the unsuspecting Pelet'.[113] But Pelet's laxity of morals is not important in a story in which he is only a minor character, and the intriguing possibility of an affair between Madame Pelet and Crimsworth is put forward in such veiled language that we find it hard to understand. When we do understand what Charlotte is saying we still find it hard to believe that Crimsworth, whose pure morals have just been praised by Mlle Reuter, would have fallen from grace so rapidly, especially in view of the progress he had made in his courtship of Frances Henri. Neither Monsieur Pelet's actual laxity nor the possible laxity of Madame Pelet and Crimsworth is developed in

The Professor; the subjects that are important, Crimsworth's progress in Mlle Reuter's school and his courtship of Frances Henri, are handled if not with delicacy, at any rate with decorum. Thus Crimsworth says,

> *Know, O incredulous reader! that a master stands in a some-*
> *what different relation towards a pretty, light-headed, probably*
> *ignorant girl, to that occupied by a partner at a ball, or a*
> *gallant on the promenade*[114]

Here and again when he declares after a somewhat tepid description of Frances Henri's charms,

> *it appeared, then, that I too was a sensualist, in my temperate*
> *and fastidious way . . .,*[115]

we can accuse Charlotte Brontë of making a mistake in choosing a man for her chief character and forcing him to utter such improbable sentiments, but it is hard to accuse her of impropriety. It is possible that the painting of Crimsworth's pupils as something very different from 'some gentle virgin head, circled with a halo, some sweet personification of innocence'[116] may have aroused qualms in sensitive breasts.

Breasts would have been naturally sensitive to *The Professor,* and indeed to *Shirley* and *Villette,* because these novels appeared after the publication of *Jane Eyre. Jane Eyre* like *Wuthering Heights* and *The Tenant of Wildfell Hall* met with strong opposition in certain quarters because of their indelicacy; indeed this is one of the many features which the novels have in common. Another common feature is that all three novels involve situations where the two central characters fall in love in spite of the fact that one of them is married to someone else. This is not of course the only aspect of the novels which aroused opposition from prudish critics who were shocked by Rochester's frankness about his mistress, Huntingdon's adultery being accepted by his wife and other incidental features of the central situation.[117] Before considering how far critics were justified in finding fault with the incautious handling of these features it is as well to consider how far the Brontë sisters dealt with the central situation. In no case does adultery take place;[118] on the contrary both Jane Eyre and Helen Huntingdon, like the most conventional heroine, flee from their lover to avoid any damage to their honour, while the less innocent Catherine receives in death the conventional reward for the Victorian heroine who had fallen from grace. The heroes of the Brontës are less conventional, but neither Heathcliff nor Rochester escapes unscathed from their adulterous or bigamous passion. It is indeed hard to find what is so shocking about the Brontë novels, and yet this did not prevent people from being shocked. One suspects that Professor Tillotson, in hailing the unconventional Brontë novels as a sign that the period in which they wrote was relatively free from prudery, was using as evidence that the Brontës were unconventional their unfavourable reception by prudish critics; this reception proves the contrary thesis that the decade was a prudish one.

7

Reviews and Reviewers

IN ASSESSING contemporary opinions of the Brontës' novels there are a number of complicating factors which have to be borne in mind. The first is the absence of any satisfactory bibliography of contemporary reviews. The two bibliographies of Butler Wood in *The Brontë Society Transactions* are incomplete.[1] Owing to the absence of any page reference it is difficult to trace all the reviews mentioned by Charlotte in her letters,[2] and this method of compiling a review of reviews cannot in any case give us the complete picture. We have to rely in part on the Shakespeare Head with all its shortcomings and, even if we did have the complete text of Charlotte's letters, this would not mean that we would have a list of all the reviews of the Brontë novels.

Comments on reviews appear mainly in the letters to W. S. Williams, and there is no particular reason for thinking that these have been badly edited. But comments also appear in letters to Ellen Nussey, and, as has been shown, Charlotte's admission that she wrote *Jane Eyre* and replies to the charge of coarseness in this and other novels are likely candidates for bowdlerisation by Ellen Nussey. The Shakespeare Head prints twenty letters from Charlotte to Williams about the reviews of *Jane Eyre*, either punctiliously thanking him for sending them to her or discussing points in the reviews. These letters last from 28 October 1847 to 16 August 1849. There are eight letters to Williams discussing reviews of *Shirley*, the first dated 5 November 1849 and the last 3 April 1850. The only letter to Williams discussing reviews of *Villette* is one dated 9 March 1853, in which Charlotte asks that unfavourable reviews should not be withheld from her, a plea echoed in a letter to George Smith, unpublished by the editors of the Shakespeare Head.[3]

Even though *Jane Eyre* is in this comparatively favoured position for information about reviews, the third edition contains selections from five reviews not mentioned in the letters.[4] Inevitably Charlotte's unhappiness at the time of *Shirley's* publication, and her position as an established author at the time of *Villette* must have affected her publishers' judgement on how many reviews to send her. There is for instance no mention in Charlotte's letters of the very hostile review of *Shirley* in *The Dublin University Magazine*.[5] Since the campaign against the indelicacy of the Brontë novels took some time to gather momentum and was conducted more in periodicals than in newspapers, on whose fiat Charlotte said that she did not wait,[6] we get a slightly too favourable impression from the letters to Williams which cover only a relatively short period after the publication of each book. Finally Charlotte's letters inevitably give us an incomplete picture of the way in which her sisters' novels were reviewed.

In the absence of any complete bibliography it is not surprising that there has been no satisfactory treatment of contemporary reviews. *The Brontë Society Transactions* have two valuable articles on American reviews,[7] emphasising their hostility to the Brontës' coarseness, but the one article on contemporary English treatment[8] is superficial, relying as it does entirely on the five reviews which were found in Emily's desk and on Charlotte's comments in her letters. Many biographers quote not from the full review, but from the publisher's advertisements which appeared in later editions of the novels;[9] since Newby quoted from reviews of *Jane Eyre* and *Wuthering Heights* to advertise *The Tenant of Wildfell Hall*, we cannot trust publishers' extracts, which give a misleadingly favourable impression. The review of *Shirley* in *Sharpe's London Journal* showed how unreliable these selections are when it commented,

The extracts appended to the publisher's advertisements, and purporting to be specimens of the opinions expressed by some contemporary journals, might lead us to fear that we were perversely singular, did we not know how to estimate at its real value such piecemeal criticism.[10]

Another complicating factor is the varying degrees of ignorance shown by reviewers of the lives of the Brontës. After the publication of Mrs Gaskell's biography few could say that the pathetic sisters were likely to be guilty of deliberate immorality, and *The Professor* escaped the charge of immorality in spite of Mrs Gaskell's fears on its account. Thus *The Athenaeum* said, 'the over-tragic life drama of Charlotte Brontë so much amazed the world that it feels disposed to err on the side of gentleness', though it adds that *The Professor* has 'the same rough bold coarse truthfulness of expression, the same . . . offence of dialogue, preference for forbidden topics' as the previous novels.[11] Before the publication of *Shirley* reviewers did not even know the sex of Currer, Ellis and Acton Bell, and this helped to prevent some, though not all, accusations of feminine immorality. Thus *The Christian Remembrancer* of April 1848 thinks that *Jane Eyre* must be by a woman, but it is not surprised that the hypothesis of a male author should have been started in view of the novel's 'masculine hardness, coarseness and freedom of expression'.[12] Between 1849 and 1857 the history of the Brontës gradually became known, but it is not clear whether their innocent life was regarded as a mitigating factor because they could not have experienced what they described, or as an additional irritant because they described what was so obviously outside their sphere. Something of this baffled feeling comes out in a review of *Agnes Grey* and *Wuthering Heights* in the *Leader* of December 1850. The critic says that it is curious to read *Wuthering Heights* and *The Tenant of Wildfell Hall*, and to remember that the authors were 'two retiring, consumptive girls'. He talks of 'books, coarse even for men, coarse in language and coarse in conception, the coarseness apparently of violent and uncultivated men', but then changes his tune to note that the books were written by two lonely girls out of a sense of duty.[13]

On the whole however the true pathos of the Brontë story was not appreciated until the publication of Mrs Gaskell's *Life of Charlotte Brontë*, and in reviews of *Shirley* and *Villette* there was little to protect Charlotte from accusations of indelicacy. Such accusations might seem hard, as there is little in either novel that seems even faintly improper. But of course *Shirley* and even, to a certain extent, *Villette* suffered through their association with *Jane Eyre*, just as *Jane Eyre* itself suffered for a time owing to Newby's dishonesty, because it was thought to be by the author of her sisters' novels. *Wuthering Heights* and *The Tenant of Wildfell Hall* add a streak of brutality to the indelicacy of *Jane Eyre*, but their unfavourable reception may owe something to the incompetence of Newby in advertising novels and his poor reputation as a publisher. In any case, it is difficult to compare the unsuccessful novels of Emily and Anne with those of Charlotte, because the latter received so many more reviews.

All these factors make it difficult to produce a complete account of the reception of the Brontë novels. A chronologically exact account is impossible, since we may know when reviews were published, but we cannot, except in rare cases, know when a particular review was written. Nor in all cases do we know the author of a review,[14] or know how much say the editor of a periodical had in determining the attitude of his reviewers. Finally there is a danger that by selecting passages which are hostile to the Brontës' alleged coarseness we may be giving a false impression of the attitude of reviewers to the Brontës. There were many reviewers who did not mention the subject of coarseness, and of those who did the majority were not blind to the merits of the Brontës. It is however possible, without exhausting the evidence, and indeed confining our survey to reviews published in England, to amass a considerable body of evidence to suggest that the Brontës offended against the canons of good taste prevalent at the time they wrote. In the first place there are more reviews hostile to coarseness than is generally allowed. In the second place even the reviews which deny coarseness acknowledge in places the existence of a considerable amount of hostile opinion. Thirdly we find a large number of individual readers either complaining about the coarseness of the Brontës or suggesting that their books are unsuitable for young readers.

Certainly *Jane Eyre* was warmly welcomed on its publication in October 1847. The *Atlas, Bath Herald, Britannia, Critic,*

Examiner, Howitt's Journal, Sun and *Weekly Chronicle* all praised it. *The Tablet* described the reading of it as 'a healthful exercise', the *People's Journal* declared that 'the moral sentiments are pure and healthy', and the *Era* said that 'the obvious moral thought' was that 'the practice of simple propriety, founded on strict morality and religious principles, is the sure road to ultimate bliss'. A slight note of caution was struck by *Douglas Jerrold's Magazine* which suggested that, 'to create emotion in the reader is too much the aim', and by *The New Monthly Magazine*, which called *Jane Eyre* 'a tale of passion', but G. H. Lewes in *Fraser's Magazine*, the first major periodical to review the novel, had no such reservations about it.[15]

But even at this stage the novelty of Jane's predicaments caused some alarm. *The Economist* in a favourable review opened the way to hostile critics when, after saying that *Jane Eyre* was 'as far removed from the namby-pamby stuff of which fashionable novels are made as from the cold unnatural and often disgusting productions of the French press', it went on to say, 'it must be said that the drawing in some cases approaches to coarseness'.[16] *The Literary Gazette* praised *Jane Eyre*, but did talk vaguely of 'ingredients of a less attractive nature'.[17] *The Athenaeum* called *Jane Eyre* 'improbable if not unpleasant',[18] and *The Spectator* said that it was reminiscent of sculptures of the Middle Ages which 'as far as delicacy was concerned were not pleasing in themselves'; although there was nothing 'of physical grossness in the book', the courtship of Jane and Rochester is described as 'a course of hardly *proper* conduct between a single man and a maiden in her teens'.[19] *The Mirror* gave *Jane Eyre* a scathing review, directed as much against Charlotte's religious and social doctrines as against her 'immorality', and referring in the process to a former work, allegedly by Currer Bell, 'quite as bold, quite as daring, quite as much distinguished for its insidious tendency, as the present volume'.[20] Charlotte thought this review unfair, and she was also not pleased with *The Observer*,[21] but the latter, though patronising, is quite favourable and contains no remarks against coarseness unless we count one rather strange allusion to sexual spite against Blanche Ingram. On the other hand *The Sunday Times* in perhaps the most prudish 1847 review said that Currer Bell was never content until she had passed 'the outworks of conventional reserve', and that the interview between Mr Rochester and his wife was 'too disgusting to quote'.[22]

In the first half of 1848 there were favourable reviews from *The Westminster Review, The Dublin University Magazine* and *Tait's Edinburgh Magazine,* which declared that 'the morality is throughout of an unexceptionable and instructive nature'. Opposition came from *The Church of England Quarterly Review,* which said that Jane Eyre had a dash of coarseness in her character, but objected to her principally because she had only morality and no religion behind her,[23] and from *The Christian Remembrancer,* which declared that it was unjust to say that *Jane Eyre* was positively immoral, but that it wore a questionable aspect with its masculine features.[24]

Meanwhile Emily's and Anne's first novels, published in December 1847, were being reviewed. Little attention was paid to *Agnes Grey,* although *The Atlas* did say that it was a 'somewhat coarse imitation of one of Miss Austin's (sic) charming stories'. Of the five reviews found in Emily's desk there is not much that is obviously prudish. *The Atlas* declares that *Wuthering Heights* gives a shocking picture of the worst forms of brutality, *Douglas Jerrold's Weekly Newspaper* claims that the reader is 'shocked, disgusted, almost sickened' by *Wuthering Heights,* and *The Examiner* thinks that the author of *Wuthering Heights* should not drag into the light all that he discovers of what is coarse and loathsome. *Britannia* calls *Wuthering Heights* 'rude', but this does not mean 'improper', and there are no accusations of impropriety in the fifth review from an unknown source, which was full of praise for Emily.[25] *The Athenaeum* said that *Wuthering Heights* was disagreeable, eccentric and unpleasant,[26] but *The Spectator,* though noting that 'the incidents are too coarse and disagreeable to be attractive, the very best being improbable, with a moral taint about them', was more complimentary about the abilities of the writer.[27] There was some praise too in the short notices in *The New Monthly Review* and *The Economist,* but the baffled feelings of reviewers of *Wuthering Heights* are best summed up by the conclusion of the review in *Tait's Edinburgh Magazine* to the effect that the novel proved that Satan was master of the law of entail.

The publication in June 1848 of *The Tenant of Wildfell Hall* appears to have acted as a catalyst. Before its publication the balance of opinion was distinctly in favour of the Brontës. Most of the few objections to the morality of *Jane Eyre* were both vague and veiled, while *Wuthering Heights* seems to have been blamed more for its brutality than any elements of indelicacy, and to have received some measure of praise as well. *The Tenant of Wildfell Hall* on the other hand attracted five exceptionally prudish reviews, and some of these reviews included the other Brontë novels in their attacks. Since, as we have shown, and as the reviewer in the *Rambler* remarked, *The Tenant of Wildfell Hall* appears a less likely book than *Jane Eyre* to arouse prudish fears, this change in the reviewers' tone calls for some explanation.

It is of course true that some reviewers had questioned the morality of *Jane Eyre* and *Wuthering Heights*, and that the suspicions aroused by these two novels could be confirmed by the appearance of *The Tenant of Wildfell Hall*. For in her views on marriage as in other spheres Anne Brontë is a much more blatant preacher of unorthodox attitudes than her sisters; she is also a much less good novelist, and therefore gave reviewers less opportunity of softening their attacks on the doctrines which she appeared to be thrusting down their throats. An additional factor is the political climate of 1848, the year of revolutions; conservative critics have ever been ready to see a connection between sexual licence and political anarchy.

In spite of these reasons for harshness on the part of reviewers the tone and the arguments used in reviews of *The Tenant of Wildfell Hall* are surprising. Thus *The Athenaeum*[28] found fault with the book because the position of the wife with regard to her husband's paramour is treated with hard indifference. Since the same reviewer also says that 'the Bells must be warned against their fancy for dwelling upon what is disagreeable', one is not quite sure of what he is complaining. *The Spectator* takes refuge in vague generalities:

There is power, effect and even nature, though of an extreme kind, in its pages; but there seems a morbid love of the coarse, not to say brutal; so that his level subjects are not very attractive and the more forcible are displeasing or repulsive, from the gross, physical or profligate substratum.

Equally vague are the comments on the Brontës in general:

There is a coarseness of tone throughout the writing of all these Bells, that puts an offensive subject in its worst point of view, and which generally contrives to dash indifferent things.[29]

But the hostility of these two reviews, emanating from periodicals which had previously found fault with the coarseness of the Bells, is as nothing when compared with that of *The Rambler*.[30] This reviewer begins by assuming that *Jane Eyre* and *The Tenant of Wildfell Hall* are by the same author. The author is said to be a clever and vigorous writer with a marked turn of mind, which has given her books a specially individual air. So far so good, but the reviewer continues,

And for the sake of the morals of the novel-reading public, we hope that this their peculiar feature has been the real cause of their attractiveness to many readers; and not that truly offensive and sensual spirit which is painfully prominent both in Jane Eyre and in the tale now before us . . . Jane Eyre is, indeed, one of the coarsest books which we ever perused. It is not that the professed sentiments of the writer are absolutely wrong or forbidding, or that the odd sort of religious notions which she puts forward are much worse than is usual in popular tales. It is rather that there is a certain perpetual tendency to relapse into that class of ideas, expressions, and circumstances, which is most connected with the grosser and more animal portion of our nature; and that the detestable morality of the most prominent character in the story is accompanied with every sort of palliation short of unblushing justification.

The Tenant of Wildfell Hall is 'not so bad a book as *Jane*

Eyre. There is not such a palpable blinking at the abominable nature of the morality of its most prominent characters.' But Gilbert Markham is described as 'a kind of gentleman farmer, whose morals, religion, cultivation, and talents are about on a par with those of Jane Eyre', and Helen Huntingdon's diary records 'with offensive minuteness the disgusting scenes of debauchery, blasphemy and profaneness'. The reviewer concludes by saying that he hopes no more works will be written by the same pen.

At about the same time as this review appeared, *Sharpe's London Magazine* produced another classic of prudish criticism.[31] The review begins ominously,

> So revolting are many of the scenes, so coarse and disgusting the language put into the mouths of some of the characters, that the reviewer to whom we entrusted it returned it to us, saying it was unfit to be noticed in the pages of SHARPE; and we are so far of the same opinion, that our object in the present paper is to warn our readers, and more especially our lady-readers, against being induced to peruse it, either by the powerful interest of the story, or the talent with which it is written.

The virtues of the book make a notice necessary; otherwise it could be allowed 'quietly to sink into the insignificance to which the good taste of the reading public speedily condemns works disfigured by the class of faults we have alluded to'. The evils of the novel which make it unfit for perusal

> arise from a perverted taste and an absence of mental refinement in the writer, together with a total ignorance of the usages of good society, rather than from any systematic design of opposing the cause of religion and morality.

On the contrary the moral of the tale is excellent, and the author seems a religious character, although his doctrines on eternal punishment are unwarranted.

What is wrong with *The Tenant of Wildfell Hall* is not the sentiments expressed, but the language in which they are expressed. In asserting this the reviewer finds himself in a difficulty.

As we are unable to support our strictures by adducing extracts
(for we must not fall into a fault somewhat too common with
reviewers, and, by polluting our pages with coarse quotations
commit the very sin we are inveighing against) we will proceed
to give a slight sketch of the story, and leave our readers to
judge whether scenes such as we shall glance at, where each
revolting detail is dwelt on with painful minuteness, each brutal
or profane expression chronicled with hateful accuracy,
can be fit subject matter for the pages of a work of fiction, a
popular novel to be obtruded by every circulating library-
keeper upon the notice of our sisters, wives and daughters.

Handicapped in this way, the reviewer can do little more than
make token gestures of horror at the liaison with Lady Lowborough, the teaching of little Arthur to swear, and the scenes
of drunkenness – gestures which are balanced by praise of the
author's depiction of character and nervous forcible style. There
are some interesting speculations on the sex of the author. 'None
but a man could have known so intimately each vile, dark fold
of the civilized brute's corrupted nature', and no woman could
have displayed 'such bold coarseness, a reckless familiarity with
the sayings and doings of the worst type of fast men'. On the
other hand no man would have emphasised the superiority of the
female characters, and thus the hypothesis of joint authorship is
advanced.

The review in *Sharpe's* concludes by regretting that the book
is

unfit for perusal of the very class of persons to whom it would
be most useful (namely imaginative girls likely to risk their
happiness on the forlorn hope of marrying and reforming a
captivating rake) owing to the profane expressions, incon-
ceivably coarse language and revolting scenes and descriptions
by which its pages are disfigured.

Since the reviewer gives no examples of these disfigurements,
nor shows why it is impossible for young girls to see them, we
may accuse him of real prudery, namely a confused and unreasonable dislike of facing facts.

The reviewer in *Fraser's* for April 1849[32] is equally confused and inarticulate about what he is discussing, but at any rate he begins by finding fault with the more ostrich-like prudes. Kingsley was the author of this review,[33] and we are not surprised to find the same strange mixture of strangled outspokenness and feminine squeamishness in this review as in Kingsley's own novels.

> *The fault of this book is coarseness – not merely that coarseness of subject which will be the stumbling-block of most readers, and which makes it utterly unfit to be put into the hands of girls; of that we do not complain. There are foul and accursed undercurrents in plenty, in this same smug, respectable, whitewashed English society, which must be exposed now and then and Society owes thanks, not sneers to those who dare to show her the image of her own ugly, hypocritical visage.*

Kingsley then emphasises once again how charitable he is in comparison with average opinion.

> *But the world does not think so. It will revile Acton Bell for telling us, with painful circumstantiality, what the house of a profligate, uneducated country squire is like, perfectly careless whether or not the picture be true, only angry at having been disturbed from its own self-complacent doze.*

This strange mixture of praise and blame leads on to a long discussion of the improbability of Gilbert Markham marrying Helen Huntingdon; not only is he her social inferior, but he is brutal to boot, although he is 'no doubt highly attractive to young ladies of his own calibre'. This straightforward snobbery may explain some of the hostility of the review in *Fraser's*, although it hardly justifies it; apart from a few ritual denunciations of 'written oaths and curses' and details of drunken scenes, Kingsley does little to show why the book is unfit for girls or what, distinct from the coarseness to which the world will object, is the additional coarseness that he himself finds so objectionable.

Another review to combine prudery with snobbery was the famous contribution of Miss Rigby to the *Quarterly* for December 1848.[34] *Jane Eyre* had escaped unscathed apart from the incidental comments in *The Rambler* for half a year after the publication of *The Tenant of Wildfell Hall*, and in October 1848, *Blackwood's* had given it a very favourable review, although noting that it was not a book for prudes.[35] Miss Rigby is commonly regarded as one of these prudes, and her hostile attitude considered both unusual and unjust. She was not however the first to condemn the Brontës for coarseness, and apart from Charlotte Brontë, whose word to the *Quarterly* was not published, and W. S. Williams,[36] there is little record of anyone objecting to her views which were influential in many quarters and by some were regarded as authoritative. Nor is she all that unjust; though both prudery and snobbery are behind her hostility she does support her strictures with arguments, and, though unfair in places, as in the notorious reference to Thackeray's governess, credit is given to the portrait of the heroine as 'a noble high-souled woman, bound to us by the reality of her sorrow, and yet raised above us by the strength of her will', when she leaves Rochester rather than become his mistress. We cannot therefore regard as exceptional the following comments by Miss Rigby.

Jane Eyre is said to be another Pamela:

> Nor is she even a Pamela adapted and refined to modern notions; for though the story is conducted without those derelictions of decorum which we are to believe had their excuse in the manners of Richardson's time, yet it is stamped with a coarseness of language and laxity of tone which have certainly no excuse in ours.

When Rochester arrives at Thornfield he pours into Jane's ears

> disgraceful tales of his past life, connected with the birth of little Adèle, which any man with common respect for a woman, and that a mere girl of eighteen, would have spared her; but which eighteen in this case listens to as if it were nothing new, and certainly nothing distasteful.

The reader may observe

> that highest moral offence a novel writer can commit, that of making an unworthy character interesting in the eyes of the

reader. . . . We would have thought that such a hero (as Mr Rochester) had had no chance, in the purer taste of the present day; but the popularity of Jane Eyre is a proof how deeply the love for illegitimate romance is implanted in our nature.

Thus in addition to the impropriety of language we have impropriety of sentiments. Yet *Jane Eyre* is a very remarkable book, far superior to *Wuthering Heights*, of which Miss Rigby says, 'With all the unscrupulousness of the French school of novels it combines that repulsive vulgarity in the choice of its vice which supplies its own antidote.' Nevertheless *Jane Eyre* is too vulgar to be written by a woman, and 'if we ascribe the book to a woman at all, we have no alternative but to ascribe it to one who has, for some sufficient reason, long forfeited the society of her own sex'.

The influence of the *Quarterly* was considerable. *The North British Review* of August 1849[37] begins by taking up the *Quarterly*'s attack on *Jane Eyre*'s vulgarity and denying it, but it does accept some of the *Quarterly*'s arguments, while at the same time moved by a violent hostility to the other Bells. Before passing on to a vitriolic attack on 'the language too disgusting for the eye or ear to tolerate' of *Wuthering Heights* and 'the conversations such as we had never hoped to see printed in English' of *The Tenant of Wildfell Hall* the reviewer has some second thoughts about *Jane Eyre:*

But there are more latent objections to the tendency of this powerful book, which we are apt to overlook on a first perusal, and of the perniciousness of which we can only judge when we have seen them developed in other works professedly proceeding from the same source. In Jane herself there is a recklessness about right and wrong which is very alarming.

Rather different is *The Dublin Review* for May 1850[38] which discusses both *Jane Eyre* and *Shirley*. This review begins by what looks like an attack on the *Quarterly*, saying that there are some for whom the books 'are too brilliant and bold', who shelter themselves under the plea that they 'are not strictly proper'. Then in the same way that *The North British* refuted the charge that Jane was vulgar, *The Dublin Review* goes on to show that Caroline Helstone is a model of propriety, and the assessment of both *Shirley* and *Jane Eyre* is a very favourable one. Doubts are mentioned when, the reviewer says, 'there is a feeling in many quarters that their morality is questionable'. These doubts are answered by the claim that adverse critics cannot appreciate originality:

> The excuse is good – the plea valid – boldness does not necessarily lead to vice, nor does originality, nor does even strong passion; but they should be dealt with only by the strong and the experienced.

Although the reviewer is favourable in general and defends the novel against the particular charge of coarseness, he is not above a reference to the cheek of the young person, when he states authoritatively, 'Undoubtedly we would give neither of these novels to very young people.'

A final reminder of the way in which *Jane Eyre* acquired its bad reputation is to be found in the opening sentence of *The Spectator* review of *Shirley* in November 1849.[39] Like *The Christian Remembrancer* review of *Villette* which, though harsher than the same periodical's review of *Jane Eyre*, yet contrives to say that *Villette* is an improvement on *Jane Eyre*, *The Spectator* before attacking the ingrained rudeness and absence of delicacy and refinement in *Shirley* compares it favourably with the other Brontë novels:

> There is less coarseness than was displayed in all of them, somewhat less questionable propriety than appeared in the best of them, '*Jane Eyre*', and nothing of the low and almost disgusting characters and circumstances that disfigured the rest.

The shocked reception of *The Tenant of Wildfell Hall* and the authoritative verdict of the *Quarterly* on *Jane Eyre* almost certainly account for the way in which *Shirley* was treated. Admittedly *Shirley* has faults unconnected with prudery, and it is sometimes difficult to distinguish between denunciations of these faults and prudish objections. The fact remains that, though as *Fraser's* rightly pointed out, 'As to the morality, it must be a very precise prude, indeed, who could ferret out an innuendo in *Shirley*',⁴⁰ a number of reviewers had no difficulty in, like *The Spectator*, ferreting out some degree of coarseness. Thus *The Dublin University Magazine*⁴¹ in a very hostile review which is in marked contrast to the same periodical's treatment of *Jane Eyre* say that, 'the coarse, the vulgar and the eccentric have no charms for us'. The reviewer accuses Robert and Louis Moore of having coarse and sensual natures, and says that Shirley is equally despicable, although her chief crime seems to be the venial one of asking Louis Moore, whether he should 'be good enough, in case hydrophobia should supervene, to smother her with a pillow'. This may not seem a very prudish objection. More serious, though still rather vague, is the following passage:

> Of all these bad qualities – these violations of good manners and sins against good taste – in this instance we accuse the writer of Shirley, and leave her to the judgement of public opinion, by which assuredly she shall be condemned.

It appears that one of the main faults of *Shirley* is its treatment of Irishmen, and this may be the reason for the sudden change of tone in *The Dublin University Magazine*, but prudery is involved in the objection. After a digression on vulgarity, and after saying that the author has not the smallest idea of what 'in our opinion is the most attractive part of woman's nature', the reviewer concludes with an attack on the whole Bell family, who 'are sadly deficient in moral tone and sound wholesome feeling'.

The most interesting comments on *Shirley* come from G. H. Lewes in *The Edinburgh Review*.⁴² As the author of the complimentary review of *Jane Eyre* in *Fraser's* Lewes can be accused of a certain inconsistency, perhaps caused by editorial policy,⁴³ in mingling praise with blame in the following comments on *Jane Eyre*.

> Faults enough the book has undoubtedly; faults of conception, faults of taste, faults of ignorance, but in spite of it all, it remains a book of singular fascination. A more masculine

book in the sense of vigour, was never written. Indeed that vigour often amounts to coarseness – and it is certainly the very antipode to 'lady-like'.

Shirley is said to be even more vigorous. 'This same over-masculine vigour is even more prominent in Shirley, and does not increase the pleasantness of the book.' Shirley is 'even coarser in texture' than Jane Eyre, while the characters are 'almost all disagreeable, and exhibit intolerable rudeness of manner'. All these remarks are sufficiently general to be considered as accusations of something distinct from sexual immodesty, and the specific examples Lewes gives of vulgarity; such phrases as 'Miss Mary, getting up the steam in her turn now asked etc.', or as 'making hard-handed worsted spinners cash up to the tune of 4 or 500%' hardly seem prudish at all. Nevertheless, though Lewes may not have ferreted out innuendoes in Shirley, he was not above making his own innuendoes in accusing Shirley of using language one would rather not hear from the lips of a lady, and saying that Schiller's remark about Madame de Stael's Corinne is equally applicable to Currer Bell. 'She steps out of her sex without elevating herself above it.'

More definitely prudish was Sharpe's London Magazine[44] which returned to the attack on the Brontës in 1849:

> The opponents of Jane Eyre (and they were legion) will find in Shirley much to cavil at – more to condemn. . . . The world complained of her last work, because the sentiments, however genuine, were too lightly veiled, and the expression of these sentiments too little suited to the taste of the age. The authoress has ill-judgingly or wilfully mistaken its opinion.

Sharpe's then denies any accusation of prudery with the words 'We are as far from being prudish as from being over-aristocratic', but the reviewer is surely being prudish when the author of Shirley is condemned for being 'such that her sex disowns her – nay will even blush for her'.

These last words suggest that the reviewer in Sharpe's may well have been a woman. Certainly the most hostile reviews were written by women, and a very typical feminine contribution came from the pen of Mrs Sara Ellis, whose Daughters of

England, Wives of England, and *Women of England* were standard manuals of feminine behaviour. Writing in *The Morning
Call, A Table Book of Literature and Art*[45] about the recent
publication of *Shirley* she begins with some speculations about
the sex of the writer of *Jane Eyre.* The hypothesis of joint authorship is not unreasonable,

> *because the work contains passages, of which the reader is
> disposed to say, that no man could have written them if he
> would; and others, of which the reader is still more disposed
> to say, that no woman would have written them if she could.*

Both books are remarkable for glaring violations of good taste.
The violations in *Shirley* appear to consist of the vulgar behaviour of Shirley in whistling and answering back, the coarseness in dragging in religious demonstrations and distinctions,
and the fact that both heroines are won before they are wooed.
Only in the last accusation is prudery involved, but in her
peroration on both books Mrs Ellis, while admitting the powerful appeal of the novels, shows how far the writer is from being
a typical wife, daughter or woman of England. She imagines
Charlotte with a mocking voice exclaiming,

> '*I have made you endure vulgarity, at which you were dis-
> gusted; boldness at which you were offended; and delineations
> of passion at which you were appalled. I have inspired you
> with hope, almost as ardent as if for yourself, that my heroes
> would succeed, even while you pronounced such men to be
> odious. I have bathed you in the sorrows of my heroines, even
> while you declared them not to be women to your taste.*'

Apart from the long and favourable notice in *The Eclectic
Review* all major periodicals reviewing *Shirley* mentioned coarseness in some form or other, even if like *The Dublin Review* and
Fraser's they rejected the charge. Newspapers were more charitable, and it seems a pity that Charlotte did not set more store by
their verdict, as she received glowing tributes, untainted by any
suggestion of coarseness, from the *Critic, Globe, Morning
Chronicle, Observer, Standard of Freedom, Sun* and *Weekly
Chronicle.*[46] *Britannia* and *The Economist* were also full of praise,

although the former thought parts of the tale not very pleasing and the latter talked of 'vigour, raciness, and freshness of style and scorn of trifling conventionalities'.[47] *The Daily News* attacked the 'vulgar, unnecessary, disgusting' opening scene, but it is probable that the reviewer like Kingsley is mainly influenced here by religious considerations.[48] For exceptions to the rule that newspapers did not made prudish attacks on *Shirley*, a rule which applied to the short notices of the cheap edition of 1852 in *The Noncomformist, Sunday Times* and *Globe*,[49] we have to look at *The Atlas, Examiner, Morning Herald* and *Times*.[50] *The Atlas* which had praised *Jane Eyre* two years before said that *Shirley* contained even more deplorable evidence of bad taste. *The Examiner* was reasonably laudatory, but it did comment, 'As well as in remarking on *Jane Eyre*, as in noticing other books from the same family, if not from the same hand, we have directed attention to an excess of the repulsive qualities not seldom rather coarsely indulged.' *The Morning Herald* said 'we find the two lady friends placed at times in rather unfeminine and unnatural positions'. *The Times*, whose main contention was that Charlotte had shot her bolt with *Jane Eyre*, was certainly invoking prudish fears when it said that *Jane Eyre* was disfigured by coarseness, but was a far better novel than *Shirley*, commented on Charlotte's fondness for 'love in a kitchen and courtship in the scullery', and declared that in *Shirley* 'lovemaking in one shape or another, is going on from the first page to the last'.

The comments of the periodicals on *Shirley*, following the falsely optimistic verdict of most newspapers, meant that by 1850 the reputation of the Brontë sisters, if not bad, was at any rate doubtful. In the next three years little occurred to alter this opinion. There was the extravagant praise of Sidney Dobell in *The Palladium* for September 1850, and the publication of a second edition of *Wuthering Heights* and *Agnes Grey* in December 1850 did produce the previously noted bewildered response of *The Leader*, and something of a recantation in *The Athenaeum*,[51] but this kinder response, prompted no doubt by Charlotte's Biographical Notice, was short-lived. *The Eclectic Review*[52] for February 1851 found *Wuthering Heights* repellent, and in August of the same year there appeared in *The North British Review* an article on 'Recent Works of Fiction' attacking the Bells for 'their coarseness of diction and even of sentiment':

> *Ellis Bell seems to revel in a gratuitous use of blackguardism in phraseology. Acton Bell affects it far too freely in Agnes Grey and The Tenant of Wildfell Hall, and Currer Bell is open to the same charge in a mitigated form.*[53]

This article is quoted in *The New Monthly Magazine*[54] a year later in an article which though in general favourable to Currer Bell, raises the charge of coarseness, and agrees with *The North British Review* in making Emily rather than Anne Brontë the chief villain:

> *Of the many among whom Jane Eyre made a sensation not a few professed themselves a little shocked. The author was so wayward, so free-spoken, so unconventional. The book was to be read gingerly, with caution, with suspicion; it was evidently by some one not used, or willing to run in harness of the old style – some one not cumbered with much serving to the prejudices, primnesses, and proprieties of genteel fiction as by law established. Especially was this antipathy in force at a time when she was the accredited author of that wild wilful wicked tale, Wuthering Heights.*

There then follows a friendly account of *Jane Eyre* and *Shirley*, in which the latter is shown to be more pleasant, but less healthy:

> *The novel that can make its favourites happy only by letting them have their own way ad libitum is perchance a little rickety in truth and morals.*

Lucy Snowe does not have her own way in *Villette*; the person who does have her own way and is flirtatious as well is Ginevra Fanshawe, and she is shown to be a despicable character. For these and other reasons one would think that *Villette* escaped the charge of impropriety, but it attracted two of the most famous prudish reviews, that in *The Daily News* by Harriet Martineau and in *The Christian Remembrancer* by

Anne Mozley. Of these the latter is the most accessible and most notorious, being commonly linked with that in *The Quarterly Review*. Thus the editors of the Shakespeare Head Brontë say that it was these two reviews which caused Charlotte the most pain, and Charlotte herself described *The Quarterly Review* and *The Christian Remembrancer* as the 'heavy Goliaths of the periodical press'.[55] The review of *Villette*[56] begins with a harsh attack on *Jane Eyre*, protesting against

> the outrages on decorum, the moral perversity, the toleration of, nay, indifference to vice which deform her first powerful picture of a desolate woman's trials and sufferings – faults which make Jane Eyre a dangerous book, and which must leave a permanent distrust of the author on all thoughtful and scrupulous minds.

It then admits *Villette* to be an improvement on its predecessor, saying that the author has gained 'both in amiability and propriety since she first presented herself to the world – soured, coarse and grumbling'. Nor are the criticisms against *Villette* directed against coarseness, so much as against religious faults and an inadequate conception of woman's role. There is the rather strange comment that Currer Bell's own morality is very faulty in allowing Graham Bretton to make assignations with Ginevra Fanshawe, although the reviewer admits that Currer Bell sees the faults in Graham. The peroration against heroines like Lucy Snowe might fairly be regarded as an example of prudery.

> We want a woman at our hearth; and her impersonations are without the feminine element, infringers of all modest restraints, despisers of bashful fears, self-reliant, contemptuous of prescriptive decorum; their own unaided reason, their individual opinion of right and wrong, discreet or imprudent, sole guides of conduct and rules of manners – the whole hedge of immemorial scruple and habit broken down and trampled upon.

This review is not all that harsh, and there is a reason for its harshness which might at first sight seem unconnected with prudery. The reviewer, Ann Mozley, was a prominent High Churchwoman; two of her brothers married two of Newman's sisters, and a third brother, J. B. Mozley, was after Newman's secession one of the leaders of the Tractarian party.[57] As representatives of the Tractarians who did not go over to Rome, the Mozleys cannot have been all that hostile to *Villette* with its emphasis on the worst features of Roman Catholicism; indeed a novel by Lady Fullerton, a Catholic convert, is not very sympathetically treated in the same review that attacks *Villette*. On the other hand the description in *Shirley* of the Puseyite curate can hardly have influenced the High Church party in Charlotte's favour, and she herself had no hesitation in attributing the hostile reviews in *The Christian Remembrancer* and other High Church papers, *The English Churchman* and *The Guardian*, to religious reasons.[58]

The Guardian indeed is much less fair than *The Christian Remembrancer*:

> It is part of the same character that she should be wanting in refinement, and that even her best characters, those she wishes to be models of purity and grace, are represented by her as consenting to situations and adopting practices no really high-minded and virtuous person would consent to. Especially this is the case with her women, who can never be accepted as real ladies.[59]

These attacks are launched against Paulina's clandestine correspondence with Graham, and one is left wondering what *The Guardian* wanted Charlotte to do, since, as we have shown, she already expresses some measure of disapproval for what is in our eyes a very innocent courtship.

It is not, however, possible to dismiss the prudish remarks in *The Christian Remembrancer* and *The Guardian* as superficial insults caused by High Church hostility. A good case can be made out for showing that Tractarianism was itself an extremely prudish movement. The curious phenomenon whereby the Evangelicals of the twenties, like the Wilberforce brothers, became the Tractarians of the forties meant that the Tractarians inherited something of the scruples of Bowdler with their zeal for celibacy as an added incentive to prudery.[60] Although Kingsley himself entered the ranks of the prudish reviewers with his eccentric attack on *The Tenant of Wildfell Hall*, we have only to compare his relatively outspoken treatment of sex in *Hypatia* with Newman's chaste *Callista* to realise that High Churchmen were less broadminded than Broad Churchmen about literary decorum.[61] Indeed there is an interesting connection here between the Brontës' latitudinarian views on religion and their emancipation from prudery, as it was Broad Churchmen like Kingsley and Stanley who took up the cudgels on behalf of *Ruth*.

Harriet Martineau's review of *Villette* in the *Daily News*,[62] though connected with the subject of coarseness by Mrs Gaskell, is not all that prudish. According to her the two faults of the book are that the author has no right to make readers so miserable and, a lesser fault, the female characters are too exclusively preoccupied with love.

> *Readers who are no prudes . . . will reject the assumption that events and characters are to be regarded through the medium of one passion only.*

Miss Martineau begins her next paragraph, 'And here ends all demur', and it seems that both the prudery and hostility in general of her review have been exaggerated as a result of Charlotte's resentment of it. Elsewhere Charlotte had little to complain about; she was pleased with the reviews, and we may note in particular the friendly reception of *Villette* by the *Atlas*, *Critic*, *Dublin University Magazine*, *Edinburgh Guardian*, *Globe*, *Leader*, *Morning Advertiser* and *Spectator*. The *Eclectic Review*, *Magnet*, *Nonconformist* and *Sunday Times* were less favourable, but not prudish, *The Westminster Review* was very favourable, although saying that Charlotte Brontë's characters outraged good taste and that propriety was not to be demanded of them, and unlike French novelists Charlotte Brontë escaped unscathed in an article by the formidable W. R. Greg in *The Edinburgh Review*. Charlotte's success in meeting the objections of her critics was not, however, quite complete. The *Athenaeum*, the most consistently hostile of the Brontës' opponents, complained, 'her talk is of duty, her predeliction of passion';[63] *The*

Literary Gazette, though full of praise of *Villette* for regaining the ground lost in *Shirley,* adds, 'Some traces too of the coarseness which occasionally disfigured Currer Bell's former books still remain.'[64] Finally *Bell's Weekly Messenger,* more out of habit, we almost feel, than from any serious conviction, still sees fit to warn Charlotte about

> *that defect – coarseness of manner – which was so painfully apparent in Jane Eyre, but somewhat softened and modified in Shirley. It is much, very much, toned down in this book but still it here and there peeps out.*[65]

By the time of Charlotte's death in 1855 we have passed from what Professor Tillotson regards the outspoken forties to the period in which prudery was at its height. Thus some of Mrs Oliphant's comments in *Blackwood's* for May 1855,[66] written at almost the same time as Charlotte's death, news of which caused Mrs Oliphant to apologise for her harshness at the end of her article, would seem to do nothing to weaken Professor Tillotson's case. When Mrs Oliphant talks of grossness and refined indelicacy and says that there are some conversations between Rochester and Jane Eyre which no man could have dared to give, she is obviously displaying mid-Victorian prudery. What is disturbing for Professor Tillotson's case is that Mrs Oliphant, as in her previously quoted 1867 article, attributes to the publication of *Jane Eyre* not the rise of prudery, but the breaking of all prudish restraints:

> *Ten years ago we professed an orthodox system of novel-making. Our lovers were humble and devoted ... and the only true love worth having was that reverent, knightly, chivalrous true love which consecrated all womankind and served one with fervour and enthusiasm. Such was our ideal, and such our system in the old halcyon days of novel-writing; when suddenly without warning Jane Eyre stole upon the scene and the most alarming revolution of modern times has followed the invasion of Jane Eyre.*

Other arguments against Professor Tillotson's case are provided by the comments of reviewers in the ten years that followed

Charlotte's death. Many of these reviews mention the subject of coarseness, but deny that Charlotte Brontë was coarse. Charlotte's death and the publication of Mrs Gaskell's life obviously made reviewers more friendly; even *The Athenaeum*, as we have shown, abated its wrath when reviewing *The Professor*. Similarly *Fraser's* for May 1857,[67] after saying, '*Jane Eyre* has been austerely condemned by austere critics. It is said that the interest depends on the terrible and immoral', and 'The charge of immorality is one easily made – still more easily repeated', eventually concludes:

> But as we recall the lone woman sitting by the desolate hearthstone, and remember all that she lost and suffered, we cannot blame very gravely the occasional harshness and impatience of the language.

In the same way *The Critic* of 15 April 1857[68] declines to reopen the old question as to where the line is to be drawn between indelicacy which is the result of corruption and the natural vigour of intellect which disdains conventional laws', but concludes that 'no purer mind ever offered its reflections to the world than Currer Bell'. Among other late notices which remarked on the accusations of indelicacy but dissociated themselves from them was that in *The Oxford and Cambridge Magazine* for June 1856,[69] which declared:

> Jane Eyre *by many has been looked upon as an immoral publication, and Currer Bell as the treacherous advocate of contempt of established maxims and disregard of the regulations of society,*

but the reviewer denied this charge. Very similar was the article by Montégut in *Revue des Deux Mondes* for 1857,[70] which although full of praise for Charlotte Brontë said, 'Plus on relit ces singulières conversations et moins on s'étonne que *Jane Eyre* ait tout effarouché les pruderies anglaises.' Finally *The Westminster Review* in 1864 in words which suggested that the peak of prudery had been passed, stated

> When Charlotte Brontë *endeavoured to do otherwise (i.e. to portray heroines who were not feeble) we can all recall that*

a prudish scream was raised against her and genteel virtue
affected to be horrified with the authoress who drew women
and girls endowed with human passion.[71]

Reviews are a good guide to the feelings of the age because
as well as their own and their editors' views they reflect the views
of the audience for whom they were written. In this connection
it is worth noting that of the best-known periodicals of the
period only *The Westminster Review* and *The Dublin Review*
did not at least once criticise one of the Brontës for coarseness;
Blackwood's, The Christian Remembrancer, Dublin University
Magazine, Eclectic Review, Edinburgh Review, Fraser's Maga-
zine, The North British Review, Quarterly Review and *Rambler*
all contained hostile articles. With the exception of Radicals
and the Broad Church all shades of opinion were represented
by these periodicals; Whig and Tory, High Churchman and
Evangelical, Catholic and Protestant, Irishman and Scot, all
united in finding something to complain about in the novels of
the Brontës, as did a whole host of less representative newspapers and periodicals. There were of course an equal number of
voices who found nothing to blame and a great deal to praise,
but we cannot dismiss the prudish hostility to the Brontës as an
eccentric aberration of a small part of the community.

This impression is confirmed when we look at those individuals
who found something objectionable in the novels of the Brontës.
The reactions of individuals are of course less valuable than the
reactions of periodicals which hope to speak for a wider audience,
nor can anything like a complete study be made. All the same an
examination of which readers found *Jane Eyre* shocking produces
some surprising results. Since we are discussing Victorian prudery
it is perhaps worth noting that Queen Victoria found nothing
wrong in *Jane Eyre.*[72] On the other hand there was surprising
hostility in a circle which one would expect to find above
prudery, that of Charlotte's literary friends. A friend of Mrs
Smith was shocked that *Jane Eyre* was left unguarded in the
house of Charlotte's publisher, G. H. Lewes called it a naughty
book,[73] and perhaps most strangely of all Mrs Gaskell's daughter
had to ask her mother's permission in 1854 to read *Jane Eyre.*[74]

Reaction in the more restricted circles in which Charlotte moved in Yorkshire was more easy to understand, although both Miss Heald's refusal to read *Jane Eyre* on the authority of the *Quarterly*,[75] and Miss Wooler's condescending remark that in spite of what Charlotte had said and done in the writing line she still retained a place in her esteem, appear a little excessive. Charlotte's indignant exclamations, both in the letter to Ellen Nussey reporting the latter remark and in a letter of rather different tone to Miss Wooler herself, claiming that only to the coarse were her works coarse,[76] suggest a considerable amount of opposition to the Brontës and, what is more important, considerable concern by Charlotte at this opposition. Two rather unlikely candidates for the role of 'persons by nature coarse, by inclination sensual' were Dean Merivale who reported in a letter to his sister Fanny in November 1848 that *Jane Eyre* made his old bachelor bones rattle.... 'It is by a young woman, and not a very refined one, from a certain want of acquired delicacy', and Elizabeth Barrett Browning, writing to Miss Mitford of 'the qualities, half savage and half free-thinking', expressed in *Jane Eyre*.[77]

We may conclude with some observations, which though they attained the dignity of print, are so individualistic that they are better considered under the heading of private views on the coarseness of the Brontës rather than public reviews of their works. The identity of W.P.P., the author of *Jottings on Currer, Ellis and Acton Bell*,[78] is still unknown. He shows a strange mixture of knowledge and ignorance about the Brontës, describing Mr Nicholls as an occasional *Edinburgh* Reviewer, giving Brontë an acute accent, and stating that the origin of the story in both *Jane Eyre* and *Agnes Grey* of an heiress being disinherited for marrying a poor clergyman lay in the circumstances of the Brontë family, but also showing that he was aware that an official life was being prepared by Mrs Gaskell. This last piece of information, when combined with the fact that the pamphlet was dedicated to 'E', might suggest that he was a friend of Ellen Nussey's, and a certain Biblical tone about his style would suggest that he was a clergyman. At all events neither his profession nor the degree of his friendship with the Brontës would explain his extraordinarily impassioned attack on prudery and defence of the Brontës against the charge of impurity. W.P.P. is worth quoting at some length, because though exceptional in his attacks on prudery, he is at the same time with his remarkably circumspect allusions, an unconscious witness to the verbal prudery he is denouncing:

The real modesty of Currer Bell is worthy of remark. It differs so agreeably from that that is common in what are called our 'fashionable novels.' For, doubtless, it is more modest and truthful to speak out on certain subjects than to pretend to ignore them. They are great facts. They cannot be denied; and, moreover, there is no need to do so, no end to be obtained in doing so. Why then simper and blush, and play the prude, when you speak of, or about things, that GOD himself, the Essence of all Purity, has thought fit to discourse of in Holy Scripture. The great Macaulay, in writing on this subject, speaks most emphatically of the folly of hiding subjects of a certain class from children, when it will be sure to reach them, and, most likely, through an impure channel; whereas, were it done properly, all this might be avoided. In the days of Fielding, these things were written, and people did not then affect to be shocked; but now you must not touch upon such subjects, without, forsooth, some Puritanical people holding up their hands in pious horror. We would ask, are people one whit better now than they were then: nay, are they so good? Did the country teem then, as it does now, with murderers of mothers, and murderers of fathers, and murderers of husbands, and of wives, and of children? Was the country flooded then with crimes of such varied kinds, and such deep dyes? Is the world more godly now, we ask, than then? We fearlessly challenge any one to the proof. No! It is too well known that we go on increasing in sin and wickedness, every day and every hour. We tax our ingenuity to invent some new way in which we may insult the Majesty of the Most High God.

We have said thus much, because it has been objected to the writings of the Bells, by some, that many subjects are far too minutely treated. But, we feel sure, that every right thinking person will repudiate such an accusation.

The Bells were highly educated, and their minds were, necessarily, well trained; of their innate purity, there can be no doubt. And, to our minds, they evidenced their true modesty most forcibly, by writing freely and truthfully on all subjects, whether they were what Mrs Grundy – detestable old bug-bear! – would call delicate, or not. Such an honest proceeding would, of course, bring down on them the puny attacks of tiny controversialists; but the reputation of Currer, Ellis and Acton Bell is built, not on the sand, but on the rock; and no feeble attempt of still feebler minds would, or could, shake it one tittle. Does it not seem passing strange, that a nation that barters her daughters for gold and rank, thus using them as those we cannot here name without sullying this fair sheet on which we write; that a people incurably overrun with vice and immorality of the worst kind, should avert its modest face, and hold up its pious hands, when a virtuous lady thinks fit to write on a subject which should be virtuous to those who are so; for 'unto the pure all things are pure: but unto them that are defiled in believing is nothing pure; but even their mind and conscience is defiled;' and again, 'evil be to him that evil thinks.'[79]

In spite of his hostility to prudery, we cannot claim W.P.P. with his coy allusion to 'those we cannot here name without sullying this fair sheet' as a representative of a new frank generation growing up in the fifties to attack the prudish forties, and in any case there is no evidence to suggest that W.P.P. was in any case a representative figure. For a major change in public taste we have to look not at the ten years between the publication of *Jane Eyre* and the publication of Mrs Gaskell's life, but at the forty years between 1867 and 1907, a change neatly summed up in the words of Rhoda Broughton: 'I began my career as Zola; I finish it as Miss Yonge.' Thereafter public taste has altered so rapidly in spite of occasional setbacks such as the prosecution of *Ulysses* and *The Rainbow*, that we now live in an age when Zola appears as innocuous as Charlotte M. Yonge. In such an age it is hard indeed to comprehend the strength of feeling against the Brontës, and it is tempting to minimise it as does Professor Tillotson, or to ignore it as do most modern critics, or to misunderstand it totally, as did the critic who thought he had detected Charlotte Brontë cocking a snook at the literary conventions of her day with an overt phallic reference. But an understanding of what these literary conventions involved and how the Brontës only gradually became aware of them can do more than save us from making ridiculous mistakes like translating the Brontës from their nineteenth-century parsonage to the campus of a progressive American university. Once the literary historian has fathomed the depths of nineteenth-century prudery the way is open for literary critics to explore several interesting questions. Is the impact of *Shirley* and *Villette* less powerful than that of *Jane Eyre*, because in an unsuccessful attempt to appease her critics Charlotte toned down the passion of her later novels? Is Anne's work unsuccessful for the same reason that contemporary critics found it so disgusting, namely that having, unlike her sisters, experienced fairly intimate relations with an ordinary family, she recorded them faithfully without paying lip service to the demands of literary decorum, and thus incidentally not paying due attention to the demands of artistic form? Finally is the intense, though curiously sexless, passion of Heathcliff and Catherine a success, because Emily Brontë, alike free from the prudery which reveals too little and the prurience which reveals too much, could give the appropriate emphasis to a subject which has baffled the prudish nineteenth century and the coarse twentieth century?

8

Snobs and Snobbery

SNOBBERY is to class, as prudery is to sex, an unnatural attitude to a natural fact of human existence. The two vices are obviously connected, as marrying and giving in marriage are two of the easiest ways of changing one's class, and sexual jealousy is at the back of much class hatred. Our own permissive society is also a relatively classless one; it was at the trial of *Lady Chatterley's Lover*, itself an interesting indication of the close link between class and sex, that the prosecuting counsel brought ridicule on himself and the cause of prudery by demanding anachronistically whether Lawrence's book was fit reading for servants.[1] By contrast the nineteenth century was conspicuous for both snobbery and prudery. It is perhaps a coincidence that the same year of 1818 saw the publication of Bowdler's *Family Shakespeare* and the attacks in *Blackwood's Magazine* on the Cockney School of Poetry, but one only has to look at Thackeray's interest in and curiously ambivalent attitude to both sexual reticence and social climbing to realise the connection between prudery and snobbery. Richardson, another important literary influence on the Brontës, has the same ambivalent attitude to both subjects as Thackeray. Because class distinctions were clearer in the eighteenth century, and because the restrictions of prudery were less harsh, Richardson was able in *Pamela* and *Clarissa Harlowe* to make the links between prudes and snobs almost brutally obvious by making his lower or upper middle class heroines painfully virtuous, and his aristocratic hero-villains libertines and rakes. Although Richardson was an author popular in the early nineteenth century, the early date of his novels shows that, though snobbery, like prudery, is a nineteenth-century phenomenon, its roots lie in the eighteenth century. The rise of a middle class, with its prosperity based on trade, not land, produced people who lacking the aristocratic confidence in their own superiority of status and conduct were abnormally conscious of the need to preserve their respectability in order to maintain their position.[2]

We would, therefore, expect to find reactions against snobbery, as well as reactions against prudery, in the works of the Brontës. It is, however, surprising that, with a few exceptions, largely dealing with *Wuthering Heights*, the hardest novel to fit into any pattern, critics have been reluctant to explore the sociological aspects of the Brontë novels.[3] This is all the more surprising because the two most famous novels, *Jane Eyre* and *Wuthering Heights*, both contain a classic case of a change of class. Heathcliff from being a friendless waif turns into the master of Thrushcross Grange and Wuthering Heights, while Jane Eyre, of more elevated birth than Heathcliff, but with just as poor prospects, becomes the wife of the prosperous Rochester, once courted as the son-in-law of Baroness Ingram of Ingram Park. The other Brontë novels also involve class-consciousness, although of a less blatant kind. In *Agnes Grey* we have the contrast between the virtuous though humble hero and heroine and the frivolous but more aristocratic Murray circle. The vulgar Bloomfields, who are retired tradespeople, and Agnes Grey's mother, disinherited by her father for marrying a clergyman, are further reminders of the class theme, although neither subject is fully developed. In *The Tenant of Wildfell Hall*, the yeoman Gilbert Markham succeeds the squire Arthur Huntingdon as Helen's husband, and the contrast is stressed when Gilbert arrives at Staningley and feels that Helen is too grand to marry anyone but a nobleman.[4] *Villette* and *The Professor* are a realistic contrast to some of the other romantic other novels, in that a career as a successful teacher and spouses like Frances Henri and Paul Emanuel, though honourable, cannot be represented as exactly aristocratic. But there is some interesting material in the early chapters of both novels, describing the fall of both Crimsworth and Lucy Snowe from an affluent to a menial position. Crimsworth is an improbable old Etonian, but his connection with Eton is stressed more than once.[5] Lucy's period of affluence is so lightly touched upon that it has entirely escaped the notice of one modern critic,[6] but Mrs Bretton is after all her godmother, and there is an interesting passage where Lucy consults a former family servant, Mrs Barrett, once her nurse, but now the housekeeper at a house of which the mistress is a former schoolfellow of Lucy's:

> *Different as were our social positions now, this child's mother and I had been schoolfellows, when I was a girl of ten and she a young lady of sixteen; and I remembered her, good-looking, but dull, in a lower class than mine.*[7]

Finally, in *Shirley* we have the most obviously sociological of the novels, although the focus on the relationship between Louis Moore, the tutor, and Shirley Keeldar, the aristocrat, on the one hand, and Robert Moore, the manufacturer, and Caroline Helstone, the Tory rector's niece, on the other, is blurred by the fact that the two heroes are so badly portrayed. By making so many of her heroes and heroines half or wholly foreign Charlotte Brontë was complicating the straightforward class issue, and by making so many of their characters bereft of one or both parents the Brontës were simplifying many marriages across class barriers by removing parental opposition. Nevertheless there is a considerable amount of evidence to suggest that the Brontës were interested in the problems arising from class distinctions.

There are thus important methodological differences between an enquiry into the Brontës' attitude to snobbery and the parallel enquiries into their views on prudery and eternal punishment. In the case of prudery we have an accepted doctrine, that of Professor Tillotson, which has to be refuted. In discussing the Brontës' religion we have to contend both against writers who take no account of the Brontës' views and writers who give the wrong account. But in assessing the Brontës' sociological ideas we have almost a clear field. Nor is this the only difference. In a consideration of prudery, as we have shown, the Brontë novels themselves are unrewarding in view of their apparent innocence, and we have to look at contemporary reviews for evidence of the Brontës' outspokenness. References to religious matters are more frequent in the text of the novels, but except in *The Tenant of*

Wildfell Hall the religious position of the Brontës is hardly clear cut, and the references need careful investigation. But the Brontës' view on social matters are both frequent and obvious, although sometimes they seem inconsistent and sometimes seem unimportant to the main theme of the novel in which they are to be found. Nevertheless the Brontës' views on snobbery would seem an easy subject for investigation, and it is perhaps as a result of a third difference between the three enquiries that so little investigation has taken place.

Victorian religion is an almost too plentifully documented area in which to find factual evidence which we can relate to the views of the Brontës. Victorian prudery is also an area not lacking evidence, although the peculiar complexity of the subject makes a very careful investigation necessary. In the case of snobbery we are on even more treacherous ground. We can say that there is a consensus of opinion on how much licence should be allowed in literature, even though it is hard to say what this consensus was. But we cannot say there was a consensus of opinion on the way to treat one's social inferiors or social superiors, for the very good reason that everybody has different social inferiors and superiors from everybody else. Twentieth-century sociologists can, with the confidence of those who have exhausted the evidence, make objective class distinctions and talk about twentieth-century class attitudes. But there were no such sociologists in the nineteenth century; instead in the words of one twentieth-century sociologist:

> The novelists and social historians of the nineteenth century emphasised time and again the wide differences which existed between the various social classes in England without attempting either to define 'social class' or to measure the numbers in each of the classes which were assumed to be in existence.[8]

What this lack of factual evidence means is that for a proper appreciation of the background against which the Brontës produced their social ideas we have to consider the views of other writers of the period and the lives of the Brontës, recognising that the ideas of other writers as well as the Brontës, must inevitably give only a partial portrait of the age even if, like the greatest novelists, their portrait is a powerful one. Following the Silver Fork school of novelists who appealed to the snobbery of the age, and the Newgate school of novelists who appealed to the reaction against this snobbery, we have a group of novelists writing in the late 1840s who tried to provide some constructive answer to the problems raised by the changes in class structure. Thus in *Coningsby* (1844) and *Sybil* (1845) we have marriages between members of different classes. More realistically *Yeast* (1848), *Alton Locke* (1850) and *David Copperfield* (1849–50) bewail the impossibility of such a marriage. In poetry *Locksley Hall* (1842) and *The Bothie* (1848) take up the theme. In all these cases, apart from *David Copperfield* where it is Steerforth's wickedness rather than his aristocratic birth which prevents him from marrying Little Emily, it is the woman who succeeds in breaking the class barrier while the man was left to curse 'the social lies that warp us from the living truth'.[9] These social lies however involved more than the rigid barriers which prevented a man from marrying above him; they involved the total confusion of society. As Ruskin said in 1851:

> The very removal of the massy bars which once separated one class of society from another, has rendered it tenfold more shameful in foolish people's, i.e., in most people's eyes, to remain in the lower grades of it, than ever it was before. . . . Now that a man may make money, and rise in the world, and associate himself, unreproached, with people once far above him ... it becomes a veritable shame to remain in the state he was born in, and everybody thinks it is his duty to try to be a gentleman ...[10]

Two of the greatest novels of this period, *Dombey and Son* (1847–8) and *Vanity Fair* (1847–8), are not so much concerned with the bridging of the gap between high and low as with characters who both bridged the gap and created a new one, self-made men who were anxious that their descendants should shake off the taint of their low birth and join the aristocracy.

In the confusion of which Ruskin spoke it is not surprising that the novelists became confused. In the general uncertainty about class distinctions[11] it is not always clear how difficult it was to break the class barrier. In Disraeli's two novels the difficulties are not very great; the gap between Millbank and Coningsby's grandfather is a political rather than a social one, and Sybil rather unconvincingly turns out to be more aristocratic than Egremont. In Kingsley's two novels and in *David Copperfield* the difficulties are too great to be overcome, although we cannot help feeling that the novelists exaggerate them by making their working-class characters so noble and the aristocrats so haughty. But this crude exaggeration, more crudely mirrored in the popular tales of Reynolds, does at any rate represent a consistent attitude to class distinctions; they are bad, lead to unhappiness and should be abolished. It is less easy to find this consistency in the more subtle *Dombey and Son* and *Vanity Fair*. Mr Osborne is obviously wrong in discouraging the marriage with the penniless Amelia Sedley. But is Mr Osborne wrong in aspiring to a better match for his son or is Mr Dombey wrong in trying to arrange a better match for himself? Mr Dombey is wrong, not because the circle represented by Mrs Skewton and Cousin Feenix is aristocratic but because it is vicious, although more realistically and sympathetically described than the aristocratic caricatures in *Nicholas Nickleby*. But all aristocrats are not vicious like Steerforth, just as all working people are not built in the heroic mould of Mr Peggotty, and though we can say that *Dombey and Son* teaches us that it is better to marry for love than money it does not seem to have anything very profound to say on the evils of snobbery, because it paints the classes in such a black and white fashion. In *Vanity Fair* the choice for George Osborne between Amelia on the one hand and Miss Swartz on the other is not a straightforward one between plebeian virtue and aristocratic vice. Miss Swartz though amiable is hardly aristocratic, and the moral squalor of the Sedley ménage is not concealed. But what Thackeray gains in realism over Dickens he loses in moral force. For we cannot help feeling that while on the one hand Thackeray is condemning Mr Osborne for recommending Miss Swartz rather than Amelia, with the other he is condemning Mr Osborne, Miss Swartz and the Sedleys together for being so vulgar.

This ambiguity lies at the root of *Vanity Fair* and does not enable us to decide whether Becky Sharp is a heroine for rising from her humble position to expose the hollowness of Vanity Fair or a villainess for dragging so many of those in her train down to her level. It is also to be found in that *locus classicus* of snobbery, *The Book of Snobs* (1848). The original title of this work, as it appeared in *Punch* (1846–7), was *The Snobs of England, by one of themselves,* and this title is an interesting reflection of Thackeray's ambivalence. Thackeray is usually credited with the invention of the word snob or rather its transference from the local Cambridge meaning of non-gownsman to the general meaning of a person of low birth who wanted to be considered grander than he really was. Most of the snobs in *The Book of Snobs* fulfil this definition, but Mr Snob, with his modest reticence about his grand relations and his well-bred hauteur as he describes the comic attempts of his low acquaintances to impress him, does not. Instead he fits the modern definition of a person who attaches undue importance to social rank, and who behaves in a different fashion to people of different classes. Of course Mr Dombey and Mr Osborne are snobs in both senses of the word, but it is a useful reminder of the confusion in which even the greatest writers found themselves in the middle of the nineteenth century to recall that the same term of snob was used to describe two very different types of people, and that it is almost impossible to use snob to mean 'a pretentious person of low birth' without being a snob in the other sense.

The *New English Dictionary*[12] conscientiously traces the change in the meaning of snob from cobbler to non-gownsman to person of low birth with no pretensions to rank or gentility, and shows that, while all three of these meanings were prevalent in the latter half of the nineteenth century, Thackeray must be credited with the first association of pretentiousness with snobbery. But it does not differentiate the snob who aspires to gentility from the snob who despises those who do not have gentility any more than Thackeray distinguishes between the two kinds of snob in *The Book of Snobs.* And yet the aristocratic snobs at the beginning of *The Book of Snobs* are very different from humble Major Ponto at the end, and to say 'The Queen is snobbish' does not mean that she 'vulgarly or meanly admires, and seeks to imitate or associate with those of superior rank or wealth'.

It is in fact difficult to write about snobbery without being snobbish. One can discuss class distinctions with the detached observation of a twentieth-century sociologist admitting that there are differences between classes, but not stating any preference for one class over another, and not suggesting any remedy for the unhappiness which class divisions bring about. The nineteenth-century novelists and social historians were not able to attain this objectivity, although Mrs Gaskell in *North and South* (1854–5) approaches it. Most novelists would have argued that such a detached view was impossible, and indeed we find many like Kingsley and Dickens taking the view that all class distinction was wrong. This attitude, although irreproachable in theory, led in practice to a considerable over-simplification of class distinctions. The fact that Steerforth is an amiable cad and Ham Peggotty a hero without reproach is not the only difference between the gentry and the working classes; indeed it is a purely incidental difference, as Dickens, who was too great a novelist to tie himself to a single social theory, showed when he portrayed Uriah Heep. But Kingsley is over-schematic; Tregarva and Alton Locke are too gentlemanly to be true, and we feel that their creator in drawing attention to their aspirations is merely falsifying the picture of the class they are meant to represent.

Thackeray takes up an intermediate position. Unlike Kingsley and Dickens at his crudest, he gives a true picture of the complex web of class distinctions which were a feature of early nineteenth-century England. Unlike the twentieth-century sociologists he was prepared to take sides and to say that class distinctions were wrong. Unfortunately, although perhaps inevitably, he found it impossible to combine his keen appreciation for social differences with the extreme view that there should be no social distinctions. Instead he took a more practical if less logical view that there was nothing wrong in having a class structure, but that it was necessary to alter the existing class structure in order that the right people should have the right amount of appreciation. In other words it was necessary to be like Mr Snob, in order to keep the snobs of England in their place.

Thackeray was Charlotte Brontë's hero, and it is not difficult to find the same kind of snobbery in her works. There are however considerable differences between the snobbery of Charlotte and Anne Brontë and that of Thackeray. In the first place, while Thackeray with his wide knowledge of the world was able to give the appearance of an objective and careful appraisal of class differences, the Brontës again and again reveal themselves woefully ignorant of some of the classes they are attempting to differentiate. Secondly, while Thackeray shared at any rate something of his contemporaries' hostility to class distinction, the Brontës, with their roots in the eighteenth century, appeared at times to accept the view that class distinctions were divinely ordained. Finally, since the ultimate criterion for what is the right social station for each individual is a purely subjective one, it is necessary to examine the rather peculiar lives of the Brontës in order to determine the reasons for their views on the social structure.

At first sight there seems little in the Brontës' lives to suggest any reason for their peculiar views. As daughters of a clergyman the Brontës should have had an established position in society. Charlotte's two closest friends, Mary Taylor and Ellen Nussey, both seemed to live in comparative prosperity; the Red House, Gomersal, and the Rydings, Birstall, are not the houses of humble men. When Charlotte became famous, she was able to hold her own with the literary lions of the day. There were periods of unhappiness in the lives of the Brontës, such as the time at Cowan Bridge or Charlotte's second year in Belgium, or the tragic years of 1848 and 1849, but these were due to special circumstances, and from the pages of Mrs Gaskell and her successors we get the impression of sad and lonely lives, but not of people discontented with, or even interested in, their station in life. The parallel case arising from the Brontës remoteness of their detachment from contemporary prudery might suggest that the Brontës were too lonely to engage in the similar vice of snobbery.

But the parallel here breaks down. The Brontës might be too poor to read contemporary novels, although the books they did read, in particular the novels of Scott and the contributions of

Thackeray to *Fraser's Magazine,* must have fed their interest in the problems of class, but they were not too poor to meet people, although until they became famous these people came from an extraordinarily limited circle. The Brontës' biographers have not given a complete picture of the Brontës' lives, only the best documented parts of them. Our first consideration when assessing the Brontës' social position must be the vexed question of Mr Brontë's Irish origins.[13] From the mass of legends which surround the Irish Brontës one or two certain facts seem to emerge. Mr Brontë came from a very poor family. After raising himself by his own exertions he had very little contact with his own family. His adoption of the patronymic Brontë, his boasts of an acquaintance with Lord Palmerston at Cambridge, the mysterious hints of noble ancestry which probably emanated from him, and his reluctance to accept Mr Nicholls, another Irish curate, as his son-in-law, all suggest that Mr Brontë was something of a snob.[14]

As opposed to these humble origins and aristocratic pretensions we have the position, not very humble, but not very elevated either, which Mr Brontë had carved out for himself as perpetual curate of Haworth. The title of perpetual curate was slightly inferior to that of vicar or rector,[15] although the stipend of £200 a year was not niggardly. The perpetual curate of Hogglestock was considerably poorer with only £120 a year, and yet, as we are reminded when his daughter is about to marry Archdeacon Grantley's son, he is as much a gentleman as the Archdeacon, whose daughter marries a duke.[16] It is likely, however that in Mr Brontë's case the title of gentleman, even if he could claim it with his humble Irish origins, was something of an empty distinction. Yorkshire was not Barsetshire, where the clergy fitted easily into a delicate hierarchy of subtle social distinctions. Although Mr Brontë had strong links with the Nonconformist movement, the presence of a large body of dissenters in the Haworth neighbourhood meant that there were fewer of his social inferiors to owe him respect as their ordained minister, and this fact would naturally weaken his standing with his social superiors. There were greater gaps between the classes in the North than in the South, and, one must add, greater gaps between members of the same class owing to difficulties of communication. Certainly there is little record of Mr Brontë introducing to his daughters many of his acquaintances, apart from a few curates, and we know what Charlotte thought of them.

The interest shown in the Rev. William Weightman by the Brontë family and by almost all Brontë biographers arises from the fact that he was almost the only person whom the Brontës met at Haworth on equal terms. Mr Brontë did have some kind of acquaintance with the family of Mr Dury, the Rector of Keighley.[17] With the Ponden House Heatons, the grandest family in Haworth, the Brontës were on visiting, if not familiar, terms.[18] Another local squire only seems to have proffered friendship because Charlotte wrote *Jane Eyre*.[19] The sole other acquaintance of Mr Brontë to make any marked impression on the Brontë children is Mr Roberson, the model for Mr Helstone in *Shirley*, and Charlotte only saw him once.[20] In contrast we may note the frequent appearances in Charlotte's correspondence of the Allbutt, Brooke, Caris, Carter, Cockhill, Haigh, Hall, Heald, Sugden, Walker and Wooler families, all of whom are in some way connected with Roe Head girls or staff, although this is of course partly explained by the fact that Ellen Nussey was Charlotte's main correspondent. Mr Brontë's friends at Thornton made when Mrs Brontë was still alive, the Atkinsons, the Franks, Miss Outhwaite and Miss Firth, seem to have remained friends in that they helped with the girls' education, but the Brontës may well have resented the element of patronage in this help, and we do not hear much of these characters after the sisters had left school.[21] Some spiteful remarks made by Charlotte about Amelia Walker, related to the Atkinsons, Firths and Franks, might suggest that it was from the prosperous friends of Mr Brontë that the authoress of *Jane Eyre* learnt how little charity was allotted to charity children.[22]

Mrs Brontë might, if she had lived, have tried to find friends for her daughters, although there is no evidence for Miss Branwell trying to do so. The Branwells may have considered themselves slightly superior to the Brontë connection, although it is hard to find anything in real life to act as a basis for the story

which appears both in *Agnes Grey* and *Jane Eyre* of an aristocratic family disowning their daughters for marrying a clergyman. One of the earliest writers on the Brontës, W.P.P., declared
that the story of Agnes Grey's parents is the story of Anne
Brontë's parents,[23] but there is nothing in the letters of Mrs
Brontë to Mr Brontë before their marriage to suggest any parental opposition, and there is evidence for contact between the
Branwells and Haworth, quite apart from the prolonged visit
to Miss Branwell.[24] Nor can the Branwells by any stretch of the
imagination be considered aristocratic.[25]

After the death of his wife the difficulties of looking after six
small children constrained Mr Brontë to send his four eldest
girls to school. Good cheap schools were hard to come by, and
the existence of Carus Wilson's school at Cowan Bridge, where
the balance of the fees was supplied by charity, must have seemed
a godsend to the hard-pressed father. The deaths of Maria and
Elizabeth Brontë have concentrated attention on the physical
discomfort of the school, but if we take *Jane Eyre* as autobiography there are indications in it, especially in the first conversations with Helen Burns and the description of Mrs Brocklehurst's visit to Lowood,[26] of Charlotte's resentment at being
treated as a charity child.

The deaths of Maria and Elizabeth Brontë lightened the
expense of educating the children. Although Mr Brontë still
needed some help with the fees, he did contrive to find in Roe
Head a school far superior to Cowan Bridge. The unhappiness of
the Brontës both as pupils, and in Charlotte's case as teacher,
seemed to have been caused more by religious than by social
anxieties, and, as has been shown, it was at Roe Head that Charlotte made most of her friends and acquaintances. Unfortunately
the correspondence with Mary Taylor has not survived, and partial bowdlerisation of the letters to Ellen Nussey leads us to
suspect the omission of proper names and personal remarks; it
would be illuminating to have more of such candid sketches as
the picture of Mrs Henry Nussey, described in the first chapter.
An additional difficulty in writing about the circle of Charlotte
Brontës acquaintances is the confusing duplication of surnames.
The Brontës did not know many people, but they knew more

than one family called Atkinson, Brooke, Carr, Carter, Green-
wood, Sugden, Taylor and Walker,[27] and it is often difficult to
be certain which family is being mentioned.

Allowing for these difficulties we can say certain things about
the Roe Head circle. In the first place the families which Charlotte met there, although slightly more prosperous than the
Brontës, cannot be regarded as aristocratic. The Allbutts, one
set of Carters and the Healds were clergymen, one set of Carrs
solicitors, and one set of Brookes members of a banking firm
which failed.[28] Charlotte's two closest friends came from families
which had strong connections with trade, and in both cases the
families were in some financial difficulty.

The idea that the Nussey family were in the words of one
modern writer '"county", Conservative and Church of
England'[29] is derived no doubt from the association, fostered by
Ellen herself, of Thornfield with Rydings, the description by
Charlotte of Rydings as one of the old family Halls of England,
and the visits made by Ellen, rather like a Jane Austen heroine,
to Bath and London.[30] The reality is a little more humble. The
ownership of Rydings by the Nussey family was always tenuous,
Ellen's mother had to leave it for a smaller house in 1837, and it
passed out of the family altogether in 1846. The visits to London
and Bath were conducted under the aegis of Ellen's brother John,
who as a court physician did have some kind of standing. But
her mother, the daughter of a corn factor, and her father in
business as a cloth manufacturer did not have much grandeur
about them, nor judging from the faint but definite indications
of financial distress, did they have much wealth either. Of Ellen's
five brothers two became clergymen, one went mad, and the
other two carried on a variety of businesses without much
success.[31]

In the case of Mary Taylor, the fictional portrait in *Shirley*
of the Yorke family is likely to be a fairly accurate one. There
seems no reason to doubt the Taylors' republicanism, to which
Mary herself bears witness, and there is also evidence to link
the Taylors with the Nonconformist movement.[32] The fact that
the Red House was built in 1660 by a William Taylor might
suggest that Charlotte had some excuse for making Mr Yorke

and Hunsden Yorke Hunsden proud of their ancient Yorkshire lineage in spite of their theoretical republicanism. But it is also possible that Charlotte is guilty of some romanticism here; in the same way that she turns Rydings into one of the old family Halls of England Mr Taylor changes from a bankrupt manufacturer of Army cloth into a Yorkshire gentleman of the old school.

But though Mary Taylor and Ellen Nussey were not aristocratic they did have the advantage of close family ties in the neighbourhood, and thus were members of a circle, from which the Brontës with their cousins in Ireland or Cornwall were excluded. We can see the way in which such circles were formed; both Mary Taylor's and Ellen Nussey's great uncles married a Miss Dixon of Gomersal and Mary Taylor's brother Joseph after thinking of marrying Isabella Nussey eventually marries Amelia Ringrose, originally engaged to George Nussey.[33] The Nussey family tree might have included Charlotte Brontë if she had accepted Henry Nussey's offer of marriage, and it is probably more correct to emphasise not the exclusion of the Brontës from the closely intertwined Nussey family circle, but to emphasise how very narrow this circle must have been. An examination of the Nussey family tree shows, as well as a series of marriages to the Walker and Clapham families, connections with both sets of Carrs, the Healds, and possibly the Dixons and Taylors.[34] The fact that so many of Ellen Nussey's friends were also her relatives might seem an unimportant one, but when Charlotte Brontë came to write novels she sacrificed probability to reproduce the circumstances of her friend's life, relating her characters by far-fetched and often unnecessary family ties.[35]

Another family connection is a clue to a period more formative than the years at Roe Head for the class consciousness of the Brontës – their years as governesses. Anne Brontë's employers at Blake Hall, the Inghams, were the second cousins of Ellen Nussey's sister-in-law; this may seem a remote connection, but relations between the two families appear to have been fairly close.[36] Charlotte Brontë's first employers, the Sidgwicks, were related to the Rev. Theodore Dury,[37] the Rector of Keighley, one of the few clerical friends of Mr Brontë with whose family the

Brontës had any kind of acquaintance. Even the Robinsons of Thorp Green were united to the Brontës by the common profession of Mr Brontë and Mr Robinson. In view of these links it is scarcely surprising that the sisters should have expected to have been treated like friends of the family, and it is scarcely surprising that when they were treated like governesses they felt bitterly hostile to the class which so despised them. The Whites of Upperwood House, Rawdon, were not, as far as can be seen, linked with any friends of the Brontës in this way, and perhaps this is why they escape comparatively lightly, although Charlotte does indulge in some straightforward snobbery at their expense.

> Well can I believe that Mrs W. has been an exciseman's daughter – and I am convinced also that Mr W.'s extraction is very low – yet Mrs W. talks in an amusing strain of pomposity about his and her family and connexions and affects to look down with wondrous hauteur on the whole race of 'tradesfolk' as she terms men of business.[38]

The move to Brussels took Charlotte away from people like Mrs White, who were both snobs and objects of snobbery, to an area where religious and racial differences were more interesting than class distinctions. The Pensionnat Heger was however a select establishment, and Charlotte's resentment against girls who were more stupid but more aristocratic than she was comes out in the Belgian novels. After returning from Belgium the Brontës were very much on their own, and Charlotte was even more so after the deaths of Emily and Anne. Her acceptance by the literary world, the first set of people outside her home and her close acquaintances to treat her properly came too late to have much influence on her novels. In general Charlotte coped surprisingly well in the new world of literature which her success opened up for her. She was not above a little harmless boasting about her grand acquaintances in letters to Ellen Nussey, which contrast oddly with the more eccentric earlier letters congratulating Ellen on remaining uncorrupted by London society.[39] On the other hand she was quick to resent any aristocratic foppery as shown by Matthew Arnold or authoritarian interference as shown by Sir James Kay Shuttleworth or man-of-the-world moral laxity as shown by Thackeray.[40] Her forays into the world of literature were comparatively few in these last years, the prevailing note of which is intense loneliness.[41]

Loneliness would seem a more obvious starting point than snobbery for investigating the social ideas of the Brontës. Loneliness is however a good breeding ground for snobbery; in the absence of any real relationships one is easily led to over-emphasise artificial barriers. Since the reading of the Brontës was as wide as their circle of acquaintance was narrow, we could blame books for the combination of enthusiasm for and hostility to the aristocracy which is characteristic of the Brontës, and also blame books for the fact that so many of these aristocrats are so unreal. The Brontës were, as has been shown, relatively ignorant of the Silver Fork school of novels, nor do they appear to have had much knowledge of the Novels with a Purpose of the 1840s,[42] and thus two promising sources of information about the aristocracy, the first largely favourable, the second hostile, were not open to them. But three obvious influences on the Brontës – Richardson, Scott and Thackeray – provide exactly the right blend of snobbery and hostility to snobbery for us to have to look no further than them in tracing the main literary sources of the Brontës' social attitude.

Although his touch occasionally deserts him in delineating the highest ranks of society, Richardson is in general an extremely subtle analyst of the various levels of social pretentiousness.[43] It is therefore probably unfair to him to say that the message of both *Pamela* and *Clarissa* is that the aristocracy is morally despicable, but socially desirable. And yet this crude message would be what the Brontës were most likely to appreciate, while the subtleties which depend on a more settled eighteenth-century social structure, in which emergent aristocrats like the Harlowes could be clearly distinguished from real aristocrats like Lovelace and parvenus like Mr Solmes, would pass them by. On the one hand in the social confusion of which Ruskin spoke these distinctions would be difficult to appreciate, and on the other hand the Brontës had little knowledge of even the *nouveau riche* class, let alone the real aristocracy.

Scott with his eighteenth-century view that everyone was happy with their station in life, and his Scottish attitude that allowed great familiarity between the classes, may seem an odd author to select as an exponent of either snobbery or anti-snobbery, especially as by removing the action of his story into the past he inevitably weakened the immediacy of his social observations. There is, however, an odd inconsistency about Scott's views on class,[44] although it is often hard to distinguish this from the more specific wavering between Whig and Jacobite, and general uncertainty about realism and romance. *The Antiquary* is a novel in which neither the more specific nor the more general ambivalence is particularly apparent, and we may therefore note how in it Scott contrives to arouse our sympathy for the supposedly illegitimate Lovel against the petty snobbery of Captain Macintyre, and then make this sympathy unnecessary by producing immensely noble ancestry for his hero.[45] Similarly the worthy if slightly plebeian Oldbuck is obviously a much more admirable character than the spendthrift Sir Arthur Wardour, and it is an unnecessary refinement to try to give the former a suitably ancient lineage.[46]

Thackeray is a much more obvious candidate for an influence likely to arouse interest in snobbery. Although there is no certain evidence that the Brontës read *The Book of Snobs*, and, although *Vanity Fair* appeared too late to have any influence on the earliest Brontë novels,[47] there is sufficient material relating to snobbery in the early stories in *Fraser's Magazine*, which the Brontës did read, for us to be fairly certain that Thackeray contributed to their views on class. Even more than Scott, Thackeray attacks snobbery with a two-edged sword. Again and again in the early Thackeray we find an account of a parvenu family being mocked by the supposedly true aristocracy for their behaviour in society,[48] and we do not know whether to condemn the parvenus for their attempt to rise above their station, or to condemn the true aristocrats for their lack of charity. Thackeray has a similarly ambiguous attitude towards sex, and here we may note another curious link between prudery and snobbery. Snobs and their opponents, like prudes and their opponents, have much in common with each other; their exaggerated interest in sex makes it easy to accuse the prudish of being prurient and vice versa, and in the same way it is easy to accuse both the snobbish and the anti-snobbish of being uncertain about their position in society, although the former make, and the latter try to break rules for defining positions in society.

The Brontës, unlike their contemporaries, are relatively immune from the charge of prudery. On the other hand they do seem to resent snobbery, and, as the only people to be hurt by snobbery are themselves snobs, it is hard to defend the Brontës against the latter charge. There does seem a strong strain of wishful thinking and romantic fantasy in the Brontës' writing about aristocrats. Allied to this there is a more sensible wish to assert the claims of the intellect, as being equal to, if not better than, those of wealth or birth. In the Brontës' lifetime it was unfortunately impossible for girls, and difficult for men to achieve this; the Brontës' efforts to found a school, where they would not be subservient to anyone but where men of wealth and fashion would be subservient to them as they sent their daughters there, foundered through lack of capital and through not knowing the right people to approach.[49] The successful school is however a recurring theme in their novels, especially in those novels with a strong anti-aristocratic bias. But the wish to be accepted by aristocrats because of intellectual attainments is very similar to a wish to be an aristocrat, and we shall find a considerable confusion of purpose in the Brontë novels as a result of this.

The juvenilia provide an obvious starting point for any discussion of Brontë snobbery. The aristocratic heroes and heroines, to be found in both Gondal and Angria, are in themselves an indication of the Brontës' social pretensions, and the multiplicity of titles with which these characters are endowed makes the point still more clearly. Charlotte's early preoccupation with the Duke of Wellington might be dismissed as a childish foible, and there is an almost democratic air about some of the exploits of the Twelve Adventurers with their plebeian-sounding names. But the magnificent figure of Arthur Augustus Adrian Wellesley, Marquis of Douro, Duke of Zamorna and King of Angria, is neither plebeian nor democratic, and the same, it would seem, is true of Emily's chief heroine, who may have a similar imposing array of names.[50]

Because it is difficult to establish the authorship of the Angrian narratives, and the story behind the Gondal poems, it is fruitless to expect any coherent social philosophy to emerge from the juvenilia. The exotic setting of both Angria and Gondal lessens the immediacy of the social comments; indeed *High Life in Verdopolis* is almost a contradiction in terms. By setting her stories in Africa Charlotte was able to escape into a realm of fantasy, where her ignorance of the aristocracy would not be too apparent, since it is hard to tell how a colony of aristocrats would behave in Africa. On the other hand it is a feature of Charlotte's early work that aristocratic trappings are described in evaluative superlatives without any attempt at accurate realism. Thus in *The Spell* we have an elaborate description of Douro Villa in the Vale of Verdopolis. After the initial shock of finding rooks cawing beside the banks of the Niger there is little to complain about in the description of the landscape, but when we approach the house the clear picture becomes blurred:

> As the huge dell descended, the foliage thickened till it became a wood in the centre, and up from its Eden bowers started the columns, the portico, and the classic casements of the fair Grecian villa, all lifted to the early sunshine by a low knoll of shaven lawn and pleasure ground, whose light, delicate green contrasted beautifully with the darker verdure of the park and woods. Nothing could be sweeter, more elegant, more Elysian. It had not the aspect of a fine old family seat, but it seemed likely the abode of taste and refinement and princely pride.[51]

Charlotte did not know much about fine old family seats or princely pride, and when it came to describing the interior of palaces in which her characters lived or the clothes they wore she had to take refuge in vague evaluations like 'a Saloon of gorgeous state'.[52]

This ignorance of aristocratic ways is a feature of the mature Brontë novels, although a less serious one there because the novels contain characters who are markedly less aristocratic.

Another feature of both the juvenilia and the novels is the particular ambivalence which is at the heart of all snobbery. The following passage is very reminiscent of Charlotte's complaints against Mrs White, the exciseman's daughter, the difference being that Charlotte was not Lord Charles Albert Florian Wellesley:

> With that love of ostentatious pomp and flashy display which circulates through the veins of every Angrian as unceasingly as his blood, the grand emigration was so contrived that at day, almost at one hour, the carriage of each oriental noble stood at the door of his VERDOPOLITAN residence, and in splendid cortège the gathered host of vehicles with their attendant out-riders went pouring from Sunrise to Sunset – a tide of thunder along the Eastern High-way.... It was hard for a steady sober Glasstowner (to say nothing of an irritable old Aristocrat) to endure the swaggering effrontery of those latter days.[53]

Charlotte is not at all sympathetic to the sneering Lord Charles, and there is a hint here of the early Thackeray's attempt to pour scorn on low-born upstarts and simultaneously to pour scorn on those who despised them. With Mina Laury, Zamorna's humble adorer, Charlotte is naturally more in sympathy, and there is a speech in *The Spell* from her to the Duchess of Zamorna, which seems to show Charlotte in a consistent if slightly emotional anti-aristocratic attitude:

> My Lady Duchess (for I know you by the Percy forehead and golden hair) it is not for an indulged daughter of aristocracy, for one who from her birth has hardly ever breathed out of the perfumed atmosphere of palace halls, or tread elsewhere than on velvet soft carpets, to talk of serving Zamorna. She may please and entertain him and blossom brightly in his smiles, but when adversity saddens him, when there are hard duties to perform, when his brow grows dark and his voice becomes stern and sounds only in command, I warn you, he will call for another handmaid; one whose foot is as familiar to wild and common as to gilded saloon, who knows the feel of a hard

*bed and the taste of a dry crust, who has been rudely nur-
tured and not shielded like a hothouse flower from every blast
of chilling wind . . . The noble and high-born cannot endure
grief. They fly with cowardly terror from the coming of mor-
tality, and when it grasps them or theirs, what wild, impious
wailings fill dome and turret, bower and hall. It is not so in
cottages. Poverty and the necessity of labour strengthen men's
souls wonderfully.*[54]

But Mina Laury is not allowed the last word. Charlotte's other
heroine, the Duchess of Zamorna, who has earlier condescend-
ingly remarked that Mina's elegance is so astonishing that 'she
might be an Earl's instead of a cottager's daughter',[55] now
proudly retaliates:

*'Miss Laury', said I, 'what right have you to rank me with
the frail painted trinkets you have described. I acknowledge
myself to be of noble blood, and I glory in my descent, for
never, either in past or present times, has a son or daughter of
the house of Percy shrunk from danger, or trembled before
affliction.'*[56]

In the passage describing the exodus from Verdopolis, Charlotte seems anxious to condemn both aristocratic hauteur and
nouveau riche ostentation; in *The Spell* she seems to admire both
peasant pride and patrician arrogance.

In her final Angrian stories Charlotte, as Miss Ratchford has
shown,[57] becomes more realistic and less aritocratic. Zamorna is
replaced as a central figure by Sir William Percy, Zamorna himself adopts some homely ways, appearing in *Caroline Vernon* at
breakfast, while the Duchess is at work in a little parlour, and
there is the final shift of scene from Angria to Yorkshire.[58] All
this prepares us for the markedly realistic tone of Charlotte's
first novel.

9

The Brontës and their Betters

IN HER preface to *The Professor*, Charlotte Brontë says that it had been her intention that her hero

> should work his way through life as I had seen real living men work theirs – that he should never get a shilling he had not earned – that no sudden turns should lift him in a moment to wealth and high station; that whatsoever small competency he might gain should be won by the sweat of his brow; that, before he could find so much as an arbour to sit down in, he should master at least half the ascent of 'the Hill of Difficulty'; that he should not even marry a beautiful girl or a lady of rank.[1]

Accordingly William Crimsworth after refusing the offer of his maternal uncle to set him up in the family living and after failing to make a career in trade under his brother, a wealthy manufacturer, sets out for Belgium, where after various difficulties he earns more than a small competency, having had the good fortune to marry a girl who if neither rich nor noble is at least capable of being the directress of a flourishing girls' school. Aristocrats like the Hon. John Seacombe, who are the patrons of rich family livings, rich millowners like Edward Crimsworth, who suddenly become bankrupt but as quickly recover and grow richer than Croesus by railway speculations, and even private school proprietors who manage to save enough in ten years to enable them to retire in comfort are hardly common in twentieth-century Britain, and for this reason *The Professor* may seem to be a novel which dates fairly rapidly. On the other hand the struggle between an aristocracy of birth, an aristocracy of wealth, and an aristocracy of intellect is a universal one, and had Charlotte Brontë really made *The Professor* a plea for the claims of the aristocracy of the intellect we would recognise *The Professor* as, if not a great novel, at any rate an important contribution to English sociological thought.

But the novelist in Charlotte Brontë overcomes the sociologist. Most of *The Professor* is occupied with the courtship of Crimsworth and Frances Henri, who is the most attractive character in the book, but also the character who is the most difficult to fit into a sociological pattern. Admittedly she is not rich, nor is it easy to make much of her obscure Anglo-Swiss ancestry, but the effort of maintaining that she is not beautiful is too much for both Crimsworth and his creator. It is equally difficult to maintain that Frances Henri represents the aristocracy of intellect in spite of the praiseworthy English compositions and spirited conversations with Hunsden, and in this connection it is worth remarking how odd it is that such an unsuccessful assistant mistress should make such a successful headmistress.

Before meeting Frances Henri, Crimsworth has his abortive affair with Zoraide Reuter. But, since both love affairs take place in Belgium, we cannot really find any valuable sociological message in the chapters which describe them and which occupy the major part of the book. We are left with the opening six chapters before Crimsworth leaves for Brussels, the last few pages when the Crimsworths return to England and the character of Yorke Hunsden who is the only person, apart from Crimsworth himself, to link the opening chapters with the rest of the book. Crimsworth's stay in X—— is too long to act as an introduction and too short to be a story in itself; unlike the rather similar opening chapters of *Villette* it does not even serve to introduce characters who, however improbably, are going to reappear in the rest of the story. The only character thus to reappear is Hunsden who arrives quite naturally to see how his protégé is getting on. But Hunsden, whose conversation is full of observations about class, is recognised to be one of the reasons for the book's failure. As Mrs Humphrey Ward says:

Great pains have been taken with him; and when he enters he promises much; but he is never truly living for a single page, and half way through the book he has already become a mere bundle of incredibilities.[2]

Finally the last few pages of The Professor, covering ten years, are of little interest or merit; as in her other novels Charlotte in seeking to tie up all loose ends merely leaves as many questions unanswered as she has tried to answer.

But, though they are the worst parts of the novel and have attracted little critical attention, the beginning and end of The Professor and Hunsden's conversations contain much interesting information about Charlotte's views on class. Indeed we can go further and say that the reason why they are the worst sections of the novel is that Charlotte's views were so confused that she lacked the courage to do more than sketch the sociological novel, and concentrated on the safer autobiographical theme.

The novel opens by stating that Crimsworth had been together with the mysterious Charles at Eton. We have a faint reminder here of Crimsworth's Angrian predecessors,[3] but it is perhaps fanciful to make too much of this particular choice of school. On the other hand, as has been shown, there is more than one reference to Eton in the course of the book, and Crimsworth contemplates sending his son there, although he anticipates that his schooldays will be no happier than his own. Eton also serves to remind us of Crimsworth's aristocratic lineage, since it is his uncles, Lord Tynedale and the Hon. John Seacombe, who send him there, and of the central theme of the sociological novel – Crimsworth's struggles to get away from his patrician heritage.

Crimsworth's ancestry is reintroduced at his brother's party on the occasion of Hunsden's first appearance. Hunsden declares bluntly that the portrait of Crimsworth's mother looks too much like that of an aristocrat to please him, as he hates aristocrats. Crimsworth asks pertinently whether the patrician descent may be read in a distinctive cast of form or features. Hunsden replies,

> *Patrician descent be hanged. Who doubts that your lordlings may have their distinctive "cast of form and features" as much as we ——shire tradesmen have ours? But which is the best? Not theirs assuredly.*[4]

He then goes on to say that the former took after his plebeian father, while William is 'the aristocrat of your family, and you are not as fine a fellow as your plebeian brother by a long chalk'. The impact of these remarks is then blunted by Hunsden admitting that William had been shabbily treated by Edward, and shortly afterwards there is a passage which suggests that the anti-aristocratic bias of both Hunsden and Charlotte Brontë was not very wholehearted.

> *The Hunsdens were of an old stem, and scornful as Yorke . . . professed to be of the advantages of birth, in his secret heart he well knew and fully appreciated the distinction his ancient, if not high lineage conferred on him in a mushroom-place like X——, concerning whose inhabitants it was proverbially said, that not one in a thousand knew his own grandfather.*[5]

In spite of this Hunsden returns to the attack in the next chapter, reproaches Crimsworth for allowing his brother to treat him like a dog, and then launches into a tirade against the gentlemanlike irony and patrician resentment with which Crimsworth meets these taunts. Crimsworth is cut out to be a nobleman and will never be a tradesman. His only chance of becoming rich (Charlotte in fact uses the same word as in her preface, and talks of getting a competency)[6] lies in marrying a rich widow or an heiress, and he is not bold or handsome enough even to do this. These words cause Crimsworth to reflect bitterly on his position in his brother's mill which is twice compared to that of a slave, and we are not surprised that he leaves a prison and a tyrant, and parts company with his brother, although it is some injudicious words of Hunsden, made in the presence of Edward Crimsworth, which cause the final breach between the two brothers. For all his praise of Edward Crimsworth's plebeian virtues Hunsden hardly approves of his tyrannical ways and, after suggesting that William should try the patronage of the Seacombes, then proceeds on finding out that this patronage has been rejected to exercise very much the same sort of patronage in recommending Crimsworth to Mr Brown of Brussels.

The move to Brussels takes us away from an examination of the class system. There are one or two remarks in the Brussels chapters which seem to suggest hostility to the aristocracy, such as the statement that Caroline, one of Crimsworth's recalcitrant pupils, was of noble birth, and none the better for it,[7] and there are the beginnings of an examination of the difference between Walloons and Flemings which dominates the Belgian class system,[8] but the main part of the novel is of little sociological significance. It would be more significant if we saw more of Crimsworth's successful efforts to carve out a position for himself. But we only learn of his successes at the end of the book. After gaining a good position through the patronage of M. Vandenhuten, aided by good fortune and his own perseverance, Crimsworth more than doubled his salary in a year and a half. This inspires his wife to set up a school of her own which is a great success owing to the Crimsworths' excellent connections. The school's prosperity is apparently indicated by the nobility of its pupils, although it is added that the directress showed no special favours to her more patrician charges.[9] But these successes are reserved for the end of the book and treated in a hurried and cursory way.[10] Even so they seem both painfully smug and tediously snobbish in spite of the disclaimers against aristocratic preference.

In marked contrast are the earlier chapters describing Crimsworth's struggles at M. Pelet's and Mlle Reuter's establishments. Here he gains nothing to account for his final success except the experience of teaching, the friendship of M. Vandenhuten and the hand of Frances Henri. The first of these advantages is hardly stressed, Crimsworth being one of those fortunate teachers who succeed from the first. The friendship of M. Vandenhuten is a stroke of good fortune arising from Jean Baptiste's clumsiness and Crimsworth's skill in swimming, acquired at Eton. From this lucky accident springs the whole of Crimsworth's success, since though reluctant to accept help from the Seacombes he has no doubts about relying upon M. Vandenhuten both to secure him his first job after leaving M. Pelet and to provide subsequent patronage for his school.

Frances Henri is with difficulty brought into the sociological novel firstly because she herself rises through her own efforts to become the directress of a fine school, and secondly because of

Hunsden's remarks about her low caste, remarks which are retracted when it is discovered how charming Frances Henri is. In neither case however does the sociological message get through very clearly. Frances Henri's efforts to improve her situation would be more impressive were it not for the unfortunate analogy drawn between her career and that of Mlle Reuter, who also began life as an assistant mistress with no prospects; she professes sympathy with Frances for this reason.[11] As for Frances Henri's low caste, but great charm, it is unfortunate that both are seen through the eyes of Hunsden. Mrs Humphrey Ward was right to lay stress on his contradictory character, and it is an appropriate touch to find him at the end of the novel entertaining both foreign intellectuals and hard-faced Manchester businessmen. But, since both his radicalism and his aristocratic pretensions grow as the novel progresses, it is hard to take seriously either his initial snobbery about Frances Henri being a lace-mender, though fortunately without any low connections, as she had no relatives, or his later admission that this snobbery was misplaced and that Crimsworth had married above him. Hunsden acquires a coat of arms when he comes to Belgium,[12] and we are not surprised that there is another passage about his ancient lineage:

> Hunsden unconsciously laid stress on the word caste and, in fact, republican lord-hater as he was, Hunsden was as proud of his old ——shire blood, of his descent and family standing, respectable and respected through long generations back, as any peer in the realm of his Norman race and Conquest-dated title.[13]

On the other hand Hunsden veers towards extreme radicalism in denouncing England as

> A little corrupt, venal, lord-and-king-cursed nation, full of mucky pride (as they say in ——shire), and helpless pauperism, rotten with abuses, worm-eaten with prejudices. . . . Examine the footprints of our august aristocracy; see how they walk in blood, crushing hearts as they go.[14]

Hunsden's confusion is shared by his creator. Three awkward questions in particular raise themselves. Firstly does Charlotte know anything about the aristocracy? It is presumably a mistake to make Crimsworth's uncle the Hon. John Seacombe a right honourable in the course of the book.[15] Secondly does Charlotte believe that ancient lineage, a misleading name for the ability to trace one's lineage through many generations, matters or not? It does not matter in the case of Frances Henri, and yet both Hunsden and Crimsworth, whose aristocratic good manners are contrasted with his brother's plebeian rudeness and M. Pelet's Gallic lapses from grace, derive much of their virtue from their ancestry. Thirdly is there any real contrast between the life Crimsworth rejects as an aristocratic hanger-on and the life he carves out for himself as a schoolmaster, dependent on aristocratic patronage?

The first two of these questions must again be asked in connection with *Jane Eyre*. Lady Eastlake was right to say that the description of the house-party at Thornfield showed that the author of *Jane Eyre* was unacquainted with the circles she was describing,[16] although nothing in these scenes rings quite so falsely as the celebrated remark of Blanche Ingram to her mother, 'Am I right, Baroness Ingram, of Ingram Park?'[17] It is however only the conversation of the supposed aristocrats that is unconvincing; their external appearance and indeed their behaviour is quite well portrayed, although there seems a little uncertainty about the exact position they occupy in the social scale. Is Rochester for instance, with his wealth and ancient name, socially superior to the Ingrams, wealthy and titled as well? On the one hand Blanche Ingram considers 'the Rochester estate eligible to the last degree';[18] on the other hand Jane Eyre thinks that Rochester is going to marry Blanche 'for family, perhaps political reasons; because her rank and connections suited him'.[19] The other members of the house-party would seem to move in the same circle of elevated aristocracy, not above trying to elevate itself still further by an advantageous match, and we are therefore surprised to find two of its members, Lord Ingram and Sir George Lynn, acquainted with the Reed family.[20] In the case of novelists like Jane Austen who were a little more sure of their footing, it might be profitable to draw a line between characters who come from the aristocracy, and characters who come from the gentry, but in the case of Charlotte Brontë this distinction almost ceases to have any meaning. We could say that the Rochesters were gentry, and the Ingrams aristocrats, but what are the Reeds?

The novel opens with some pointed remarks by the Reeds to the effect that Jane is their humble dependent, and we subsequently learn the reasons for Jane's dependence. Her father had been a poor clergyman, her mother had married against the wishes of her friends 'who considered the match beneath her',[21] and she had been cut off without a penny by the Reeds. On the death of Jane's parents her Uncle Reed had taken pity on her, her Eyre relatives being presumably too poor; indeed they are described by Mrs Reed as poor, low relations.[22] But since the Reeds are so unsympathetically described, we are not surprised to find that their pretensions to superiority over the Eyres are quite unjustified; in the opinion of Bessie the Eyres 'are as much gentry as the Reeds are',[23] although Mrs Reed still claims superiority by calling Jane's uncle 'a sneaking tradesman', because he has some connection with the wine trade.[24] Later the Reeds' fortunes suffer owing to the extravagances of John, and it is perhaps because of this that Georgiana fails to marry into a Lord's family; indeed it is odd that they should even be known by the respectable Lord Ingram and Sir George Lynn.

As the prosperity of the Reeds decreases, so that of John Eyre increases. Like Crimsworth in *The Professor* he is fortunate enough to secure a competency,[25] although it is not clear how he does this, the exact nature of his connection with the wine trade and Madeira never being revealed; the statement that he is the Funchal correspondent of Richard Mason's house hardly clarifies the situation.[26] Earlier in his life he had been engaged in unfortunate speculations which had impoverished his brother-in-law, the father of St John Rivers. As a result the Rivers family lose touch with John Eyre, although it is not clear why they should also have disowned Jane Eyre. With a paternal aunt married into such a distinguished family Jane might well feel that she was fully the equal of the Reeds.

The cousinship of St John Rivers with Jane Eyre is useful for establishing Jane's credentials as a gentlewoman, but would otherwise seem to be an unnecessary coincidence, although it does enable Jane to show her generosity by sharing her wealth, and serves to emphasise the fact that St John Rivers can never be more than a brother to Jane. It is however only one of several wild coincidences resulting from Charlotte Brontë's social naïveté. In the narrow circles in which she moved it was quite natural to feel that everybody was related to or acquainted with everybody else; we have seen evidence of such a tightly-knit circle of acquaintances and relatives among Charlotte's schoolfellows. Nor is such a closed circle surprising among people prevented by poor communications from travelling far from their homes, and prevented by fairly rigid class barriers from knowing people whose station was much above or below them. But Jane Eyre does travel far; the length of the journeys from Gateshead to Lowood, from Lowood to Thornfield, and from Thornfield to Morton is emphasised. Nor do the inhabitants of these places have much in common with each other. It is therefore exceedingly surprising that at every place to which she goes Jane finds that her former acquaintances are known. Naturally the Reeds are known at Lowood, fifty miles from Gateshead,[27] and Mr Brocklehurst punishes Jane Eyre for her alleged ingratitude to Mrs Reed. She is rescued from this ignominy by the testimony of Mr Lloyd, the apothecary at Gateshead, who is known to Miss Temple.[28] This is strange, especially as we are told that the status of Mr Lloyd is not very high, as he is only summoned to tend to the servants and the likes of Jane Eyre.[29]

Although Thornfield is at least seventy miles from Lowood, the profession, if not the character, of Mr Brocklehurst is known to Mr Rochester, who has also heard of Mr Reed in the same way that his guests have heard of the Reed children, although the distance between Gateshead and Thornfield is a hundred miles.[30] The journey from Thornfield to Morton is another long one, occupying thirty-six hours,[31] and at Morton Jane is safe for the time from enquiries about her immediate past, although we are not surprised that St John Rivers knows Mr Brocklehurst,[32] with whom indeed he has much in common. These devices for linking the various parts of the story are clumsy, and show what a very unrealistic novel *Jane Eyre* is.

Another unrealistic touch is provided by the emphasis on the ancient lineage of both St John Rivers and Rochester; it is about the one thing they have in common, apart from the wish to marry Jane. Mrs Fairfax introduces the subject by saying that, 'Almost all the land in this neighbourhood, as far as you can see, has belonged to the Rochesters time out of mind.'[33] Later she suggests that his wealth and good blood are sufficient compensations for his lack of looks to make him a general favourite in society,[34] and Jane is naturally worried that he will marry Blanche Ingram. Instead Rochester falls in love with Jane, and since Baroness Ingram of Ingram Park would hardly be likely to put up with a bigamous son-in-law the whole courtship of Blanche and Rochester seems to serve little more purpose than the aristocratic charade which forms part of it. Just before the abortive wedding to Jane we hear of 'the old time-stained marble tomb, where a kneeling angel guarded the remains of Damer de Rochester, slain at Marston Moor in the time of the civil wars'.[35]

St John Rivers lacks Rochester's wealth, but there is even more emphasis laid on his ancient lineage, which is introduced in very much the same way as that of Rochester. It is the housekeeper Hannah who declared loyally that 'th' Rivers' wor gentry i' th' owd days o' th' Henrys, as onybody might see by looking into th' registers i' Morton Church vestry'.[36] In contrast the much richer Mr Oliver is the son of a journeyman needle-maker, and perhaps this explains why he is prepared to welcome St John Rivers as a son-in-law. For it is in connection with the propsect of his marrying Rosamund Oliver that the good birth and name of St John Rivers are again stressed,[37] and we are reminded of the parallel situation between Rochester and Blanche Ingram.

Although less realistic than *The Professor*, *Jane Eyre* does make some attempt to describe the conditions of the working classes, about which *The Professor* for all its emphasis on the Crimsworths being a working couple,[38] is singularly reticent. Writing only two years after the publication of *Sybil*, Charlotte

Brontë does seem aware of Disraeli's 'two nations'. Although a governess could hardly be described as rich and would indeed be despised by most members of the rich, there was a great gulf fixed between even this lowest section of the Rich and the Poor. This is shown by Jane's inability to fend for herself among the Poor on her arrival in Morton, and by both Hannah and Rosamund Oliver suggesting that the natural place for Jane's talents was a post as a governess.[39] Instead she works in the village school at Morton, St John Rivers having apologised for the fact that her scholars will be 'only poor girls – cottagers' children – at the best, farmers' daughters'. Towards her new pupils Jane's attitude is frankly condescending:

> I must not forget that these coarsely-clad little peasants are of flesh and blood as good as the scions of gentlest genealogy; and that the germs of native excellence, refinement, intelligence, kind feeling, are as likely to exist in their hearts as in those of the best-born.[40]

In spite of her claim to St John Rivers that she is not ambitious Jane is not happy with her work originally, saying, 'I felt degraded. I doubted I had taken a step which sank instead of raising me in the scale of social existence',[41] although the life of a village schoolmistress is better than becoming Mr Rochester's mistress. Later she finds teaching more congenial, but on coming into her inheritance has no hesitation about giving up her post.

Life as a lady of independent means is more attractive for Jane than life as a village schoolmistress, just as the prospect of being Rochester's wife is preferable to being the unpaid curate of an Indian missionary, which is what St John Rivers offers when he proposes marriage to her. We can hardly blame Jane for her choice any more than we can blame Charlotte for forsaking realism for romance, and making marriage into the aristocracy rather than an independent career her heroine's aim. After all it was very difficult for a woman to contemplate any career apart from marriage in 1847 and, given this fact and an additional bonus of being able to marry for love which not many girls of 1847 could look forward to, why should not one marry as advantageously as possible? All the same we feel that

Jane should not stress what she has gained as much as she does when she finds her wedding-veil:

> I smiled as I unfolded it, and devised how I would tease you about your aristocratic tastes, and your efforts to masque your plebeian bride in the attributes of a peeress. I thought how I would carry down to you the square of unembroidered blond I had myself prepared as a covering for my low-born head, and ask if that was not good enough for a woman who could bring her husband neither fortune, beauty, nor connections. I saw plainly how you would look; and heard your impetuous republican answers, and your haughty disavowal of any necessity on your part to augment your wealth, or elevate your standing, by marrying either a purse or a coronet.[42]

Admittedly this wedding-veil is never worn, nor does this marriage for which it was bought take place for some time. By the time it does take place Jane has her share of her uncle's competency, and has discovered that her relatives are not as plebeian as she had once imagined.[43] There is no more talk of her preserving her independence by continuing to act as Adèle's governess, and Adèle goes to school, while Jane settles down to being a wife and a mother. It is difficult to represent the marriage of Jane Eyre and Rochester as an act of reconciliation between the Rich and the Poor.

Shirley, on the other hand, is a novel devoted to effecting a reconciliation between the two nations. Unlike other novels of the same period, such as *Sybil* and *North and South*, it loses much of its immediate effect by looking back at the events of the Luddite riots rather than considering the contemporary Chartist disturbances. Mr Helstone, as an old-fashioned Church and State Tory, is a rather out-of-date figure, though as late as the Reform Bill there were probably many clergymen like him.[44] On the other side of the ecclesiastical fence we have the dissenting radicals, but it would have been difficult to find many such characters as late as 1849. Finally the introduction of machinery as the central bone of contention between masters and men gives the novel an anachronistic air.

Even allowing for these limitations *Shirley* is still weak when

it comes to appreciating the problems of the workers and offering solutions for them.[45] All the main characters come from the
middle and upper classes, and the only member of the working
classes to be treated in any depth is William Farren, the rioter
who becomes a gardener with the help of Mr Yorke and Mr
Hall. Some attempt is made to prevent William from becoming a
character out of Hannah More's tracts, the poor but honest
labourer, pleased with God's dispensations; he is reluctant to
accept charity, and when Caroline is convalescing helps to restore
her by his conversation. Mrs Pryor, who feels that a great gulf
lies between her caste and his, is shocked by these conversations,
and is afraid that William may presume. Caroline replies,
'William presume, mamma? You don't know him. He never
presumes: he is altogether too proud and sensitive to do so.'[46]

There is a certain presumption of superiority in Caroline's
remark, and we may suspect the same in the attitude of a
writer who paints William Farren as an exceptional member of
the working classes, other members of whom appear as dangerous
revolutionaries.[47] Two other remarks 'Eleemosynary relief never
yet tranquillized the working-classes', and, 'There's nothing the
lower orders like bettter than a little downright good-humoured
rating'[48] seem to suggest a similar superior attitude. In fact the
first remark, made by Robert Moore, does suggest that charity is
not enough, although the charitable project for the relief of the
poor occupies an important place in the book. The second
remark, made by Charlotte Brontë, suggests another point, not
noticed by the Hannah Moore school of Social reformers,
namely that kind words are useless without some respect for the
working person's individuality. The latter remark leads to the
observation, 'Taken as they ought to be, the majority of the
lads and lasses of the West-Riding are gentlemen and ladies,
every inch of them: it is only against the weak affectation and
futile pomposity of a would-be aristocrat they turn mutinous.'[49]

There are several would-be aristocrats in the book, and they
are all unattractive people. 'Mr Malone's father termed himself a
gentleman'; his son is despised for his arrogance and for not
being a real gentleman.[50] Mr Donne laments 'the want of style,
the absence of elegance' in Yorkshire, but his 'somewhat under-

bred manner and aspect'[51] suggest that he has not been accustomed to either style or elegance. One suspects that out-raged Yorkshire pride is the driving force behind these criticisms of opponents of Yorkshire, but the criticism of Sam Wynne, the first claimant to Shirley's hand, appears to be dictated by straightforward snobbery. The Wynnes were Briarfield gentry, and Mr Wynne senior was a magistrate, but he makes mala-droit malapropisms.[52] His son has twice Shirley's money but, significantly, only 'equal connections' and 'equal respecta-bility'[53] and is decidedly inferior to Shirley's most serious suitor, Sir Philip Nunneley, the baronet.

Opposed to these are the novel's heroes and heroines, the Moores, Caroline Helstone and Shirley Keeldar. Robert Moore in his capacity as a member of the mercantile classes who have 'no good feeling for any class but their own'[54] begins the novel by getting on very badly with the working classes, and the re-straining influence of Caroline is needed to temper his cut-throat capitalism. There is perhaps a hint in the closing sentence of the book, pointing to the change from oak-trees and nut-trees and fairies to stone and brick and ashes that the Industrial Revolu-tion, led by such capitalists as Robert Moore, was not wholly beneficial.[55] On the whole however Charlotte Brontë was not interested in the sociological and political events which formed the framework of her novels. She was much more interested in the marriage of her middle-class heroes and heroines.

Even here there is ample scope for sociological comment. The actual marriages of Shirley and Caroline to the brothers Moore are by most standards not ill-assorted. Charlotte has taken good care to give the Moores an obscurely patrician background, and hints that neither Shirley nor Caroline is particularly aristo-cratic. Thus Hortense Moore can boast proudly of the ancient lineage of the Moores and the Gerards, and her grandmother with her château on the Scheldt,[56] while Mr Yorke, another version of Hunsden Yorke Hunsden, with his republican views and pride in his ancestry, can claim that the blood of the Moores is as pure as that of Shirley.[57] Shirley is attacked for marrying Louis Moore who occupies the servile position of tutor, but is told by Mr Sympson when she refuses Sam Wynne that she

cannot aspire to marry into the peerage.[58] Caroline is in fact
related to the Moores, and the only obstacles to her marriage
with Robert Moore are the latter's Whig views, anathema to the
Tory Mr Helstone, and the fact that both partners are poor.
With the end of the war against the French these unromantic
objections are removed, and the marriage takes place without
any opposition from Caroline's family.

By modern standards Louis might seem a better husband than
Robert. He has not proposed marriage to anyone else or been
shot at or been near bankruptcy, and if he is not rich his prospective wife is. It is hard to understand the excessive violence
of Mr Sympson's antipathy to the idea of Shirley marrying the
tutor. One suspects a certain amount of exaggeration in this
violence and in the emphasis laid on the servility of Louis's
position. A tutor was better paid than a governess,[59] and Louis
had gained a position of trust in the Sympson household. It
looks as if Charlotte was introducing with a new twist her
favourite theme of the downtrodden governess, a theme which
is already sufficiently discussed in Mrs Pryor's anecdotes of her
life with the Hardmans.

These anecdotes gain an added piquancy, as they come from
Mrs Pryor, who apparently without any irony believes that,
'The aristocracy are decidedly a very superior class'.[60] They are
examples of the same anti-aristocratic prejudices that we found
in *The Professor*. But when Miss Hardman is made to say in
connection with the necessity of a well-bred governess:

> *The daughters of tradespeople, however well educated, must
> necessarily be underbred, and as such unfit to be inmates of
> OUR dwellings, or guardians of OUR children's minds and
> persons . . .,*[61]

the irony of the attack on her is lessened by the fact that Charlotte, like Mrs Pryor and that other savage, though very
different, critic of the aristocracy, Hunsden, appears herself to
have some belief in the advantages of good birth.

A more serious spokesman against the aristocracy of birth is
Shirley Keeldar. Not only does she speak up for the depressed
governess class, she marries into it, and in refusing other suitors

stresses the claims of the intellectual.[62] It is of course not just intellectual superiority that Shirley is looking for in a husband, it is any form of superiority of character; the Duke of Wellington as well as Socrates is among her list of heroes.[63] She does however reject the claims of superiority of rank, twice acknowledging that Sir Philip Nunneley is of far higher rank than she is, and yet saying that he is not worthy of her.[64] It would indeed be a telling point against the worldly views of Mr Sympson to maintain that it was no more unfitting for Shirley to marry beneath her than for Sir Philip to marry beneath him.

This is a point that Shirley does not make, and it is doubtful if Charlotte Brontë or her readers would have thought it a valid one. Shirley does, however, make several pronouncements against the follies of rigid class divisions. She defends Robert Moore against the insinuations of Mrs Helstone that he is a greasy tradesman, claiming that he looks a gentleman and heroic.[65] On the one hand 'by fits she was even elated at the notion of being lady of the manor', but on the other 'her exultation being quite undisguised was singularly inoffensive; and for her serious thoughts, they tended elsewhere'.[66] To Mr Yorke, that bogus radical, she says,

> all ridiculous, irrational crying up of one class, whether the same be aristocrat or democrat – all howling down of another class, whether clerical or military – all exacting injustice to individuals, whether monarch or mendicant – is really sickening to me: all arraying of ranks against ranks, all party hatreds, all tyrannies disguised as liberties, I reject and wash my hands of.[67]

Finally, in denouncing the worldly ideas on marriage of Mr Sympson, Shirley launches into a great tirade against marriage for worldly motives.

> Your God rules at the bridal of kings – look at your royal dynasties! Your Deity is the deity of foreign aristocrats – analyse the blue blood of Spain! Your God is the Hymen of France – what is French domestic life?[68]

Shirley is enthusiastic about playing at being the lady of the

manor, does use the term gentleman for expressing her approbation of Robert Moore, and is aware of the class differences while
saying that they do not matter. In spite of this she is the nearest
approach in Charlotte Brontë's novels to the advocate of a classless society, and it is presumably this feature of her character
which led Charlotte to say that Shirley was based on her sister
Emily.[69] Emily had of course none of Shirley's near-aristocratic
airs and graces, but as we shall show in examining *Wuthering
Heights*, she did have something of the same objective hostility
to snobbery shown by Shirley. It may be as a result of Emily's
influence that Charlotte is less snobbish in *Shirley* than in
previous novels; she had also emerged a little from her Yorkshire naïveté, and is more deft and sure in portraying subtle
class distinctions.

In *Villette*, although most of the novel is set in Belgium, and
therefore relatively free from pictures of the English class system,
Charlotte is at pains to give clear hints of the social position of
each character, while in making Lucy Snowe marry Paul Emanuel
rather than John Bretton she seems to be speaking, as in *Shirley*
and *The Professor*, against the worldly doctrine that one should
try to marry above one's station. There is however the usual
ambiguity about whether good birth matters. Exception has
been taken to Shirley for being too vulgar a heroine;[70] not only
is Lucy Snowe a model of decorum but care is taken, as it is
with Jane Eyre, to sketch in for her a shadowy background of
gentility, even though she has fallen on evil days. In addition to
the previously mentioned connection with Mrs Bretton and Mrs
Barrett we have the revealing statement when Lucy goes to
London that the waiter remembered her uncles, Charles and
Wilmot, and becomes full of respect as a result.[71] One wonders
what exactly was the calamity which fell upon Lucy's family in
such a disastrous fashion that neither her godmother nor her
aristocratic-sounding uncles were able to rescue her. Presumably
it involved a family quarrel as well as financial loss, similar
to the quarrel that severed relations between Jane Eyre's uncle
and St John Rivers's father.

Mrs Bretton's social position is stated in the second sentence
of the book:

Her husband's family had been residents there for generations, and bore, indeed, the name of their birthplace – Bretton of Bretton; whether by coincidence, or because some remote ancestor had been a personage of sufficient importance to leave his name to the neighbourhood, I know not.[72]

Dr Bretton had been a physician, but had left his widow in sufficient prosperity to be able to maintain a fairly handsome establishment at Bretton. This prosperity had lessened in the three years when Lucy had lost sight of the Brettons, and fortune had retrenched her once ample gifts. But John Bretton's success as a doctor had set the family on their feet again; they are able to take La Terrasse, a small château, Mrs Bretton sees her old Bretton agent with a view to regaining part of what her husband had left, and, though M. de Bassompierre says that John Bretton is not the equal of his daughter, the young doctor is able to convince him that he is in a position to marry.[73]

In spite of being Bretton of Bretton, there is nothing particularly aristocratic about John Bretton, and Lucy is certainly not degrading herself in turning to Paul Emanuel, also from a rich family which had lost its fortune, and another person to have built up a powerful position for himself by his own exertions.[74] As in *The Professor*, the central and best part of the book, the love affair between Lucy Snowe and Paul Emanuel, is of little sociological significance, and most of the class interest is to be found in a relatively minor character. Although Ginevra Fanshawe is unlike Hunsden in a great many ways she does perform some of the same functions. She is the means of Lucy's going to Mme Beck's in the same way that Hunsden is the indirect cause of Crimsworth's joining M. Pelet's staff. Just as Hunsden is the one person apart from Crimsworth to be present in both Belgium and X——, so Ginevra Fanshawe is the one link, apart from Lucy Snowe and John Bretton himself, between the Brettons and de Bassompierres on the one hand and Mme Beck on the other. Finally Hunsden's jibes against the aristocracy are a less effective form of Ginevra's petulant pronouncements in favour of the aristocracy. In both cases there is a certain confusion in the character's attitude towards the aristocracy, and in the attitude of Charlotte Brontë.

Ginevra first appears on board the packet which is taking Lucy Snowe to Boue-Marine. She is immediately contrasted with another group of passengers, the Watsons:

> *The Watsons were doubtless rich people ... the women were dressed richly, gaily, and absurdly out of character for the circumstances. ... The men were of low stature, plain, fat and vulgar.*[75]

Besides these four characters, 'two males, two females', there was but one other passenger, 'a young lady, whom a gentlemanly, though languid-looking man escorted'. The Watsons show their vulgarity by offering Lucy a camp stool which is of course declined, whereas Ginevra shows her good breeding, after a sour look of disdain at the flaunting silks and velvets of the Watsons, by approaching Lucy in conversation, although she had previously curled her lip at her father's recommendation to do so. In her conversation she reveals that her father

> *is an officer on half pay, but well descended, and some of our connections are great enough, but my uncle and godpapa De Bassompierre, who lives in France, is the only one that helps us.*[76]

This flaunting of grand relations seems more in keeping with the silks and velvets of the women Watsons than with the simple print dress of the other lady passenger, and the contrast between the *nouveaux riches* Watsons and the aristocratic Miss Fanshawe is further blurred when the Watsons, perhaps aided by the stewardess who prefers wealth to grand connections, behave better when attacked by seasickness than the selfish Ginevra.

Ginevra quickly reappears at Madame Beck's where she is equally blatant about her advantages and Lucy's disadvantages.

> *In the first place I am the daughter of a gentleman of family, and though my father is not rich, I have expectations from an uncle. ... I suppose you are nobody's daughter, since you took care of little children when you first came to Villette.*[77]

In addition Ginevra with the aid of her chaperone, Mrs Chol-

mondeley, finds admirers in the shape of the aristocratic Count
de Hamal and John Bretton. They give her a further opportunity for displaying her snobbery, since she prefers Colonel de
Hamal, a gentleman of excellent connections, to a man who 'is
bourgeois, sandy-haired, and answers to the name of John!'[78]
This contrast between the bourgeois and the aristocrat is
obviously meant to be absurd, as Dr John is so manifestly a better
man than de Hamal. And yet Charlotte Brontë is not content
with showing that Ginevra's snobbery is wrong; she must also
show that she is wrong in her snobbery. The Brettons are not an
ignominious family, and it is silly of Ginevra to laugh at Mrs
Bretton who is correctly described as an English middle-class
gentlewoman. Her own parents occupy 'such a station and
possess such connections as, in their opinion, demand display',[79]
but they are poor, and Ginevra does not seem to have much to
boast about. She might boast about M. de Bassompierre, but he
turns out to be a friend and even a distant connection of the
despised Brettons. On discovering this Ginevra becomes less
enthusiastic about M. de Bassompierre, who is described in the
same way as Dr Bretton as looking like a bear.[80] When, however,
she elopes with Alfred de Hamal, it is M. de Bassompierre who
provides Ginevra with her portion, and in spite of an earlier sneer
at her uncle's coarse Scotch breeding she christens her son by
the imposing title of Alfred Fanshawe de Bassompierre de Hamal.

The elder Alfred de Hamal appears to have nothing but his
title to recommend him, but Charlotte contrives to pour scorn
even on this title. The dislike of Belgium, shown in such contemptuous titles as Boue-Marine, Labassecour and Villette, is
also shown in the attitude to the aristocracy of that country.
On going into her first class Lucy Snowe says that she knows
that some of her pupils were of noble family 'as nobility goes in
Labassecour'.[81] Later she remarks that

> equality is much practised in Labassecour; though not repub-
> lican in form, it is nearly so in substance, and at the desks of
> Madame Beck's establishment the young countess and the
> young bourgeoise sat side by side.[82]

Nor was it always easy to tell the difference between the two
except that the young aristocrats tended to be less courteous;
this was often due to the admixture of French blood. There are
further sneers in the chapter entitled 'The Concert'. The King
and Queen of Labassecour are a disappointment, some of the
Villette aristocracy are fat and stupid, and Dr John simultaneously notes the humble nature of the Labassecour court and
the humble position of Ginevra Fanshawe in it in the following
devastating outburst:

> Mrs Cholmondeley is there with a very grand party. Yes:
> Ginevra was in her train; and Mrs Cholmondeley was in Lady
> ——'s train who was in the Queen's train. If this were not
> one of the compact little minor European courts, whose very
> formalities are little more imposing than familiarities, and
> whose gala grandeur is but homeliness in Sunday array, it
> would sound all very fine.[83]

Finally both Lucy Snowe and M. de Bassompierre, whose title is
fortunately a French one, are agreed that John Bretton would
make an infinitely better husband than any of the ducs, barons,
or vicomtes of Villette.[84]

Thus Ginevra is foolish in thinking it is better to be a countess
than plain Mrs John Bretton, and she is also foolish in being
unable

> to conceive how any person not bolstered up by birth or
> wealth, not supported by some consciousness of name or con-
> nection, could maintain an attitude of reasonable integrity.[85]

Indeed her strange friendship with Lucy Snowe, which might
seem unlikely in one who sneers at Mrs Bretton in her pursuit of
social success, is to be explained by her thinking Lucy an aristocrat in disguise. Lucy in the same passage says that she is content that she was known,

> where it imported that known I should be; the rest sat on
> me easily: pedigree, social position, and recondite intellectual
> acquisition, occupied about the same space and place in my
> interests and thoughts; they were my third-class lodgers.

We feel this is partly true of Lucy Snowe, who is annoyed that on her travels she is treated with scant respect, but admits that this lack of respect is justified, is pleased that she has risen from being an old lady's companion to being a school teacher, but hardly thinks the achievement a great one, and is pleased at the success of her school, measured like that of Frances Henri by the growing nobility of her pupils, but is far more interested in Paul Emanuel.

With Charlotte Brontë one cannot be so sure of the exact status which she allotted to pedigree and social position, let alone intellectual attainment. To continue the metaphor, as she herself continues it in *Villette*, sometimes she seems to be for throwing them out of her house altogether, at other times allotting them at any rate the second-best bedroom. The highest place is obviously allotted to Love, but it is possible to bear social rank in mind even when loving. This is less true of *Villette* than of the other novels, but even in *Villette* Charlotte's most explicit statement of her attitude to the importance of good birth is essentially ambiguous. After saying that she would allot pedigree, social position and recondite intellectual acquisition to the small sitting room and the little back bedroom even if the dining and drawing room stood empty, Lucy Snowe adds that the world thinks differently. Charlotte then surprisingly defends the world's attitude.

> If a man feels that he would become contemptible in his own eyes were it generally known that his ancestry were simple and not gentle, poor and not rich, workers and not capitalists, would it be right severely to blame him for keeping these fatal facts out of sight – for starting, trembling, quailing at the chance which threatens exposure? The longer we live, the more our experience widens, the less prone are we to judge our neighbour's conduct, to question the world's wisdom: wherever an accumulation of small defences is found, whether surrounding the prude's virtue or the man of the world's respectability, there, be sure, it is needed.[86]

We must not be too harsh on Charlotte Brontë. By laying emphasis on the flaws in her social philosophy we must not lose sight of the virtues of her novels which are more concerned with the individual than with society. Because of their lack of relations and friends Jane Eyre and Lucy Snowe are in a social vacuum: this emptiness heightens the pathos of their struggle in the world, although it is a rather odd world in which they struggle. Indeed we are reminded of the strongly religious element in the Brontë works; the people Jane meets who all seem to know each other, and the people Lucy meets whom she has so often met before, are realistically improbable people but useful symbols, as in *Pilgrim's Progress*, of the struggles of the individual soul. Moreover, in giving her heroes and heroines a vaguely respectable ancestry, in dividing the world into those who were gentlemen and those who were not, and in having little time and sympathy for the working classes, she was after all merely considering the tastes of her readers. Some of her critics found a heroine who was a governess and a heroine who whistled too much to stomach; they would hardly have put up with anything more vulgar. But Jane Austen, without any wish to change the social order, contrived by her accurate focus on social behaviour to make several valid points about how we should behave to those who are differently situated from ourselves; the same cannot be said of Charlotte whose message is a blurred one, marred by inconsistency and ignorance. Jane Austen could portray with knowledgeable detachment climbing snobs like Mrs Elton, disdainful snobs like Lady Caroline de Burgh, and dissolute snobs like Mr Yates; her needle-sharp denunciations of aristrocratic and would-be aristocratic bad manners are a valuable guide to human behaviour. Charlotte on the contrary uses a bludgeon, and her portraits are spoilt by autobiographical rancour or parvenu ignorance or a hankering after aristocratic birth. Darcy and Mr Rochester both comment on the inferiority of their prospective brides; Elizabeth Bennet sends Darcy packing, but Jane Eyre falls into Rochester's arms.

Autobiography, ignorance and inconsistency are also features of the work of Anne Brontë. We do not know a great deal about the life of Anne, and it is perhaps too easy to represent *Agnes Grey* as straight autobiography with the Inghams of Blake Hall portrayed by the Bloomfields of Wellwood House and the Mur-

rays of Horton Lodge standing for the Robinsons of Thorp
Green. Anne's experiences with the children of the two house-
holds may be accurately mirrored in her account of the fiendish
young Bloomfields and frivolous young Murrays. But the Inghams, coming from a well-established Yorkshire family, were
unlike Mr Birdwood, a retired tradesman who had realised a
considerable fortune; Blake Hall was not a new house, surroun-
ded by mushroom poplars, and one of the Ingham girls in later
life was scorned for marrying beneath her into trade.[87] If we are
looking for models for the Bloomfields, Charlotte's employers,
the Whites of Upperwood House, seem a much more likely
prospect.[88] The Robinsons of Thorp Green were an aristocratic
family, being related to the Marquess of Ripon, but Mr Robinson
was a clergyman with Evangelical sympathies.[89] Since Anne
Brontë three times in the novel draws a pointed distinction
between a bad worldly match and a good marriage to a poor
man, and in each case the poor man is a clergyman, we must
regard Mr Robinson's profession as in some sense detracting
from his worldliness. There is a fourth clergyman who is himself worldly, Mr Hatfield, whose seven hundred a year, though
not enough for Miss Murray, was three and a half times Mr
Brontë's salary; unlike Agnes Grey's father or her brother-in-law,
Mr Richardson, or Mr Weston, he is not a good man, and may
possibly be modelled on Mr Robinson. At all events Anne cannot
resist making even him an example of the danger of putting
wealth before virtue, since Miss Murray in marrying Sir
Thomas Ashby obviously suffers far more than if she had become
Mrs Hatfield.[90] There is no parallel here with the fate of Lydia
Robinson who eloped with an actor called Henry Roxby, and
was cut off without a penny.[91]

Nor can there be any biographical parallel between the marriage of Agnes Grey's parents and that of Anne Brontë's parents
in spite of the theory to this effect of W.P.P. Mr Grey is a
clergyman, and when he marries has some private means as well
which he loses through rash investment. Unlike St John Rivers
and even Mr Helstone, who have no private means but are
considered quite eligible, Mr Grey is not considered good enough
by his wife's family who refuse to give them any part of their

fortune, and only reappear in the story to send a hard-hearted letter on the occasion of Mr Grey's death.

Unlike the very similar story of Jane Eyre's parents which at least serves to explain Jane's orphaned state, the story of Agnes Grey's parents serves no useful purpose unless it be to give Agnes a vaguely aristocratic lineage while at the same time providing material for a little anti-aristocratic propaganda. There is thus the same ambiguity as we found in Charlotte's works, and this impression is strengthened in a significant passage where Agnes Grey's mother compares the treatment suffered by Agnes at the hands of the vulgar Bloomfields with the treatment to be expected from a more aristocratic family.

> This time, you shall try your fortune in a somewhat higher family – in that of some genuine thorough-bred gentleman, for such are far more likely to treat you with proper respect and consideration than those purse-proud tradespeople and arrogant upstarts. I have known several among the higher ranks who treated their governesses quite as one of the family; though some, I allow, are as insolent and exacting as anyone else can be: for there are bad and good in all classes.[92]

But though there are bad and good in all classes we do not see much good in the aristocrats of *Agnes Grey*, although the aristocratic Murrays are slightly better than the upstart Bloomfields.

The satire against the Bloomfields is crude and obvious. The children behave badly, Mr Bloomfield is rude to his wife about the food, and Uncle Robson is not a gentleman. The mushroom poplar groves of Wellwood House, an appropriate name for a mansion of a would-be gentleman, symbolise the *nouveau riche* atmosphere of the Bloomfield household.[93] By contrast the wide park, stocked with deer, and beautiful old trees of Horton Lodge, shows that the Murrays are proper gentlefolk, although their behaviour both in general and towards their governess still leaves much to be desired.

The trouble with the Murrays is that though themselves well up on the aristocratic ladder they are anxious to climb still further, by a more aristocratic match. As a result Rosalie Murray spurns her more attractive suitors in order to become Lady

Ashley, although she would have much preferred to have become a Peeress.[94] Her delight in her title is reminiscent of Ginevra Fanshawe, but is even more short-lived. Also reminiscent of Ginevra Fanshawe is Rosalie's contempt for the humble nature of Agnes's sister's marriage to Mr Richardson, who is neither handsome nor young, but only good.[95] Mr Richardson is of course but a pale shadow of the novel's hero, Mr Weston, whose origins are not touched upon, although he is eventually wealthy enough to marry Agnes. Mr Weston's condescending kindness to the poor, in notable contrast to the *brusquerie* of the socially ambitious Mr Hatfield, gives the novel a democratic air, and it is unfortunate that this impression is spoilt by clumsy pieces of snobbery. Agnes Grey's family are proud of their aristocratic origins, although her maternal grandfather, described vaguely as a squire, behaves worse than the Murrays. Cast off by this squire's family 'our only intercourse with the world consisted in a stately tea party, now and then, with the principal farmers and tradespeople of the vicinity (just to avoid being stigmatised as too proud to consort with our neighbours)'.[96] And yet Agnes is curiously ignorant of aristocratic ways. Was Mr Grey with a snug little property of his own as well as a small incumbency really such a bad match for a squire's daughter?[97] Why was he so much inferior to the rich nabob who married Agnes's aunt and who inherited Agnes's mother's portion? In the same way it is not clear why Mr Hatfield should be so unsuitable a husband for Rosalie Murray. Rosalie's enthusiasm for titles and determination to have one herself is frankly vulgar, and the distinction between the Bloomfields and the Murrays, like the similar distinction between Ginevra Fanshawe and the Watsons, becomes blurred. Finally the authentic note of rancour from the unnoticed governess comes out without any concealment in the following passage:

Nota-bene – *Mr Hatfield never spoke to me, neither did Sir Hugh or Lady Meltham, nor Mr Harry or Miss Meltham, nor Mr Green or his sisters, nor any other lady or gentleman who frequented that church: nor, in fact, any one that visited at Horton Lodge.*[98]

The obvious contrast between the humble and virtuous Mr Weston and Agnes Grey, and the richer and more vicious world of the Bloomfields and Murrays, is repeated in *The Tenant of Wildfell Hall*. In the part of the novel that centres around Wildfel Hall we see a humble but on the whole happy society, whereas Helen Huntingdon's narrative reveals the corrupt dissipation which ruined the more elevated society of Grassdale Manor. Whereas *Agnes Grey* had been too slight a work to attract critical attention, *The Tenant of Wildfell Hall*, deriving notoriety from *Jane Eyre*, was attacked for its bold social doctrines. The reviewer in *Fraser's*[99] had no objection to the exposure of the ugly hypocritical visage of Society, but thought it both improbable and wrong that Gilbert Markham should marry Helen Huntingdon. Against the straightforward snobbery of comments such as the remark that Gilbert 'is no doubt highly attractive to young ladies of his own calibre' it is difficult to argue, but the gap between Helen Huntingdon and Gilbert Markham is smaller than the reviewer in *Fraser's* thinks. There is a curious mystery about Helen's origins. She only sees her father once, and he does not leave her much money. Her brother is the squire of the Wildfell Hall neighbourhood, but not too grand to contemplate marriage with Jane Wilson and to converse on easy terms with Gilbert Markham. Gilbert, who introduces himself as the son of a sort of gentleman farmer, and is described with a trace of sarcasm by Helen as 'the fine gentleman and beau of the parish',[100] is not deterred by thoughts of his presumption in aspiring to marry above his station until he arrives at Staningley. By this time Helen's husband and uncle have both died, and it is Helen's wealth which causes Markham's neighbour in the coach to suggest that 'she'll marry none but a nobleman' and Markham himself, as deferential as *Fraser's* to 'the fitness of things', to ask himself:

> And could I bear that she should think me capable of such a thing? – of presuming upon the acquaintance – the love, if you will – accidentally contracted, or rather forced upon her against her will, when she was an unknown fugitive, toiling for her own support, apparently without fortune, family or

connections; to come upon her now, when she was reinstated
in her proper sphere, and claim a share in her prosperity,
which, had it never failed her, would most certainly have kept
her unknown to me for ever.[101]

Helen does think Gilbert capable of such presumption, and
he marries her, apparently without meeting either the antici-
pated slights and censures of the world, or the sorrow and dis-
pleasures of those she loved. Indeed both Helen and her aunt
seem enthusiastic that the marriage should take place, and it is
perhaps this enthusiasm which raised the hackles of the reviewer
in *Fraser's*. But we can easily understand the readiness of Helen
and her aunt to accept Gilbert, since the whole book is aimed
at showing how much better his world is than the society from
which Helen had chosen her previous husband. Anne Brontë is
less blatant than in *Agnes Grey* in drawing the contrast between
the two worlds. In *Agnes Grey* we are actually told that Mr
Richardson is good and Sir Thomas Ashby bad, but in *The
Tenant of Wildfell Hall*, we are left to judge for ourselves the
difference between the healthy society described in the first part
of the book and the evil atmosphere surrounding Grassdale
Manor. Nor does Anne Brontë make the mistake of painting the
humbler society in too rosy colours. Unlike Mr Weston and the
Grey family who are almost too good to be true, the Markham
family and their friends are not without faults. Fergus and even
Gilbert are boorish, although their antics are but pale shadows
of the dissipation of Huntingdon and his friends, and the Mark-
hams do work for their living. Mr Markham and Rose interfere
too much in the affair between Gilbert and Mrs Graham,
although this slight excess of over-protectiveness is much better
than the complete failure of Helen Huntingdon's family to prevent her from making a foolish match. Eliza Millward and Jane
Wilson indulge in scandalous gossip about Mrs Graham and
Lawrence, but this gossip, although unpleasant and rewarded by
Jane and Eliza losing the respect of Gilbert and Lawrence, is a
more venial fault than the real adultery of Annabella and
Huntingdon, a sin which might have been nipped in the bud
with a little more frank speaking. Finally, Jane Wilson, the least

attractive figure among Markham's acquaintances, is the worst type of snob, aspiring to marry Lawrence and, when she fails, retiring into the country town to avoid living with her rough brother Robert. Here she lives.

> in a kind of close-fisted, cold, uncomfortable gentility, doing no good to others, and but little to herself; spending her days in fancy work and scandal; referring frequently to her 'brother the vicar', and her 'sister, the vicar's lady', but never to her brother the farmer and her sister, the farmer's wife; seeing as much company as she can without too much expense, but loving no one and beloved by none – a cold-hearted, supercilious, keenly, insidiously censorious old maid.[102]

But this brutal portrait is more than balanced by that of the hard, pretentious, worldly minded Mrs Hargrave earlier in the book,[103] whose anxiety to make good matches for her daughters is partly the result and partly the cause of her determination that her son should be enabled to hold up his head with the highest gentleman in the land. Whereas Jane Wilson merely does no good to anyone, Mrs Hargrave does positive harm to the character of her son Walter, and her wish to gain a rich man as a son-in-law almost ruins the lives of both her daughters.

Jane Wilson and Mrs Hargrave are minor characters, and it is perhaps unfair to compare the narrative of Gilbert Markham with the diary of Helen Huntingdon by taking these two characters from the two sections of the novel. But the passage decribing the eventual fate of Jane Wilson, although it occurs in a rather clumsy disposal of minor characters,[104] does reveal that Anne Brontë, whose knowledge of English families outside her own was greater than that of Emily and Charlotte,[105] did have something of an ear for some of the delicate gradations of social snobbery. Jane Wilson's willingness to speak about one brother and reluctance to mention the other is a touch worthy of *Middlemarch*, and we sometimes regret that Anne Brontë abandoned her portrait of middle-class provincial life for her account of the aristocracy, of which she knew so little. There are several features of life at Grassdale Manor which would strike a hostile critic like Miss Rigby as unconvincing. In the first place we may note the narrow canvas on which Anne chooses to paint her unflattering portrait. With the exception of the unimportant Mr Boarham and Mr Grimsby all the characters in Helen Huntingdon's narrative are related to each other. Huntingdon has two friends apart from Grimsby, namely Hattersley and Lord Lowborough, and they marry Helen's two chief acquaintances, Milicent Hargrave and Annabella Wilmot, who are both nieces of Helen's first admirer. Milicent's sister marries Helen's brother, and the novels ends by announcing a marriage between Helen Hattersley and the young Arthur Huntingdon. Now it would be possible to find parallels for this closely knit circle of acquaintances both in other novels of this period and in families known to the Brontës.[106] But to limit the characters in this way, while it may be suitable for a novel of provincial life, is not suitable to a portrait of the aristocracy. It is inherently improbable that Huntingdon, who whatever his faults is an eminently sociable man, should limit his acquaintances to two or three boon companions, especially when he spends half the year in London. It is also improbable that two of these boon companions should choose a wife out of the very small circle of Helen Huntingdon's female acquaintances.

Anne Brontë's ignorance of the aristocracy is hard to distinguish from her inability as a novelist to develop a wide range of characters, but if *The Tenant of Wildfell Hall* is meant to show us the superiority of the honest yeomanry over the dissolute squirearchy then it is certainly a failing that life at Grassdale Manor seems very like the life of a yeoman, apart from some incidental and not very convincing idleness and dissipation. *Wuthering Heights* has a similar stark economy of characters but we do not accuse Emily Brontë of being either a bad novelist or an undiscriminating observer of the social scene for this reason. We do sometimes wonder why Edgar Linton became so withdrawn from his neighbours after his wife's death, although Emily gives some explanation in drawing some attention to his melancholy and making Lockwood comment on the remoteness of the locality. In general, however, *Wuthering Heights* succeeds, where *The Tenant of Wildfell Hall* fails, in painting a realistic contrast between two ways of life, the rough hard farming life of Wuthering Heights, and the more comfortable squire's life of Thrushcross Grange.

Because the difference between the two ways of life is obviously meant to stand for something deeper than a mere cultural difference at a particular moment of time, critics have tended to concentrate on the metaphysical differences between the two houses[107] and to ignore the more obvious differences. And yet, as many critics have pointed out,[108] Emily is at some pains to date her novel accurately. She also fixes her novel in a definite place by her careful rendering of the Yorkshire accent, and indeed in one place makes Linton sneer at Hareton's Yorkshire accent.[109] All the other Brontë novels with the obvious exception of *Shirley* try to conceal the location of the English part of their story.

It is easy to pick out the salient points of the difference between Thrushcross Grange and Wuthering Heights. In spite of its forbidding situation and name, Wuthering Heights has a comparatively cheerful interior with shining pewter dishes and silver jugs on the vast dresser beneath the beamed roof. The floor is uncarpeted and the chairs high-backed primitive structures, painted green or black, but 'the apartment and furniture would have been nothing extraordinary as belonging to a homely northern farmer',[110] In contrast we have the first description of Thrushcross Grange as it appears to the young Heathcliff, 'a splendid place carpeted with crimson, and crimson-covered chairs and tables, and a pure white ceiling bordered by gold, a shower of glass-drops hanging in silver chains from the centre, and shimmering with little soft tapers'.[111]

Between the rugged homeliness of Wuthering Heights and the lavish splendour of Thrushcross Grange there may seem little to choose between the unhappiness suffered by the inhabitants of each house. We may note however one significant feature which distinguishes the two houses on our introduction to them, and is repeated at the end of the book. On the occasion of Lockwood's second visit to Wuthering Heights he leaves Thrushcross Grange because there is no proper fire, only a servant girl 'raising an infernal dust as she extinguishes the flames with heaps of cinders'.[112] On reaching Wuthering Heights,

Lockwood finds a warm cheerful apartment which 'glowed delightfully in the radiance of an immense fire, compounded of coal, peat and wood'.[113] On his final visit to Thrushcross Grange Lockwood finds it cold and damp, whereas Wuthering Heights has a fine red fire illuminating the chimney although the windows and doors are open.[114] It is natural for an inhabited house to be warmer than one that is let to an irregular tenant, but even when Edgar Linton is alive there is a chilly air about Thrushcross Grange which compares unfavourably with the roaring fire which always seems to be blazing at Wuthering Heights.[115] Even when fire is mentioned in connection with Thrushcross Grange there is not much warmth about it. Thus when Heathcliff is conducting his strange courtship of Isabella, Catherine pulls a chair to the fire, saying, 'Here are two people sadly in need of a third to thaw the ice between them.'[116] When she recovers from the shock of Isabella's elopement Edgar orders Nelly Dean to light a fire in the many-weeks'-deserted parlour.[117]

The difference between a warm and cold house may not seem of immediate sociological importance. More obviously important is the different attitude to servants in the two houses. At Wuthering Heights the servants are part of the family, Nelly being Hindley's foster-sister, and Joseph and Zillah being allowed to speak their mind to members of the family. When Hindley returns home with his wife he banishes Nelly and Joseph to have their meals in the kitchen, and soon sends Heathcliff to join them.[118] At the time of Isabella's visit to Wuthering Heights, Hindley still seems to have his meals separately, but Joseph is indignant at Isabella's refusal to share his rough food.[119] When Heathcliff is in complete control at the time of Lockwood's visits, it is not wholly clear whether the servants have their meals with the family or not. At the time of Lockwood's second visit we do not hear of Joseph or Zillah at the table, and on the occasion of his third visit Catherine is told by Heathcliff to get her dinner with Joseph and to remain in the kitchen. On the other hand Nelly Dean reports that in the closing months of Heathcliff's life, 'We always ate our meals with Mr Heathcliff', and Hareton, whom Heathcliff wants to degrade to a menial position, always seems present at the same table.[120]

At Thrushcross Grange the servants apart from Nelly are anonymous and conventional. They are accommodated in a kitchen wing.[121] When Edgar needs help against Heathcliff he tells Nelly to summon two men out of the hall.[122] In spite of Nelly's respect for Edgar Linton and her antipathy to Heathcliff her account of the conversations she has with the two men clearly reveal Heathcliff as the more friendly. Heathcliff calls his old childhood friend Nelly, whereas Edgar makes remarks like, 'It is nothing, is it, Ellen Dean? . . . You shall account more clearly for keeping me ignorant of this!', and 'The next time you bring a tale to me you shall quit my service, Ellen Dean.'[123] Edgar is even more haughty to Heathcliff, suggesting that the kitchen is a more suitable place for his reception than the parlour and forcing Catherine to say 'Set two tables here, Ellen: one for your master and Miss Isabella, being gentry; the other for Heathcliff and myself being of the lower orders.'[124]

This is a clear indication that the contrast between Thrushcross Grange and Wuthering Heights is in part a contrast between the hierarchical society and a classless society. Other references make it clear that a contrast is intended between a society that works for its living and a society that relies on the work of others. Whereas Edgar mopes in his library Heathcliff takes an interest in his sheep and horses.[125] The younger Catherine is criticised because she does nothing to earn her bread.[126] Isabella and Linton despise the porridge that they are offered at Wuthering Heights, and Joseph on the latter occasion comments pertinently 'His mother wer just soa – we wer a'most too mucky to sow t'corn for makking her bread.'[127] Mrs. Leavis sees the action of Hareton and the younger Catherine in replacing the currant bushes with flowers as a final victory of the nineteenth-century capitalist over the eighteenth-century yeoman,[128] but it is hard to see stocks and wallflowers as symbols of capitalism. On the other hand, though it is hard-working Hareton Earnshaw, last of the ancient line, who succeeds in getting control of both properties, his decision to move the younger Catherine to Thrushcross Grange does seem to indicate the passing of the old way of life.[129]

Where Mrs Leavis is undoubtedly right is in suggesting that

Emily gives definite indications that life at Wuthering Heights is preferable to life at Thrushcross Grange. Since the permanent inhabitants of Wuthering Heights, Hindley, Heathcliff, Hareton and Joseph, seem so boorish it may seem to be a flaw in the novel that the life which has produced them should be so recommended, and yet the apparent flaw is really a virtue, as can be seen by looking at the parallel case of *David Copperfield*. In this novel, Dickens wants to show that humble fishermen like the Peggottys are better than haughty aristocrats like Steerforth and Dartle, and accordingly paints the Peggottys in the most heroic colours and the Steerforths as treacherous figures full of the most outrageous pride. But these black and white caricatures have the effect of making us lose sight of the original distinction between aristocrats and fishermen; Steerforth is bad, not because he is an aristocrat, but because he is Steerforth, and the same is true in reverse of the Peggottys. How much better is the method of Emily Brontë, in showing us the attractive way of life in spite of the unattractive features of those who live this life, and the unpleasantness of another way of life in spite of the superficially pleasant nature of the characters enjoying it. There is of course still a problem connected with Heathcliff. Though he is the product of the healthy Wuthering Heights environment and lives at Wuthering Heights for most of his life, he cannot be considered as a representative of what Wuthering Heights stands for. Indeed our first introduction to Heathcliff makes this clear. Mr Heathcliff forms a singular contrast to his abode and style of living. He is a dark skinned gipsy in aspect, in dress and manners a gentleman.'[130] Heathcliff's transition to a gentleman is an object of some wonder to Nelly Dean, and when she visits Wuthering Heights on Isabella's invitation she comments, 'So much had circumstances altered their positions, that he would certainly have struck a stranger as a born and bred gentleman; and his wife as a thorough little slattern.'[131] Although Nelly is observant enough to notice that the metamorphosis of Heathcliff has not resulted in any improvement in Wuthering Heights which presents a dreary, dismal scene, she does not seem to notice that after the metamorphosis she seems to lose any sympathy she once had with him. Like Hindley who returns from his three years' absence with different dress and speech and different ideas about the place of the servants, the years of Heathcliff's absence do see him change from being a Marxist hero to a capitalist villain.[132]

The problem of Heathcliff has led many critics to assume that *Wuthering Heights* is essentially a non-moral document, and in this climate of critical opinion it may seem shocking to suggest that the novel has the narrow political meaning that old-fashioned yeomanry is better than new-fangled capitalism although, when Nelly Dean urges Catherine to consider Edgar's worldly advantages insufficient reason for marrying him, Emily is using her as a mouthpiece against the values of the new capitalist Vanity Fair. But the choice between Heathcliff and Edgar has more levels of meaning than the mere choice between two kinds of life, and here we may compare Emily with her two sisters. Charlotte Brontë has a message for society; this message is easy to extract from her novels, but it is a confused message, marred by exaggerated caricature and several inconsistencies; we are glad to extract this part of her work and to be left with her portrait of individual emotions, sincere and passionate. With Anne Brontë it is even easier to extract the social comment from the novel, but in her case there is very little left when we have made the extraction. Emily Brontë intermingles social and moral comment with even richer insight into the nature of the universe to such an extent that we cannot as with her sisters select passages from her novel and say that they compose the social and moral message. To do so would be an insult to a great novel. At the same time it would be a mistake to say that *Wuthering Heights* is without social or moral bias. What Emily Brontë appears to have done in *Wuthering Heights* is to have used the whole novel to express a preference for a particular way of life, and to have given a purely objective account of this way of life. This is not the sum of her achievement, but it is a considerable achievement in itself.

Appendix A
T. J. Wise and the Brontës

T. J. WISE was president of the Brontë Society in 1926–7, and vice-president from 1897 to 1936; he acted as adviser to the Society on a number of occasions, and it is an ironic comment on his role in the Society's affairs that he is listed in the index to the *Transactions of the Brontë Society* as Sir Thomas Wise. There are useful hints of Wise's activities on behalf of the Society in *Letters to J. H. Wrenn*, ed. Ratchford (New York, 1944), p. 478, and in letters from C. K. Shorter to W. T. Field, and H. E. Gorfin to J. J. Stead, recorded in Sotheby's Catalogue for 5 December 1967 (Nos. 477, 473).

As editor and bibliographer of the works of the Brontës Wise exerted a still more powerful influence. His lavishly produced *A Bibliography of the Writings in Prose and Verse of the Members of the Brontë Family* (London, 1917), and *A Brontë Library* (London, 1929), are incomplete and out of date but the bibliographical notes on the poems at the end of S.H.E.A. and S.H.C.B.P. are more useful; they do however owe more to Symington than to Wise, who as the principal bibliographer as well as the principal editor and owner of the Brontë material had a formidable opportunity of altering the record in his own interests.

Even these defective bibliographies cannot conceal the extent to which Shorter and Wise cornered the Brontë market. Apart from a few Branwell poems, either published by Leyland in *The Brontë Family* (London, 1886) or in the *Brontë Society Transactions* for 1927, the limited edition of poems by Charlotte, Emily and Anne Brontë (New York, 1902), *The Spell* by Charlotte (Oxford, 1931), edited by MacLean with acknowledgements to Shorter's executors, *A Leaf from an Unopened Volume* printed

in *Derby Day and other Stories* (Boston, 1934), by A. E. Newton, a friend of Wise, occasional poems by the sisters in nineteenth-century periodicals or the *Brontë Society Transactions*, the
notable *Legends of Angria*, edited by Fannie Ratchford (New-
haven, 1933) with thanks to Wise in the preface, most of the
poems and stories were first published by either Wise or Shorter. These publications fall into three distinct categories. We
have the expensive limited editions of individual poems or
stories, such as *The Adventures of Ernest Alembert*, edited by
Wise (London, 1896), or *The Four Wishes*, edited by Shorter
(London, 1916). There are the inaccurate and incomplete *Complete Poems* of Charlotte (London, 1923), Emily (London, 1910,
and revised edition, London, 1923), and Anne (London, 1920)
and the *Twelve Adventurers* (London, 1925), all edited by Shorter with considerable assistance from C. W. Hatfield. Then there
are the more comprehensive, but by no means complete Shakespeare Head editions of the *Poems by Charlotte and Patrick Branwell Brontë, Emily and Anne Brontë,* and the *Miscellaneous and
Unpublished Writings of Charlotte and Patrick Branwell Brontë,*
edited by Symington and Wise (Oxford, 1934–8), Miss Gerin's
recent edition of *Five Novelettes* by Charlotte Brontë, which
appeared after this study was complete, draws attention to the
incompleteness of the Shakespeare Head edition.

Wise was also the author of Part I, *The Autograph of Charlotte Brontë*, of *A Reference Catalogue of British and Foreign
Manuscripts* (London, 1893). He wrote this before he had
acquired his biggest haul of Brontë manuscripts through the visit
of Shorter to Mr Nicholls in Ireland. As purchaser of Brontë
manuscripts Wise's role is also a dominating one. He secured
from Mr Nicholls almost all the juvenilia apart from a few which
Nicholls retained, and which were sold at his death, Wise being
among the purchasers (these manuscripts are listed in *Book
Auction Records* (London, 1907, p. 682), and a few bought in
Brussels by Professor Ernest Nys, and subsequently sold to the
British Museum (these manuscripts are recorded in S.H.C.B.M.
p. 470). But there is something of a mystery about the way he
made this extensive purchase.

In the account which appears in *Charlotte Brontë and her*

Circle and the two later Life and Letters collections Shorter and
Mr Nicholls come to an understanding, stress is laid on the sim-
plicity of the Nicholls's life, but there is no mention of the sordid
subject of money. In the *Times Literary Supplement* of 3 April
1924 Shorter said that a friend gave him a blank cheque to
secure the Brontë relics. In a letter of 1917 to C. W. Hatfield
Shorter said that he had bought the little books from Nicholls for
£400, and in two letters to J. H. Wrenn on 10 and 22 September
1907 Wise said that the Brontë collection had cost him £1100 and
£1500. These figures are confused and confusing, and one has to
take into account Wise's desire to impress his Transatlantic
clients, but it is obvious from the printed record that money
changed hands, that Shorter and Wise were in partnership, and
that copyright as well as actual manuscript material was sold.

These three points are confirmed by the correspondence of
Mr Nicholls with Shorter preserved in the Brotherton Collection,
Leeds. Nicholls thanks Shorter three times for cheques, with some
reluctance allows practically all the letters to be published, and
in a rather naïve letter of 10 July 1895 surrenders the copyright.
On 24 June 1895 Nicholls in thanking Shorter for Mr Wise's
cheque says that he has understood the ultimate destination of his
manuscripts to be the South Kensington Museum. To this letter
Wise has pencilled a note saying that he never made such a suggestion, and that such a destination did not appeal to him at all.
On 28 December 1895 Nicholls wrote that he was quite satisfied
with Mr Wise's assurance that the letters would be given to the
nation and felt sure that he had received full value for them.
Again Wise has added that he gave no such assurance. Finally
and rather sharply on 21 January 1896 Nicholls asks Shorter for
the return of some letters without letting Mr Wise appropriate
them.

In the preface to *The Four Wishes*, pp. iii–iv, Shorter makes
a fairly frank confession of the way in which he and Wise
divided the spoils they had obtained from Nicholls. After saying
that he had paid several hundreds of pounds for Mr Nicholls's
collection he said that he retained the copyright, but that a
friend took the manuscripts. It is not difficult to guess the
identity of the friend. What is perhaps worth more investigation

is Shorter's claim to own the copyright, a claim which he seems to have extended to include all the Brontës' unpublished works although, on the evidence of Mr Nicholls's letters to Shorter in the Brotherton Collection, Mr Nicholls either did not know what he was surrendering or did not surrender it. As late as 1970 Shorter's family were still claiming the copyright of Charlotte's unpublished works, and the Brontë Society apparently endorsed their claim in spite of the clause in the Copyright Act of 1956, freeing manuscripts over a hundred years old in museums from the restrictions of copyright.

Copyright was an important issue, as it enabled Shorter and Wise to print Brontë material they had secured from other sources. Most of this material consisted of letters written by Charlotte. Some collections of letters passed into the safe custody of museums, as for instance the letters of Miss Wooler which are in the Fitzwilliam Museum, Cambridge, and the letters to G. H. Lewes which are in the British Museum. Wise did obtain letters to other correspondents, such as W. S. Williams, and J. Taylor, but there is no particular reason to attribute to such acquisitions anything that smacks of dishonesty or that would lead to inaccuracy.

This is not the case with the letters written by Charlotte to Ellen Nussey. Although not all the evidence relating to the dispute between Wise and Ellen Nussey has been made available, there is sufficient material both in the Brotherton Collection, Leeds, and the Brontë Parsonage Museum to damn Wise even more definitely than in the case of the purchase from Nicholls. On 18 November 1892 Ellen Nussey wrote a letter, beginning 'Dear Sir', in which the recipient of the letter was thanked for his enclosure and for the promises he had given in connection with the possession of Charlotte's letters. It is obvious what the promises are from a later note on an envelope, in which Ellen Nussey states that the original letters are in safe keeping until they are finally lodged in the National Museum. This note was provoked by someone, described as 'A dreadful man', fairly obviously Horsfall Turner, claiming that letters were in circulation; when it became obvious that letters were in circulation, because a Mr John Waugh was offering them to the newly

founded Brontë Society, it was against Horsfall Turner that
Ellen Nussy turned in rage.

The Waugh correspondence reveals a different villain. Waugh,
worried at Ellen Nussey's claims that he had not acquired the
letters fairly, found out from the booksellers, Pearsons and Co.
of Grange-over-Sands, that they had secured them from a Mr
T. J. Wise. Ellen Nussey in a letter of 12 July 1895, cast doubt on
this, calling Wise 'that unprincipled man'; to this Wise replied
in the same strain saying he could produce receipts, letters hag-
gling over the price and the counterfoil of a cheque dated 17
November 1892.

It is thus obvious that Wise is the recipient of the letter of 18
November 1892, and that he had not kept his promise to reserve
the letters for a national collection. This is made quite clear in a
rather pathetic note from Ellen Nussey, dated 26 July 1895,
and probably occasioned by Wise's threat of legal proceedings. In
this letter she admits that she has sold the letters, but says they
were a sacred deposit with Mr Wise, to be eventually deposited
in Kensington Museum. She also gives the price of the letters as
£125.

This was not the end of the quarrel, as various references in
Ellen Nussey's letters to her friends make clear. These letters to
people like Mrs Cortazzo, though dreary reading, are useful
correctives to the impression that Ellen Nussey was hysterical or
that she had found everyone her enemy, and the same is true of
letters from people like Wemyss Reid acknowledging that she
had been badly treated. No doubt the Birstall correspondence
will reveal the full story of Ellen Nussey's efforts to bring Wise
to book for breaking his promise.

What the Birstall letters may also do is to reveal the extent
to which the honesty or dishonesty of the various editors is reflected in the accuracy or inaccuracy of the various editions.
Horsfall Turner's edition had been produced before the dispute
between Ellen Nussey and her editors, and Wise's edition was
to be produced long after it. The only edition likely to be directly
affected by the controversy was Shorter's *Charlotte Brontë and
her Circle*, published in 1896. The copyright of Mrs Gaskell was
still in force, but this could hardly be a great restriction. A

restricting factor was likely to be the dearth of manuscripts which Wise had already begun to sell or exchange. It is not even clear whether he possessed more than a part of Ellen Nussey's collection. Wise has written on a letter from J. Waugh to Ellen Nussey's solicitor a note to the effect that Ellen Nussey squeezed him into paying twenty-five shillings for each letter. This would suggest that the hundred and twenty-five pounds was only paid for one hundred letters.

Wise's dishonesty in other literary matters is now an established fact, and it may seem superfluous to catalogue his misdeeds in Brontë affairs. This may be the reason why Wise's infamy in Brontë matters has yet to be exposed; the matter is a complicated one, and the two chief experts on Wise, Carter and Pollard, as typographical authorities, may well have felt reluctant to enter this fresh circle of Wise's inferno. Miss Ratchford's silence is harder to explain; she is an expert both on Brontë manuscripts and on T. J. Wise, although if she had studied Wise before studying the Brontë juvenilia, she might have felt a little less confident about her findings on the Brontës.

Nevertheless, it is vital that Wise's misdeeds should be exposed. Compared with his production of bogus first editions and his clumsy pillaging of the treasures of the British Museum his handling of Brontë manuscripts has had a far greater effect on English literature. Had Wise kept the promises he seems to have made to Nicholls and Ellen Nussey, our knowledge of the Brontës would have been considerably enriched. As it is we have to fight against the fog of uncertainty which his dishonesty has engendered.

Once it has been established that financial gain rather than the disinterested pursuit of knowledge was the mainspring behind Wise's activities, a whole area of uncertainty is opened up, since Wise exercised such a monopoly in Brontë affairs. Moreover the purchase and sale of Brontë manuscripts was an area in which there was a wide opportunity for profit, as can be seen from the following example. At the sale of Mr Nicholls's property in 1907, 77 pages of poems by Branwell were bought by Wise for £6 6s od. Five years later, at the sale of William W. Allis of Milwaukee 22 pages of *Corner Dishes*, allegedly by

Charlotte Brontë, were sold for 700 dollars. The next item in this sale was a copy of the bogus 1847 edition of E. B. Browning's *Sonnets from the Portuguese*, and this is evidence, if evidence is needed, for the source of Allis's purchase. Another tantalising indication of the value of Branwell's and Charlotte's manuscripts and of a possible attempt by Wise to substitute one for the other is to be found in a letter from J. J. Stead to H. C. Gorfin, recorded as part of lot 473 in Sotheby's catalogue for 5 December 1967. The letter on behalf of the Brontë Society rejects some Brontë manuscripts emanating from Wise, on the grounds that they are by Branwell. By selling Branwell's manuscript's as Charlotte's, by selling manuscripts which he had promised to bequeath to the nation, by binding manuscripts together which had no connection, but which might result in a more profitable sale, and by editing inefficiently the Brontë manuscripts he had squandered Wise has surely won himself an immortal place in Brontë studies.

Appendix B

The Needham Copies of Charlotte Brontë's Letters to Ellen Nussey

THE LETTERS are printed exactly as they appear in the copies owned by Sister Needham. Variations to be found in the manuscripts where available (MSS), in the Shakespeare Head Brontë (SHLL), in Shorter's 1908 *Life and Letter's* (S), and the suppressed Horsfall Turner edition (HT) are printed below each letter, but variations of punctuation are not included. The numbers of the letters in the Shakespeare Head edition are given for the purposes of identification.

Letter 854

Dear ——[1]   [2]

I am better now – as usual the reduction of strength was rapid – and the convalescence equally so. The very dreadful pain in my head is almost gone and so is the influenza. Papa too is better – but I was frightened about him – not that he has in the least lost appetite or thought himself ill – but the eyes etc. betrayed those symptoms that fill me with alarm.

I have written to Mrs Gaskell to ask her for next week[3] – when I get her answer I will tell you what is its purport – and your coming can be arranged accordingly.

I am glad dear ——[4] you are having a little enjoyment. Stay at O——[5] if you can wait[6] till you hear from me again[7] – You had better come direct here if we can arrange it[8] – we shall see.

Yours faithfully
C. Brontë

1. Ellen, HT, S, SHLL, MSS.
2. June 16th '53, HT, S. June 16th, 1853, SHLL, MSS.
3. SHLL, MSS add, 'I do not know whether she will be at liberty before August or Septb., but'.
4. Nell, HT, S, SHLL, MSS.
5. Oundle, HT, S, SHLL, MSS.
6. SHLL, MSS omit 'wait'.
7. SHLL, MSS add, 'as if Mrs Gaskell does not come'.
8. SHLL, MSS omit, 'if we can arrange it' and add, 'but'.

The manuscript of this letter is at Haworth.

Letter 855

Dear ——[1]   [2]
I have been very much vexed to find that Martha forgot to post my letter till too late – consequently as we have no post on Sunday it will not reach you till today at the earliest. I now write a line to tell you to be sure & arrange your departure from O——[3] according to your own convenience. My health has nothing to do with the question, as I am now about in my usual condition – only thin as I always am after illness. Be sure however to let me know the time of your arrival that I may arrange to send for you ···
I do trust it may be fine healthy weather while you are here. The enclosed is from A.[4] to you – I have not read it though it was sent to me open. It takes two posts from O—— to Haworth. I shall *expect you by next Thursday.*

Yours faithfully
C. Brontë

I trust you will get through your journey all right.

1. Ellen, HT, S, SHLL.
2. June 20th, '53, S, SHLL.

3. Oundle, HT, S, SHLL.
4. Amelia, S, SHLL.

The manuscript has not been traced, and it is obviously this copy that has been used by all editors.

Letter 870

Dear ——[1]   Haworth   [2]
I duly & safely reached home with my purchases at about 5 o'clock yesterday afternoon. I found Papa &c very well. The mops – the carpet & rug all give satisfaction. The other purchases[4] I kept from observation[5] but they will be appreciated I dare say when they appear in their proper time and place – I hope you all reached home all right but I fear the fatigue you underwent will leave its effects today. It was not a very good preparation for the long walk to S.[6]

Write soon & tell me how you are – I have some headache today, but not violent – a general jaded, weary feeling was to be expected. With love to all at ——[7] and kind regards to Mr ——[8]

I am dear ——[1]

Yours fagged but faithfully
C. Brontë

1. Ellen, HT, S, SHLL, MSS.
2. Haworth, HT, Thursday morning S, MSS. Thursday morning (8 October 1853), SHLL.
3. SHLL, MSS omit, 'the'.
4. SHLL, MSS, the crockery and glass.
5. SHLL, MSS read 'out of sight' instead of 'from observation'.
6. Scholes, HT, S, SHLL MSS.
7. 'Your mother and Mercy' for 'all at —', HT, S. SHLL, MSS.
8. Clapham, S. C-, HT, SHLL, MSS.

The manuscript is at Haworth. The variations here are small but the coincidence between Shorter, Horsfall Turner and the Needham copies on the one hand and the manuscript and SHLL on the other is impressive.

Letter 880

My dear ——[1]   [2]
I am sorry to hear that Mrs R—— N——[3] has had a paralytic stroke – is this true or is it an exaggerated account? At her age one would have scarcely expected an attack of that nature but I believe paralysis attacks more persons and younger persons than formerly. A clergyman of not more than 35 in the neighbourhood of S.[4] is entirely disabled from duty by the effects of a paralytic stroke. How does your mother continue to get on? Papa has so far borne the winter surprisingly well on the whole – though now and then he still complains of muscular weakness and other slight symptoms which renew anxiety. Still I have more reason for gratitude than fear in his case. Is Mrs C better for Mr Teale's advice?[5] *Last* but not *least* how are you yourself?[6]

Yours affectionately
C. Brontë

1. Ellen, HT, S, SHLL.
2. Haworth, March 1st, 1854. HT, S, SHLL.
3. Richard Nussey, HT, S, SHLL.
4. Skipton, HT, S, SHLL.
5. Your sister Anne it seems has consulted Mr Teale – is she better for his advice. S, SHLL.
6. No italics, HT, S.

The manuscript of this letter is not extant. Apart from the single sentence about Ann Nussey and Mr Teale all versions are very similar; this sentence looks like an explanation by Ellen Nussey, and since it is the unreliable Shorter who first introduces it, we cannot be very confident that any editor saw the manuscript.

Letter 881

Dear ———[1]   [2]

I am very glad to hear that Mrs R———[3] is presumed out of danger.[4] It is well too that the brain has so far escaped serious injury – it seems to me perhaps the worst of all dooms for the death of the mind to anticipate that of the body, yet sometimes when these attacks fall directly on the nervous system a state of irritation follows which is found very trying not only for the poor patient – but more especially for friends. You do not say that such is the case in the present instance, and I hope it will not prove so ·[5] So far I have been so favoured as to escape *severe* colds – but my headaches do at times harass me and keep me thin. I am truly glad to hear that your Mother keeps[6] well[7]. Papa still continues well. Believe me my dear ———[1]

Yours affectionately
C. Brontë

1. Ellen, HT, S, SHLL, MSS.
2. Haworth, March 7th, 1854, S. Haworth, March 7th '54, SHLL, MSS.
3. Richard, S, SHLL.
4. for I think and believe her loss would probably be severely felt by your brother – and he could not be much disturbed without evil coming more or less home to you all at Brookroyd, SHLL, MSS.
5. I trust and believe your brother John is right in his opinion of your own ailment. On no account let it alarm you – for I imagine that comparatively few people are wholly free from some such inconvenience as you describe. An over-sedentary life producing a confined state of the bowels – I suppose is at the root of it. Remembering the effect that iodine produced on you long since – I cannot help being glad that you have given up that remedy. It seems to me that reducing drugs must be hazardous when the constitution is not robust. It is strange that I have never heard of you as looking ill – but I have no doubt it was owing to the low state to which the pills etc had brought you – that that cold you

caught in the winter took such hold on your system, SHLL, MSS.:

6. S, SHLL and MSS omit, 'keeps' and insert, 'Mr Clapham and Mercy are'.
7. SHLL and MSS add, 'and that your sister Anne is better. Mr Teale will really do a good deed if he suceeds in curing her'. HT and S omit 'really'.

The manuscript of this letter is in the Henry Huntington collection. The divergence between versions following it and versions following the Needham copies is a striking indication of the unreliability of the latter, although we are not greatly enriched by Charlotte's advice on Ellen Nussey's ailment.

Letter 883

My dear ——[1]   [2]
I put off writing yesterday because I had a headache – I have it again today – not serious but depressing – however I will write a few lines – and if they are inefficient you will know the reason.

Miss W.[3] kindly asked me likewise to go and see her at Hornsea – but I had a prior engagement this month – which, however, it seems very doubtful whether I shall keep – it would have given me true pleasure to have joined Miss W – had not my previous promise stood in the way.

I was *very* glad to hear of Miss C's[4] engagement – offer her my sincere congratulations on the subject. I don't know J—— B——[5] but if he only prove as kind a husband as I feel sure she will be a good wife – they have a good chance of happiness. Mrs R—— N——'s[6] convalescence was good news also – I trust she will steadily improve – & many years may elapse before she has any return. The third stroke of paralysis or apoplexy is generally said to be fatal – but there is an instance in this neighbourhood of three strokes recurring within a period of twenty years – and the patient lives still – and is indeed almost entirely recovered from the effects of the third attack. One leg only is stiff and unmanageable but he can walk pretty well.

Be sure & look after yourself dear ——[1].[7] Mind cold and the night air. Tell me if you are pretty well & in good spirits[8] when you write again.[9]

Yours affectionately
C. Brontë

1. Ellen, HT, S, SHLL, MSS.
2. March 22, 1854. HT. March 22nd, 1854, S. Wednesday morning (March 2nd, 1854), SHLL. Wednesday morning, MSS with Mar. 22 – 54 in Ellen Nussey's hand.
3. Wooler, HT, S, SHLL, MSS.
4. Cockhill, HT, S, SHLL, MSS.
5. John Battye, SHLL, MSS.
6. R. Nussey, HT. Richard Nussey, S. R-d Nussey, SHLL, MSS.
7. SHLL, MSS add, 'take exercise – keep your spirits up'.
8. are in good spirits. HT, S. are in pretty good spirits, SHLL, MSS.
9. SHLL, MSS (after a lacuna, in which something has been cut out) add, 'How does your sister Ann go on? – and what treatment is prescribed by Mr Teale'.

The manuscript of this letter is at Haworth.

Letter 884

My dear ——[1]   [2]

The enclosure in yours of yesterday puzzled me at first for I did not immediately recognize my own handwriting – when I did the sensation was one of consternation and vexation as the letter *ought*[3] by all means to have gone on Friday. It was intended to relieve ——[4] of great anxiety. However I trust he will get it today – and on the whole – when I think it over – I can only be thankful that the mistake was no worse and did not throw the letter into the hands of some indifferent and unscrupulous person. I wrote it after some days of indisposition & uneasiness and when I felt weak and unfit to write. While writing to him – I was at the same time intending to answer *your*[3] note – which I suppose accounts for the confusion of ideas – shewn in the mixed and blundering address.

I wish you *would*[3] come about Easter rather than another time for this reason. Mr N——[4] if not prevented proposes coming over then – I suppose he will stay at Mr G's[6] as he has done two or three times before – but he will be frequently coming here – which would enliven your visit a little – perhaps too he might take a walk with us occasionally – altogether it would be a little change – such as you know – I could not always offer.

If all be well he will come under different circumstances to any that have hitherto[7] attended his visits before – were it otherwise I should not ask you to meet him – for when aspects are gloomy and unpropitious – the fewer there are to suffer from the cloud – the better.

He was here in January and was then received but not pleasantly. I think it will be a little different now.

Papa breakfasts in bed[8] & has not yet risen – his bronchitis is still troublesome. I had a bad week last week – but am greatly better now for my mind is a little relieved though very sedate and rising only to expectations the most moderate.

Sometime perhaps in May – I may hope to come to B——[9] but as you will understand from what I have now stated I could not come before.

Think it over dear ——[1], and come to Haworth if you can. write as *soon*[3] as you can decide.

Yours affectionately
C. Brontë

1. Ellen, HT, S, SHLL.
2. Haworth, March 28th, 1854, S. Haworth, March 28th, '54, HT, SHLL.
3. No italics, HT, S, SHLL.
4. him, HT, S, SHLL.
5. Nicholls, HT, S, SHLL.
6. Grant's, S, SHLL.
7. HT, S, SHLL omit, 'hitherto'.
8. SHLL inserts, 'today'.
9. SHLL replaces this sentence by 'I may be in your neighbourhood and shall then come to Brookroyd!'.

Alterations 7, 8, 9 may arise from a consultation of the manuscript, now not extant, but the punctuation and absence of any

italics (a feature of Charlotte's style when she was agitated) in
the printed versions suggest that the manuscript was not copied.

Letter 885

My dear ——[1]   [2]
    You certainly were right in your second interpretation of my
note, I am too well aware of the dullness of Haworth for any
visitor – not to be glad to avail myself of the chance of offering
even a slight change. But this morning my little plans have all[3]
been disarrayed by an intimation that Mr N——[4] is coming on
Monday – I thought to put him off, but have not succeeded. As
Easter now consequently seems an unfavourable period both
from your point of view and mine – we will adjourn it till a
better opportunity offers. Meantime I thank you dear ——[1] for
your kind offer to come in case I wanted you. Papa is still very
far from well – his cough very troublesome and a good deal of
inflammatory action on the chest. Today he seems somewhat
better than yesterday – and I earnestly hope the improvement
may continue. With kind regards to your mother and all at
B——[5].
    I am dear ——[1]

Yours affectionately
C. Brontë

1. Ellen, HT, S, SHLL.
2. April 1st '54, HT, SHLL. April 1st, 1854, S.
3. HT, S. SHLL omit, 'all'.
4. Nicholls, HT, S, SHLL.
5. Brookroyd, HT, S, SHLL.

The manuscript of this letter is not extant.

Appendix C

Reviews of the Brontë Novels

(i) Reviews Consulted for this Study

Athenaeum
1.   23 Oct 1847, pp. 1100–1, on *Jane Eyre*.
2.   25 Dec 1847, pp. 1324–5, on *Wuthering Heights* and *Agnes Grey*.
3.   8 July 1848, p. 671, on *The Tenant of Wildfell Hall*.
4.   3 Nov 1849, pp. 1107–9, on *Shirley*.
5.   28 Dec 1850, pp. 1368–9, on *Wuthering Heights* and *Agnes Grey*.
6.   12 Feb 1853, pp. 166–8, on *Villette*.

Atlas
1.   23 Oct 1847, p. 719, on *Jane Eyre*.
2.   22 Jan 1848, p. 59, on *Wuthering Heights* and *Agnes Grey*.
3.   3 Nov 1849, pp. 696–7, on *Shirley*.
4.   12 Feb 1853, p. 106, on *Villette*.

Bath Herald
1.   20 Nov 1847, p. 4, on *Jane Eyre*.

Bells Weekly Messenger
1.   11 Dec 1852, p. 6, on *Shirley*.
2.   12 Feb 1853, p. 6, on *Villete*.

Blackwood's Magazine
1.   Vol. 64 (Oct 1848), pp. 473–4, on *Jane Eyre*.

Britannia
1.   6 Nov 1847, p. 710, on *Jane Eyre*.
2.   15 Jan 1848, pp. 42–3, on *Wuthering Heights*.

3.   10 Nov 1849, pp. 714–15, on *Shirley*.

Christian Remembrancer
1.   N.S. Vol. 15 (April 1848), pp. 396–409, on *Jane Eyre*.
2.   N.S. Vol. 25 (April 1853), pp. 423–43, on *Villette*.

Church of England Quarterley Review
1.   Vol. 23 (April 1848), pp. 491–2, on *Jane Eyre*.

Courier
1.   1 Jan 1848, pp. 9–10, on *Jane Eyre*.

Critic
1.   31 Oct 1847, p. 277, on *Jane Eyre*.
2.   15 Nov 1849, pp. 519–21, on *Shirley*.
3.   15 Feb 1853, pp. 94–5, on *Villette*.

Daily News
1.   31 Oct 1849, p. 2, on *Shirley*.
2.   3 Feb 1853, p. 2, on *Villette*.

Douglas Jerrold's Magazine
1.   Vol. 6 (July–Dec 1847), pp. 471–4, on *Jane Eyre*.

Douglas Jerrold's Weekly Newspaper
1.   15 Jan 1848, p. 77, on *Wuthering Heights* and *Agnes Grey*.

Dublin Review
1.   Vol. 28 (March 1850), pp. 209–23, on *Jane Eyre* and *Shirley*.

Dublin University Magazine
1.   Vol. 31 (May 1848), pp. 608–14, on *Jane Eyre*.
2.   Vol. 34 (Dec 1849), pp. 680–9, on *Shirley*.
3.   Vol. 42 (Nov 1853), pp. 612–15, on *Villette*.

Eclectic Review
1.   Vol. 26 (Dec 1849), pp. 739–49, on *Shirley*.

2. N.S. Vol. 1 (Feb 1851), pp. 223–7, on *Wuthering Heights* and *Agnes Grey*.
3. N.S. Vol. 5 (March 1853), pp. 305–20, on *Villette*.

Economist
1. 27 Nov 1847, pp. 1376–7, on *Jane Eyre*.
2. 29 Jan 1848, p. 126, on *Wuthering Heights*.
3. 10 Nov 1849, pp. 1251–3, on *Shirley*.
4. 4 Jan 1851, p. 15, on *Wuthering Heights*.

Edinburgh Guardian
1. 3 Dec 1853, pp. 4–5, on *Villette*.

Edinburgh Review
1. Vol. 91 (Jan 1850), pp. 153–73 on *Shirley*.
2. Vol. 97 (April 1853), pp. 380–90, on *Villette*.

Era
1. 28 Nov 1847, p. 9, on *Jane Eyre*.

Examiner
1. 27 Nov 1847, pp. 256–7, on *Jane Eyre*.
2. 8 Jan 1848, pp. 21–2, on *Wuthering Heights*.
3. 3 Nov 1849, pp. 692–4, on *Shirley*.
4. 21 Dec 1850, p. 815, on *Wuthering Heights*.
5. 5 Feb 1853, pp. 84–5, on *Villette*.

Fraser's Magazine
1. Vol. 36 (Dec 1847), pp. 690–4, on *Jane Eyre*.
2. Vol. 39 (April 1849), pp. 423–6, on *The Tenant of Wildfell Hall*.
3. Vol. 40 (Dec 1849), pp. 692–4 on *Shirley*.

Globe
1. 9 Nov 1849, p. 1, on *Shirley*.
2. 6 Dec 1852, p. 1, on *Shirley*.
3. 7 Feb 1853, p. 1, on *Villette*.

Guardian
1. 23 Feb 1853, pp. 128–9, on *Villette.*

Howitt's Journal
1. 20 Nov 1847, p. 333, on *Jane Eyre.*

Leader
1. 28 Dec 1850, p. 953, on *Wuthering Heights* and *Jane Grey.*
2. 12 Feb 1853, pp. 163–4, on *Villette.*

Literary Gazette
1. 23 Oct 1847, pp. 748–9, on *Jane Eyre.*
2. 5 Feb 1853, pp. 123–5, on *Villette.*

Magnet
1. 28 Feb 1853, p. 6, on *Villette.*

Mirror
1. 4th Series, Vol. 2 (Dec 1847), pp. 376–80, on *Jane Eyre.*

Morning Advertiser
1. 4 Feb 1853, p. 6, on *Villette.*

Morning Chronicle
1. 25 Dec 1849, p. 7, on *Shirley.*

Morning Herald
1. 16 Nov 1849, p. 6, on *Shirley.*

New Monthly Magazine
1. Vol. 81 (Nov 1847), p. 374, on *Jane Eyre.*
2. Vol. 82 (Jan 1848), p. 140, on *Wuthering Heights* and *Agnes Grey.*
3. Vol. 95 (July 1852), pp. 295–305, on *Jane Eyre* and *Shirley.*

Nonconformist
1. 15 Dec 1852, p. 992, on *Shirley.*
2. 16 March 1853, p. 224, on *Villette.*

North British Review
1. Vol. 11 (Aug 1849), pp. 482–8, on *Jane Eyre, Wuthering Heights* and *The Tenant of Wildfell Hall*.
2. Vol. 15 (Aug 1851), pp. 422–3, on the Brontë Novels.

Observer
1. 1 Nov 1847, p. 2, on *Jane Eyre*.
2. 4 Nov 1849, p. 7, on *Shirley*.

Palladium
1. No. 3, Sept 1850, pp. 161–75, on Charlotte Brontë's novels and *Wuthering Heights*.

People's Journal
1. 13 Nov 1847, pp. 269–72, on *Jane Eyre*.

Quarterly Review
1. Vol. 84 (Dec 1848), pp. 162–76, on *Jane Eyre*.

Rambler
1. Vol. 3 (Sept 1848), pp. 65–6, on *The Tenant of Wildfell Hall*.

Sharpe's London Magazine
1. Vol. 7 (Sept 1848), pp. 181–4, on *The Tenant of Wildfell Hall*.
2. Vol. 11 (June 1850) pp. 370–3, on *Shirley*.

Spectator
1. 6 Nov 1847, pp. 1074–5, on *Jane Eyre*.
2. 18 Dec 1847, p. 1217, on *Wuthering Heights* and *Agnes Grey*.
3. 8 July 1848, pp. 662–3, on *The Tenant of Wildfell Hall*.
4. 3 Nov 1849, pp. 1043–5, on *Shirley*.
5. 12 Feb 1853, pp. 155–6, on *Villette*.

Standard of Freedom
1. 10 Nov 1849, p. 11, on *Shirley*.

Sun
1.   6 Nov 1847, on *Jane Eyre.*
2.   14 Nov 1849, on *Shirley.*

Sunday Times
1.   5 Dec 1847, p. 2, on *Jane Eyre.*
2.   2 Jan 1853, p. 2, on *Shirley.*
3.   13 March 1853, p. 2, on *Villette.*

Tablet
1.   23 Oct 1847, p. 675, on *Jane Eyre.*

Tait's Edinburgh Magazine
1.   N.S. Vol. 15 (Feb 1848), pp. 138–40, on *Wuthering Heights.*
2.   N.S. Vol. 15 (May 1848), pp. 346–8, on *Jane Eyre.*

Times
1.   7 Dec 1849, p. 3, on *Shirley.*

Weekly Chronicle
1.   23 Oct 1847, p. 3, on *Jane Eyre.*
2.   11 Nov 1849, p. 3, on *Shirley.*
3.   12 Feb 1853, pp. 105–6, on *Villette.*

Westminster Review
1.   Vol. 48 (Jan 1848), pp. 581–4, on *Jane Eyre.*
2.   Vol. 52 (Jan 1850), pp. 418–19, on *Shirley.*
3.   N.S. Vol. 2 (July 1852), pp. 129–41 on the Brontë novels.
4.   N.S. Vol. 3 (April 1853), pp. 474–91, on *Villette.*

(ii) Some important posthumous reviews

Athenaeum
1.   13 June 1857, pp. 755–7, on *The Professor.*

Blackwood's Magazine
1. Vol. 77 (May 1855), pp. 554–68, 'Modern Novelists, Great and Small'.
2. Vol. 82 (June 1857), pp. 77–94, 'Currer Bell'.
3. Vol. 102 (Sept 1867), pp. 257–80, 'Novels'.

Dublin University Magazine
1. Vol. 50 (July 1857), pp. 88–100, on *The Professor.*

Critic
1. Vol. 16 (15 April 1957), pp. 168–71 on *The Life of Charlotte Brontë*

Edinburgh Review
1. Vol. 106 (July 1857), pp. 124–6, 'The Licence of Modern Novelists'.

Fraser's Magazine
1. Vol. 55 (May 1857), pp. 569–82, 'Charlotte Brontë'.

Oxford and Cambridge Magazine
1. June 1856, pp. 328–35, 'Thackeray and Currer Bell''.

Sharpe's London Magazine
1. N.S. Vol. 5 (June 1855) pp. 339–42, 'A Few Words about Jane Eyre.'

Westminster Review
N.S. Vol. 26 (July 1864), pp. 24–9, 'Novels with a Purpose'.

(iii) Reviews not consulted

1. On *Jane Eyre*
   Morning Advertiser: notice mentioned, 28 Oct 1847. (SHLL. Vol. II, p. 151).

   Glasgow Examiner: notice mentioned, 27 Nov 1847. (SHLL. Vol. II, p. 156).

Church of England Journal: favourable notice mentioned, 23 Dec 1847. (SHLL. Vol. II, p. 166).

Scotsman: notice mentioned, 31 Dec 1847. (SHLL. Vol. II, p. 170).

Oxford Chronicle: notice mentioned, 4 Jan 1848. (SHLL. Vol. II, p. 174).

Morning Herald: favourable notice mentioned, 22 Jan 1848. (SHLL. Vol. II, p. 181).

Morning Chronicle: favourable notice mentioned, 12 May 1848. (SHLL. Vol. II, p. 212).

Guardian
Liverpool Standard   favourable extracts quoted
Morning Post   in the third edition of Jane
Nottingham Mercury   Eyre (April 1848)
Sheffield Isis

2. On Shirley
Church of England Quarterly Review: unfavourable notice mentioned, 3 Jan 1850 (SHLL. Vol. III, p. 63).

3. On Villette
Morning Herald: notice mentioned, ? 1853 (SHLL. Vol. IV, p. 57).

Appendix D

Nussey family tree, showing connections with the Walker, Carr, Clapham, Heald and Ingham families. Information supplied by Mr J. T. M. Nussey of Chester.

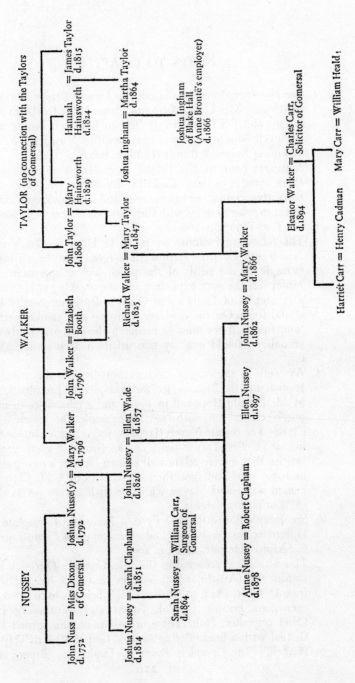

NOTES TO CHAPTER 1

1. See the very different attitudes to Cowan Bridge shown in the articles by Mrs E. M. Weir and Dame Myra Curtis in B.S.T. 56 (1946) and B.S.T. 63 (1953), and to Branwell Brontë in Gerin, *Branwell Brontë* (London, 1961) and du Maurier, *The Infernal Genius of Branwell Brontë* (London, 1960).

2. Margaret Lane in *The Brontë Story* (London, 1953), a sympathetic study of Mrs Gaskell's difficulties, but also a useful corrective against her inaccuracies and omissions, does make some effort to come to terms with Charlotte's and Branwell's love affairs.

3. B.S.T. 77 (1967), p. 169.

4. The following footnote on p. 18 of Elliot B. Gose's article in *Nineteenth Century Fiction* (June 1966) provides an interesting example of the perils of the psychological approach. 'Thomas Moser sees the guns exploding and the breaking of Hareton's pipe as examples of Emily's and Cathy's depriving him of his male sexual force. On the contrary, hunting and smoking with male companions, if one must be Freudian about it, are clearly inverted sexuality (should one say masturbation or homosexuality) etc. etc.'

5. As well as showing a distinct hostility to the psychological approach to the Brontës (see, for example, the presidential address by Mr Donald Hopewell in 1954), and a reluctance to admit the purely critical approach (see, for example, the review of W. A. Craik's *The Brontë Novels* (London, 1968) by Sir Linton Andrews in 1968), *The Transactions of the Brontë Society* are full of articles that merely relate well known facts in a new guise. Thus in 1952, 1963 and 1968 there are articles by C. T. Clay, Charles Lemon and Isabel Mayne which do little except précis the story of *Wuthering Heights*.

6. See Joseph Prescott, 'Jane Eyre: a Romantic Exemplum with a Difference' in *Twelve original essays on great English novels*, ed. C. Shapiro (Detroit, 1960), p. 100.

7. This attitude is reflected in the title, *Gondal's Queen: a novel in manuscript* (Austin, 1955), and in sentences like, 'The period from October, 1845, to January, 1848, belongs to her two literary excursions outside Gondal, *Poems* and *Wuthering Heights*. Cruel tragedies, both! These ordeals over, she turned again to Gondal with a final offering to her "God of Visions".' (p. 35).

8. Hatfield's *The Complete Poems of Emily Jane Brontë* (Oxford,

1941) is a great improvement on any previous edition of Brontë poems, but it cannot be relied on absolutely.

9. W. D. Paden in *An Investigation of Gondal* (New York, 1958) makes out a good case against Miss Ratchford on both scores.

10. An exception is the review by Professor Barbara Hardy in *Nineteenth Century Fiction*, 23 (2), (September 1968), pp. 240–3.

11. Robert Blake in *The Sunday Times*, 3 December 1967.

12. See Chapter 4 for a detailed discussion of these errors.

13. *Charlotte Brontë: The Evolution of Genius* (Oxford, 1967), p. 614.

14. Ibid., p. 398.

15. Ibid., p. xiv.

16. The dates of the letters written by Charlotte Brontë between 1836 and 1838 are uncertain, and Shorter and the Shakespeare Head edition give them in a very different order. Miss Gerin has no hesitation about giving conjectural dates as if they were certain and adopts an eclectic attitude in following both Shorter and the Shakespeare Head at different times, Nor does she even do this with any consistency. On p. 109 she cites for a letter of 29 December 1836, the Shakespeare Head Life and Letters, II, 149; this should read I, 149, and is interesting to note that Shorter dates this letter 29 December 1837. On p. 113 she cites Shorter, I, 138 for a letter dated 2 October 1837, and says that the letter is in the Brontë Parsonage Museum. The letter is not in the Brontë Parsonage Museum and, though Symington and Wise date this letter 2 October 1837, Shorter dates it 2 April 1837. Finally, on p. 114, Miss Gerin follows the text of Shorter who is the only authority cited, although on this occasion the manuscript is in the Brontë Parsonage Museum, and the Shakespeare Head, unlike Shorter, follows the manuscript faithfully reproducing Charlotte's agitated punctuation.

17. Op. cit., p. xiii. The above examples would suggest that Miss Gerin's consultation of the manuscripts in the Brontë Parsonage Museum has not been very thorough and, though she acknowledges the help of many American collections, she rarely cites them.

18. See my article in *Notes and Queries* (January 1970) on 'Charlotte Brontë and Calvinism'.

19. It is invidious to single out Miss Gerin for making mistakes which she shares in common with other Brontë biographers without recognising her merits, which are such that her life of Charlotte is likely to become the standard Brontë biography. Her earlier books on Anne and Branwell are less ambitious; her

Emily Brontë (London, 1971) appeared after this study was virtually complete, but it appears to follow the same pattern as the books on Anne and Branwell with many of the same errors repeated.

NOTES TO CHAPTER 2

1. Even in the Shakespeare Head Life and Letters which delves into the remote past of Mr Brontë, and includes several letters written after Charlotte's death, over a third of the letters are to Ellen Nussey, and in Shorter's edition the proportion is over half.

2. See for example, Winifred Gerin, *Charlotte Brontë: the Evolution of Genius*, p. 75.

3. Dr Phyllis Bentley in *The Brontës and Their World* (London, 1969), p. 37, states authoritatively, 'To Ellen Nussey we owe an eternal debt of gratitude, for she kept every letter that Charlotte wrote to her ... more than four hundred of the precious documents remain available.' It is not clear whether Dr Bentley means that Ellen kept every letter until Charlotte's death (hard to prove), or for all time (plainly false). It is not clear whether she means that more than four hundred manuscripts or more than four hundred letters in some form are available to us: both statements are false. Daphne du Maurier in *The Infernal World of Branwell Brontë*, is an exception to the usual rule, for she says (p. 226) that Ellen destroyed many letters.

4. This difficulty in sending letters from Brussels may explain the gaps noted by Miss Margaret Rhodes, in B.S.T. 78 (1968), p. 250 in the correspondence with Ellen Nussey.

5. Even this letter (S.H.L.L., Vol. IV, p. 97) is uncertainly dated.

6. S.H.L.L., Vol. IV, p. 157.

7. The manuscript is in the Brotherton Collection, Leeds. See Appendix A., for the identification of Ellen Nussey's correspondent as T. J. Wise.

8. S.H.L.L., Vol. IV, pp. 103–4.

9. Ibid., Vol. IV, pp. 247–9, and B.S.T. 8 (1898), pp. 23–42, and 68 (1958), pp. 220–32.

10. *The Story of the Brontës, their Home, Haunts and Friends and Works, part second – Charlotte's letters* (Bingley, 1885–9).

11. It is a tedious task to count up the exact number of letters, especially as editors both combine two letters into one (Shakespeare Head, 270) and print one letter as two (Shorter, letters 27 and 40). There is, however, nothing to suggest that instances of the

former kind of mistake so outnumber the latter that the printed total of about 370 represents a manuscript total of 500.

12. At Oakwell Hall there are two envelopes, dated October 8th, 1847 and October 15th, 1847, of which the latter has the pencilled note on it in the handwriting of Ellen Nussey, 'To destroy cf A—— Mr. Nicholls'. This would seem to refer to the letter at Oakwell Hall mentioning both Amelia Ringrose and, in a not very complimentary fashion, Mr Nicholls. The manuscript of this letter is dated by Ellen Nussey, October '47, and by the Shakespeare Head editors is allocated to 15 October, presumably on the authority of the envelope.

13. e.g. Miss Mildred Christian in *A Guide to Victorian Fiction*, ed. Stevenson (Cambridge, Mass., 1964), p. 223, for the number of letters in the Horsfall Turner edition.

14. See letters from Sidney Biddell and Alpheus Wilkes in S.H.L.L., Vol. IV, 273 and 275, and the articles by Scruton and Mrs Cortazzo cited above, note 9.

15. Mrs Gaskell herself uses the figure 350 (see Chapple and Pollard, p. 372); this may be an approximation for 380, but the presence of manuscripts with proper names not censored would appear to suggest that Ellen Nussey retained some of them.

16. There is no way of proving when Ellen Nussey censored the names; she may have indulged in further censorship for the benefit of Horsfall Turner, but the close coincidence between manuscript expurgations and Mrs Gaskell's omissions would suggest considerable censorship at this early date.

17. S.H.L.L., Vol. IV, pp. 247–95. It is distressing that so untrustworthy an account should be the only one in print, as it has now become established as the truth. See for instance, the ready acceptance of Ellen Nussey's supposed desire for money in Annette B. Hopkins, *Elizabeth Gaskell: Her Life and Work* (London, 1952), p. 189.

18. For a fuller account of these copies see my article in *Durham University Journal*, December 1970.

19. *Hours at Home*, Vol. 2 (1870). The order of the letters in the *Hours at Home* series for the difficult Roe Head period is, using the Shakespeare Head numbers, 36, 46, 52, 51, 53, 58, 48, 54, 66; this, allowing for the fact that *Hours at Home* was only printing a selection, is very similar to the Needham order of 36, 38, 44, 45, 46, 47, 52, 51, 62, 65, 48, 54, 53, 58, 64, 55, 43, 66. The differences in the text between the Needham copies and the *Hours at Home* selections are minimal.

20. *Charlotte Brontë: A Monograph* (London, 1877). Reid's book,

though it does not quote the letters accurately, misquoting indeed from the letter it reproduces in facsimile, gives a fuller version than the Needham copies, and indeed the correspondence between Reid and Ellen Nussey as recorded in the Shakespeare Head edition would suggest that he used the originals.

21. Three of these are at Haworth, one in the British Museum, one in the Bodleian, and one in the Houghton Library, Harvard. Some copies have notes in the handwriting of Ellen Nussey.

22. See Appendix A.

23. Part of the correspondence between Horsfall Turner and Ellen Nussey is accessible in the Brontë Parsonage Museaum, and in it there is mention both of copies and originals. Since Turner's edition follows the order of the Needham copies, and he was accused of stealing the originals, he must have had access to both.

24. For a comparison of some of the Needham copies with the printed editions, see Appendix B.

25. In the British Museum (Ashley B. 169).

26. Shorter's two other books on the Brontës, the popular *Charlotte Brontë and her Sisters* (London, 1905), and the revised *Charlotte Brontë and her Circle* (London, 1914), contain no important textual variations, although the latter volume does contain, without apology, the letters to M. Heger which in 1908 Shorter declared to have been destroyed.

27. Wise in *A Bibliography of the Writings in Prose and Verse of the Brontë Family* (London, 1917), p. 190, gives the false information that Reid printed everything in *Hours at Home*, and that Shorter printed every letter published by Reid. In fact, with exact numbers difficult to calculate owing to editors' printing fragments of letters, it would seem that Reid printed a fifth of the letters in *Hours at Home*, and Shorter a third of those published by Reid.

28. 750 copies were printed, and the difficulty of getting hold of a copy has driven many Brontë biographers to rely on the obviously less accurate edition of Shorter, or even the totally unsatisfactory *The Brontë Letters*, (London, 1960), edited by Muriel Spark.

29. Some of the correspondence relating to this quarrel, which involved several missing items from the Society's possession, is to be found in the Brontë Parsonage Museum.

30. To be found in the Symington Papers at Haworth.

31. The editors of the Shakespeare Head Brontë claim to have consulted the Henry Huntington Library, the Pierpont Morgan Library, The New York Public Library, the Historical Society of

Pennsylvania and the Buffalo Public Library, but Professor Christian notes that divergences between editorial readings and manuscript readings are especially prevalent in the case of manuscripts in the Henry E. Huntington Library.

32. For an example of Wise's inaccuracy as a copyist, see Partington, *Thomas Wise in the Original Cloth* (London, 1946), p. 250.

33. These three letters are discussed in detail pp. 19–21, 24–5.

34. A few names still remain undeciphered, especially in the early letters, but Ellen Nussey was able to supply most names to Shorter.

35. Professor Christian notes that letters 85, 106, 184, 189, 294, 457, 586, 599, 753 and 814 are inaccurately transcribed.

36. For the Needham versions of these letters, see Appendix B.

37. In letter 880, the Needham copies omit the statement 'Your sister Anne it seems has consulted Mr Teale', and in letter 885 the Shakespeare Head adds the word 'all' in the phrase 'all too well aware'. For a debate on letter 884, see Appendix B.

38. The Needham version of letter 842 gives no indication that it is omitting the first paragraph or the important postscript of the Shakespeare Head version.

39. This may be seen by an examination of the errors noted by Miss Christian and indeed by an examination of letters written to people apart from Ellen Nussey.

40. Letter 886 in the Shakespeare Head contains very close similarities to the Needham version, but the important last sentence is omitted in the Needham copy, and 'to esteem – and if not love – at least affection' becomes 'to esteem and affection'.

41. For a preliminary investigation of T. J. Wise's role in Brontë affairs see Appendix A.

42. For an account of this copy see B.S.T. 74 (1964), p. 50. Shorter purchased this copy, identifiable by its missing title page, from Mr Nicholls but Wise refused to believe that it had any association with Emily. In the correspondence relating to this transaction, preserved in the Brotherton Collection, Leeds, there is no mention of any annotations.

43. We may note in particular the clumsily large signature of *The Foundling* in the Ashley Library (facsimile in S.H.C.B.M., Vol. I, p. 221, and the suspicious multiplicity of signatures in *Corner Dishes*, as recorded by Professor Christian in *The Trollopian*, 2 (1947), pp. 189–90.

44. Note the coarse stanzas beginning 'Eamala is a gurt bellaring bull, shoo swilled and swilled till shoo drank her full' (S.H.C.B.M., Vol. I, p. 228) in *The Foundling*, and the pugilistic

Zenobia Percy in *Corner Dishes* (S.H.C.B.M., Vol. I, p. 358).

45. S.H.C.B.M., Vol. II, pp. 469, 472. Wise already broken by the disclosures of Carter and Pollard had only a nominal share in the first volume of the *Miscellaneous and Unpublished Writings of Charlotte and Branwell Brontë*, published in 1936, and no share at all in the second volume published a year after his death.

46. S.H.C.B.P., p. 441, gives a list of poems by Branwell, once attributed to Emily. Although these attributions were made at a time when Emily's stock was rising, Emily's extreme sensitivity about the discovery of her poems, her reluctance to lose her anonymity, the vague rumours about the authorship of *Wuthering Heights*, and the fact that Gondal seems to start when Angria is finished are all arguments in favour of Branwell's being the author of more of the poems that are regarded as being Emily's. It is difficult to get round the evidence of the birthday notes that Gondal is the creation of Emily and Anne. Daphne du Maurier in *The Infernal Genius of Branwell Brontë*, pp. 65, 66, makes out a good case for some collaboration between Branwell and Emily.

47. The rarity of Anne's manuscripts might make them valuable, and there is a possible hint of confusion between Anne's handwriting and Charlotte's in a letter to Wise from W. F. Prideaux, recorded in Sotheby's catalogue for 5 December 1967, lot 461,

48. Wise has yet to be proved guilty of forging manuscripts. For his own attempts at poetry, see Partington, *Thomas Wise in the Original Cloth*, pp. 30–31.

49. Dr Phyllis Bentley in *The Brontës and their World*, pp. 27–39, 42–3, gives a very fair summary of the contents and importance of the juvenilia, but when considering individual pieces she comes badly adrift, drawing on p. 34 some highly speculative conclusions about Emily from the rude poem about Eamala, of which we have shown even the authorship to be uncertain.

50. Professor Christian in *The Trollopian*, 3, (1948), pp. 57–9 records some examples of letters, allegedly by Charlotte, which she could never have written. Examples of replicas of manuscripts posing as the original are rarer, but one such letter, an early photostat of a letter in the Shakespeare Head, was recorded as being at Haworth, although the original was in the Henry Huntington Museum.

51. *The Letters of Mrs Gaskell*, edited by J. A. V. Chapple and A. E. Pollard (Manchester, 1966), pp. xxvi, xxvii, 944.

52. See A. Kyle Davis Jr., *The Letters of Matthew Arnold: A Descriptive Checklist* (Charlottesville, Virginia, 1968), and the

review of this by K. Allott in *The Modern Language Review*, Vol. 63 (2) (April 1970), pp. 401–3.

53. See Annette B. Hopkins, *Elizabeth Gaskell: Her Life and Work* (London, 1952), p. 356.

54. B.S.T. 74 (1964), p. 47.

55. I discuss this letter (S.H.L.L., Vol. I, p. 147) in *Notes and Queries* (January 1970).

56. Harrison and Stanford, *Anne Brontë: Her Life and Works* (London, 1959), pp. 49–50, mention the first theory, but support the second.

57. Some facts about Henry Nussey's diary are mentioned by Mrs Chadwick in *In the Footsteps of the Brontës* (London, 1914).

58. These two quotations are to be found under the headings 23 February and 7 March 1839 in the diary (Egerton MSS. 32684).

59. S.H.L.L., Vol. I, p. 308.

60. This envelope is in the possession of Sister Margaret Needham. I have not been able to trace the manuscript of this letter. The envelope has the words 'Jane Eyre and the Taylors' on it as well as the date June, 1848 in Ellen's handwriting. Winifred Gerin in *Charlotte Brontë: The Evolution of Genius*, p. 357 assumes that Charlotte in this letter is referring to *Jane Eyre*, but does not state her evidence.

61. See S.H.L.L., Vol. II, pp. 207, 211 for other denials of authorship. We have no trace of a letter in which Charlotte confessed authorship; there may have been one censored by Ellen Nussey.

62. An article by Fran Carlock Stephens published in T.L.S., 14.5.70.

63. Add. Mss. 39, 763.

64. S.H.L.L., Vol. II, pp. 156, 180, 200, 204, 206–7, 209–10.

65. This novel and its possible debt to *Jane Eyre* are discussed in detail in Chapter 7.

66. S.H.L.L., Vol. II, p. 288.

67. *Jane Eyre*, p. 453.

68. S.H.L.L., Vol. II, p. 60.

69. Two words are illegible at this point.

70. In Sotheby's Catalogue for 9 April 1968, lots 457, 458, 459, three letters of Charlotte Brontë to Ellen Nussey, formerly belonging to Viscount Astor, were sold to three different purchasers, The figure paid for one of these letters, dated 16 May 1853, was £450, nine times more than the figure Ellen Nussey had been offered for all the letters in 1891. This letter contains a different text from that printed in the Shakespeare Head version.

71. Sixty-four envelopes are at Haworth, most of them a gift from Mrs Needham, who bought a collection of envelopes at the sale of

Ellen Nussey's possessions. A further 36 envelopes, are still in the possession of Mrs Needham's daughter. There are also numerous envelopes in America recorded by Professor Christian.

72. Among such works we must name W. Wright, *The Brontës in Ireland* (London, 1893), J. Malham Dembleby, *The Confessions of Charlotte Brontë* (Bradford, 1954), A. Law, *Emily Brontë, and the Authorship of Wuthering Heights* (Altham, 1925), R. Wilson, *All Alone: the Life and Private History of Emily Jane Brontë* (London, 1928), V. Moore, *The Life and Eager Death of Emily Jane Brontë* (London, 1936).

73. The three books by Miss Gerin on Anne, Branwell, and Charlotte Brontë, and three other standard biographies, Phyllis Bentley, *The Brontës* (London, 1947), L. and E. Hanson, *The Four Brontës* (Oxford, 1949), and Margaret Lane, *The Brontë Story*, all fall into this category.

74. The best examples of this contempt for biography are to be found in articles in *Nineteenth Century Fiction*, although four recent critical works on the Brontë, I. S. Ewbank, *Their Proper Sphere: a Study of the Brontë sisters as Early Victorian female novelists* (London, 1966), R. B. Martin, *The Accents of Persuasion: Charlotte Brontë's Novels* (London, 1966), W. A. Craik, *The Brontë Novels* (London, 1968), and E. A. Knies, *The Art of Charlotte Brontë* (Ohio, 1969), all eschew the biographical approach Mrs Craik is especially vigorous in her contempt for biography.

75. The forthcoming Clarendon edition of the Brontë novels will, it is to be hoped, clear up the remaining sources of confusion about the text, mainly concerned with Charlotte's revisions of her sister's works. For practical purposes the Haworth edition, edited by Mrs Humphrey Ward (London, 1899–1900), is satisfactory.

NOTES TO CHAPTER 3

1. A notable exception is Blondel, *Emily Brontë: Expérience Spirituelle et Création Poétique*, (Paris, 1955) a useful source of information about the religious background of all three sisters.
2. Grace E. Harrison, *The Clue to the Brontës* (London, 1948).
3. B.S.T. 67 (1957), pp. 131–40.
4. Mary Robinson, *Emily Brontë* (London, 1883), p. 158.
5. Maurice's thought is hardly clear at the best of times, but there can be no doubt of the rejection of eternal punishment in *Theological Essays* (London, 1853) and *The Word 'Eternal' and*

the *Punishment of the Wicked: a letter to the Rev. Dr. Jelf*
(London, 1853). In works published before 1848, Miss Oram
can only adduce vaguely universalist views.

6. B.S.T. 74 (1964), pp. 28–38.
7. *The Four Brontës* (revised edition, Hamden, Conn. 1967); *Anne
    Brontë* (London, 1959); *Branwell Brontë* (London, 1961) and
    Charlotte Brontë: the Evolution of Genius.
8. *The Four Brontës*, p. 24.
9. See *The Methodist Magazine*, 1801, p, 22, 1807, p. 505, and
    1810, p. 161 for arguments against Calvinists, and Chapter I,
    note 16, for Miss Gerin's mistake about the 1810 passage.
10. *Charlotte Brontë, the Evolution of Genius*, p. 36. See also Mrs
    Gaskell's *Life*, p, 124.
11. *The Four Brontës*, p. 24.
12. *Shirley*, p. 400.
13. S.H.L.L., Vol. IV, p. 254.
14. Margaret Lane, *The Brontë Story*, is a fair specimen of such a
    biography.
15. W. A. Craik, *The Brontë Novels*, makes a few passing references
    to Charlotte's religion, dismisses Emily's religion a little cavalierly
    with the statement that she had laid aside Christian morals
    although still using Christian references, and makes no allusion
    to Anne's religion.
16. 'The Incest Theme in Wuthering Heights', by E. Solomon in
    Nineteenth Century Fiction, 14, (June, 1959), p. 80.
17. A card index file of such books, prepared by Professor M. Chris-
    tian and Miss A. Forster, is to be found in the Haworth Parson-
    age Museum.
18. For the evidence connecting these libraries with the Brontës see
    Chapter 6.
19. The catalogues of the Robinson Library and the sale of Ellen
    Nussey's possessions by Messrs Firth and Wright on 18 and
    19 May 1898, are to be found in the Haworth Parsonage
    Museum.
20. The Branderham-Bunting equation is fairly obvious with the
    similarity in Christian names and the close resemblance between
    the disturbance in Gimmerden Sough chapel and an incident in
    Bunting's life. St John Rivers obviously owes something to Henry
    Nussey (see Chapter 2), but his more heroic exploits in the East
    would appear to be derived from the missionary endeavours of
    Henry Martyn.
21. Mrs Gaskell's *Life*, pp. 142, 236, S.H.L.L., Vol. I, p. 99.
22. There are frequent comparisons, some of them far-fetched, made

between the Wesleys' hymns and the poetry of the Brontës in *The Clue to the Brontës*. A useful comparison can be made between *No Coward Soul is Mine* and *The Prayer of Humble Access*.

23. See Joseph E. Baker, *The Novel and the Oxford Movement* (Princeton, 1932) and Margaret Maison, *Search Your Soul, Eustace* (London, 1961).

24. See *The Report to the General Board of Health of a Preliminary Inquiry into the Sewerage, Drainage and Supply of Water and Sanitary Condition of Haworth* (Benjamin Herschel Babbage, 1850), p. 10.

25. See Halévy, *The Triumph of Reform* (London, 1950), p. 154, for some unworldly exhortations of the Wesleyan Conference, such as that in 1831, 'Let not worldly politics engross too much of your time and attention'.

26. *Wuthering Heights*, Preface, p. liv gives Charlotte's comments on 'the practice of hinting by single letters those expletives with which profane and violent persons are wont to garnish their discourse'. Expletives of course can refer to both sex and damnation, but Emily Brontë's only involve the latter.

27. Newman, *Apologia*, ed. Svaglic (London, 1967), p. 71.

28. The Wesleyan Hymn-book of 1780 contains only one hymn, albeit a horrible one, on the subject of hell, and in 1744 John Wesley regretted that so many preachers emphasised the wrath rather than the love of God.

29. See Newsome, *The Parting of Friends* (London, 1966) for links between the Evangelical Revival and the Oxford Movement.

30. S.H.L.L., Vol. III, p. 208.

31. For such 17th and 18th century preachers see D. P. Walker *The Decline of Hell* (London, 1964).

32. This point is made by A. O. J. Cockshut in a review of Mrs Ewbank's *Their Proper Sphere* (*Essays in Criticism*, 17, (1967), p. 110). Mr Cockshut says that it would be impossible for the same man to gabble through the service and to be a ritualist, but does not offer any evidence for his claim.

33. A book by Woodlaw on The *Socinian Controversy* is listed in this library, but I have been unable to trace it.

34. *Villette*, p. 495.

35. S.H.L.L., Vol. III, pp. 177, 290. Dr Arnold is, in a sense, the founder of the Broad Church tradition, from which the authors of *Essays and Reviews* derive their inspiration, but with his keen sense of juvenile sinfulness and his hatred of Unitarians he cannot, unlike the reviewers and F. D. Maurice, be really

reckoned an opponent of hell. For the remarks to Mrs Gaskell on
Maurice and eternal punishment see below.

36. D. Thom, Memoir prefaced to *Sermons preached in Bold Street
and Crown Street Chapels* (Liverpool, 1863), p. xxxix.

37. *The Universalist* (London, 1850–2), Vol. I, p. 135.

38. Ibid., Vol. I, pp. 49–51, Vol. II, pp. 41–6, 65–71.

39. Winifred Gerin's books on *Anne Brontë and Charlotte Brontë:
the Evolution of Genius,* and *A Man of Sorrow* (London, 1965),
written by her husband, John Locke and Canon W. T. Dixon,
are all favourable to Mr Brontë and hostile, as are most
biographers of the Brontës, to Miss Branwell and the Rev. Carus
Wilson.

40. See S.H.L.L., Vol. I, p. 169 for the good old plan. On p. 85 he
suggests moderate reform of the Church and State, but on p. 131
he is anxious about reform.

41. A. B. Hopkins, *The Father of the Brontës* (Baltimore, 1958),
pp. 6–14.

42. For a useful account of Grimshaw's position see F. E. Baker,
William Grimshaw, 1708–1763 (London, 1963).

43. S.H.L.L., Vol. I, p. 66. For other references to the next world in
this eccentric correspondence see Vol. I, pp. 61, 63.

44. Right at the end of his life he still talks of both the worlds
(S.H.L.L., Vol. IV, p. 237). The remark in a letter to Mrs Gaskell,
'the prospect of eternal annihilation will give but little support
to feeble humanity', cited in B.S.T. 43 (1933), would seem to
be a denial of Socinian doctrines rather than an agreement,
similar to that of Charlotte in her letter to Mrs Gaskell, with the
position of F. D. Maurice.

45. *Collected Works of the Rev. Patrick Brontë,* edited by J. Horsfall Turner (Bingley, 1898), p. 66.

46. Ibid., pp. 114, 115, 123.

47. Ibid., pp. 36, 49, 73.

48. Ibid., p. 63.

49. Ibid., pp. 21, 50, 74, 82, 93, 99.

50. Ibid., p. 218.

51. Ibid., p. 254.

52. The Bible is in the Brontë Parsonage Museum. The New Testament quotations are Matthew VII, 13 and 14 and XXV, 46.

53. These counter arguments do in fact both appear in *The Seeker of
Salvation* (London, 1835), a Calvinist tract written by the Rev.
John Angell James, p. 86.

54. Ibid., p. 27 for the evil thoughts (unchaste thoughts are adultery)
and p. 65 for the doubts.

55. *The Tenant of Wildfell Hall*, p. 178.
56. S.H.L.L., Vol. I, p. 212. See also Chapter 6.
57. S.H.L.L., Vol. I, p. 71.
58. See *A Man of Sorrow*, p. 235, for Simeon's remarks about Carus Wilson's Calvinism, and Clement Carus-Wilson Shepheard-Walwyn, *Henry and Margaret Shepheard – Memorials of a Father and Mother* (London, 1882), p. 34 for the possible defence of Carus Wilson.
59. See Ford K. Brown, *Fathers of the Victorians* (Cambridge, 1961) pp. 170–9.
60. Baker, pp. 233–4.
61. Brown, pp. 452–7, though making a surprising defence of Carus Wilson, is in no doubt about his Calvinism for this reason.
62. *The Children's Friend* (Kirkby Lonsdale, 1826–34), Vol. II, p. 8, III, p. 1, VIII, p. 282, VI, p. 214.
63. Ibid., Vol. XI, p. 257.
64. Harrison, pp. 59, 213 and pp. 18–29 for a somewhat sentimental account of the influence of Mrs Fletcher.
65. Gerin, *Anne Brontë*, pp. 231–2 for the behaviour of the Robinsons at Scarborough.
66. Many Evangelical authors are represented in the library, notably Wilberforce, Hannah More, Scott, Venn, Simeon, Gisborne, Milner, Bickersteth, Bradley, and (a nice touch) Carus Wilson. Most of these authors have more than one work or more than one copy of the same work catalogued. Miss Gerin suggests that the books were collected by Mr Robinson's parents, but Mr Robinson's father had died when he was an infant, and many of the books were written after 1800.
67. *Sermons on Select Subjects* (London, 1825), p. 205.
68. *The Doctrines of Election and Final Perseverance, stated from Scripture* (5th edition, London, 1822), p. 16.
69. *Death Bed Scenes* (4th edition, London, 1830), Vol. II, pp. 17–18.
70. *Villette*, p. 96.
71. Mrs Gaskell's *Life of Charlotte Brontë*, p. 317. For the many similarities between *Wuthering Heights*, *The Tenant of Wildfell Hall* and *Jane Eyre* see below.
72. Gerin, *Charlotte Brontë: the Evolution of Genius*, p. 33: 'it must be a matter of wonder to any student of Brontë juvenilia to note the absence of all reference, either direct or indirect, to religious or clerical influences shaping their minds'. The absence of references to religion is not quite as complete as Miss Gerin makes out, but is nevertheless impressive. A possible partial explanation is that Branwell, obviously the least religious of the

Brontë children, had more hand in the juvenilia than is generally allowed.

73. S.H.C.B.P., pp. 264–85. As has been shown in the first chapter more poems may have been written by Branwell than are some-times ascribed to him, but the text and date of those that are ascribed to him are fairly easy to obtain, as the manuscripts are mainly in England and are unlikely to have been tampered with.

74. Ibid., p. 282.

75. Ibid., p. 344. Manuscript in Brontë Parsonage Museum.

76. Compare S.H.L.L., Vol. I, p. 199 with p. 264. Other letters of interest are Vol. I, p. 273 and Vol. II, p. 113.

77. Ibid., Vol. I, p. 265.

78. *And the Weary are at Rest* (London, 1924), pp. 44–57.

79. S.H.C.B.P. gives the wrong date. The manuscript in the Brontë Parsonage Museum shows that the poem was written on 30 April 1838, and transcribed on 12 May of that year.

80. S.H.C.B.P., p. 407.

81. Ibid., p. 418.

82. S.H.L.L., Vol. II, p. 263.

83. S.H.C.B.P., p. 138.

84. Ibid., p. 192. There is also a poem looking more like one of Bran-well's ending 'I'm going to the pit of sulphur blue, and my name is Thomas Aird' (S.H.C.B.P., p. 220).

85. Ibid., p. 23 and p. 240.

86. Ibid., p. 211.

87. Cited in *Charlotte Brontë: the Evolution of Genius*, pp. 121–3.

88. S.H.C.B.M., Vol. II, p. 156.

89. S.H.L.L., Vol. II, p. 166.

90. Ibid., Vol. I, pp. 137, 267.

91. Ibid., Vol. II, p. 242, 267.

92. Annette B. Hopkins, *Elizabeth Gaskell: Her Life and Work*, p. 356 gives the full text of this letter.

93. B.S.T. 74 (1964), pp. 46–7.

94. *Shirley*, p. 308.

95. S.H.L.L., Vol. II, pp. 39, 131, 193, 225.

96. There is a mild complaint about Mr Nicholls's refractory attitude towards Dissenters in S.H.L.L., Vol. IV, p. 154, but no bitterness in this complaint.

NOTES TO CHAPTER 4

1. S.H.L.L., Vol. I, p. 220.

2. *Shirley*, p. 334.
3. Ibid., pp. 10, 131.
4. S.H.L.L., Vol. III, pp. 2–3, Vol. I, pp. 218–19, where Mr C is presumably Mr Collins.
5. S.H.L.L., Vol. III, p. 249, *Villette*, p. 495.
6. *Shirley*, p. 180.
7. *The Professor*, p. 23.
8. *Jane Eyre*, p. 167.
9. *The Professor*, pp. 99, 103, 110, 120, 123.
10. *Villette*, p. 505.
11. S.H.L.L., Vol. I, p. 267.
12. *Jane Eyre*, p. 283, *Shirley*, p. 3.
13. Charlotte speaks rather tartly of her cousin Eliza Williams who can talk of nothing but the Evangelical Clergy (S.H.L.L., Vol. I, p. 214).
14. *Shirley*, p. 556.
15. *Jane Eyre*, Author's Preface, p. xliv.
16. Namely the Evangelicals. For examples of their insistence on divine providence being shown to work in this world, see Quinlan, *Victorian Prelude* (New York, 1941), pp. 195–201.
17. Even the slight doubt about the fate of Paul Emanuel is only a concession made by Charlotte to her father's plea that the novel should not end in unrelieved gloom.
18. S.H.L.L., Vol. II, p. 95.
19. Ibid., p. 101.
20. *Jane Eyre*, p. 287.
21. Ibid., p. 65.
22. S.H.L.L., Vol. III, p. 75.
23. *Jane Eyre*, pp. 358, 375.
24. Ibid., pp. 355, 358.
25. But Carus Wilson's eldest daughter was an invalid (Shepheard-Walwyn, op. cit.).
26. *Jane Eyre*, p. 33.
27. Compare Ibid. pp. 31 and 68 with pp. 480 and 495.
28. Ibid., pp. 430, 442, 457.
29. Ibid., p. 510.
30. S.H.L.L., Vol. II, p. 149.
31. Ibid., p. 236.
32. *Jane Eyre*, p. 509.
33. Ibid., pp. 90, 390.
34. *Shirley*, pp. 359, 401.
35. Ibid., pp. 419, 427.
36. Ibid., p. 449.

37. S.H.L.L., Vol. IV, p. 95, 'some were appointed beforehand to sorrow and much disappointment'. See also Vol. III, pp. 124, 328.
38. *Villette*, pp. 148, 503.
39. Ibid., p. 503.
40. Ibid., p. 571.
41. Ibid., p. 573.
42. S.H.L.L., Vol. IV, p. 178. The evidence presumably comes from Mr Nicholls.
43. See Hewish, *Emily Brontë* (London, 1969), pp. 103–5 for some doubts about the usual story of Emily's death, although even he wonders whether she wished to prolong her life. Anne's willingness to die is better documented in S.H.L.L., Vol. II, pp. 333–8.
44. B.S.T. 4 (1898) gives an account of Anne's conversation with the Moravian bishop.
45. Charlotte is contemptuous of Mr Langweilig, a Moravian who lived up to his name, in *Shirley*, p. 112, and another reference (p. 602) links Moravians as the favourite sect of Mr Yorke with Quakers, to whom we know Charlotte had an antipathy.
46. These are the titles given in the Shakespeare Head edition of the *Poems of Emily and Anne Brontë*, which prints facsimiles of the dated manuscripts of *If This Be All* and *Vanitas Vanitatum, Omnia Vanitas*. The manuscripts of *To Cowper* and *A Word to the Elect* are recorded by Miss Christian as being in the J. Pierpont Morgan library, and she gives the same dates as the Shakespeare Head edition.
47. Charlotte's letters give very few hints of this, although plenty of information about Willie Weightman's other romances. There is some sad love-poetry, written by Anne, but there is more written by Emily, for whom attempts to find a lover have been singularly unsuccessful. Mr Weightman did resemble Mr Weston in more respects than mere similarity of surname, for he was a merciful preacher and obviously an attractive character, but this is little evidence on which to build a hypothesis which over the years has been allowed to grow into a certainty.
48. Mrs Gaskell's *Life of Charlotte Brontë*, p. 141. ' "Mary" says, "Cowper's poem, 'The Castaway,' was known to them all, and they all at times appreciated, or almost appropriated it".'
49. S.H.E.A., p. 221.
50. Ibid., p. 232.
51. S.H.L.L., Vol. II, p. 52.
52. S.H.E.A., p. 243.

53. Ibid., p. 258.
54. There is no evidence for this beyond the fact that Anne had finished the second volume of *Passages in the Life of an Individual* by the time of the 1845 birthday fragment, but there is a change of mood between the chapters based on Blake Hall and those dealing with Thorp Green, and if Anne had started her novel late there would have not been much point in including the section about the Bloomfields.
55. *Agnes Grey*, p. 374.
56. Ibid., pp. 438, 445–7, 449.
57. *Sharpe's London Magazine* (Sept. 1848), p. 184 comments grimly on Anne's adoption of the doctrine of universal salvation 'alike repugnant to Scripture and in direct opposition to the teaching of the Anglican church'. In general, however, reviewers were remarkably reticent about the Brontës' eschatology, though W.P.P. in *Jottings on Currer, Ellis and Acton Bell* (London, 1856), p. 22 comments, 'It was the opinion of all the Bells that everyone would be finally saved: that, though the soul was sinful at death, yet it would afterwards be so purified, as to be fitted to inhabit the city of Many Mansions.'
58. *The Tenant of Wildfell Hall*, pp. 178–9.
59. There are other references, mainly in the Epistles, which can be interpreted as indications of universal salvation. On the other hand, the passages suggesting eternal punishment are more numerous, and it is a little difficult to weaken 'eternal' into 'long-lasting', when the original Greek has phrases like εἰς τοὺς αἰῶνας τῶν αἰώνων intended to strengthen the force of αἰώνιος.
60. *The Tenant of Wildfell Hall*, p. 193.
61. Ibid., p. 200.
62. Ibid., p. 345.
63. Ibid., pp. 319–20.
64. Ibid., p. 339.
65. Ibid., p. 306.
66. Ibid., p. 452.
67. Ibid., p. 459.
68. Ibid., p. 366.
69. S.H.L.L., Vol. I, pp. 124–5, 239, Vol. II, pp. 52–3.
70. For an interesting discussion of the resemblances between *Wuthering Heights* and *The Tenant of Wildfell Hall* see Sir Linton Andrews, 'A Challenge by Anne Brontë', in B.S.T., 75 (1965), pp. 29–30. In arguing that *Jane Eyre* was influenced by *Wuthering Heights* in *Novels of the 1840s* (Oxford, 1954), pp.

282–4. Professor Kathleen Tillotson has little to support her except the obvious fact that the *Professor* is far less full of fire and passion than *Jane Eyre*, and the less certain fact that *Jane Eyre* was started after *Wuthering Heights* was finished.

71. *Five Essays Written in French by Emily Jane Brontë*, translated by Lorine White Nagel (Austin, 1948), pp. 18–19.

72. S.H.L.L., Vol. I, p. 137.

73. Miss Ratchford in *Gondal's Queen*, p. 31 tries to get round the first of these objections by arguing that many of the poems in the untitled notebook are definitely of Gondal, but this has hardly been established.

74. Although, as has been suggested in chapter 1, there is still the possibility of doubts about the authorship of some of Emily's poems, we can, thanks to the existence of C. W. Hatfield's *The Complete Poems of Emily Jane Brontë*, be confident about their date and text.

75. Ibid., pp. 36, 59.

76. Ibid., pp. 39, 40, 121, 122, 135.

77. Ibid., pp. 132, 133.

78. Christina Rossetti was also worried by this problem; although eventually coming down on the side of orthodoxy, and perhaps refusing various suitors because of her orthodox views, she shows traces of unorthodoxy in her notebooks to be found in the Bodleian which contain unpublished poems and the first drafts of poems later revised for publication.

79. Hatfield, p. 121.

80. Ibid., p. 138.

81. Ibid., p. 138.

82. Ibid., pp. 131, 145.

83. Ibid., p. 150.

84. Ibid., pp. 151, 152.

85. Ibid., p. 151.

86. Ibid., p. 220.

87. Ibid., p. 243.

88. Ibid., p. 239.

89. Ibid., p. 196.

90. Ibid., p. 198.

91. Ibid., p. 225.

92. Miss Daphne du Maurier in *The Infernal Genius of Branwell Brontë* dates the occasion, on which Branwell is alleged to have read Wuthering Heights to 1842, and (pp. 91, 104) gives persuasive, if not convincing parallels between *Wuthering Heights* and poems and letters of Branwell; we can accept the force of

these parallels without swallowing the story that Branwell wrote *Wuthering Heights*.

93. *Wuthering Heights*, pp. 1, 21, 245.
94. Ibid., p. 257.
95. See Lord David Cecil, *Early Victorian Novelists* (London, 1934), p. 166; in spite of his warning that Emily does away with the ordinary antithesis of good and evil (p. 154) Lord David Cecil appears to be able to find plenty of 'bad' characteristics in Linton, and it is not difficult to do so. What is difficult to justify is his contention that these bad characteristics are a result of Linton's combining the bad qualities of both storm and calm. It would be a great deal easier on the evidence of this passage to say that Linton is all calm, and the Emily Brontë disapproved of calm.
96. *Wuthering Heights*, p. 47.
97. Ibid., p. 96.
98. Ibid., p. 160.
99. Ibid., p. 155.
100. Ibid., p. 166.
101. Ibid., p. 300.
102. Ibid., p. 341.
103. Ibid., p. 88, a distortion of Romans, VIII, 28.
104. The religious loyalties of the two are clearly indicated in the passage (p. 306) in which Nelly Dean says that in the absence of any church she usually goes to the chapel attended by Joseph. This chapel is either Methodist or Baptist, but she is not sure which.
105. Ibid., p. 172.
106. Ibid., p. 66.
107. Ibid., p. 298.
108. *Dr Faustus*, ed. Greg (Oxford, 1950), 11, 117–24.
109. *Wuthering Heights*, p. 43.
110. The nature of Heathcliff's and Catherine's love remains unchanged by the onset of puberty and the onset of death.
111. *Wuthering Heights*, p. 82.
112. Ibid., p. 350.
113. Ibid., p. 126.
114. Ibid., p. 99.
115. e.g. James Haffley, 'The Villain in Wuthering Heights' in *Nineteenth Century Fiction*, 13 (December 1958), where the villain is Nelly Dean.
116. *The Letters of Matthew Arnold, 1848–1888*, ed. Russell (London, 1895) Vol. I, p. 29.

117. *The Poems of Matthew Arnold*, ed. Allott (London, 1965), p. 395.
118. Ibid., p. 48.
119. *The English Common Reader* (London, 1925), 1st Series, p. 225.

NOTES TO CHAPTER 5

1. *Novels of the 1840s*, pp. 54–73.
2. M. J. Quinlan in *Victorian Prelude* is the best guide to this period. N. Perrin in *Dr Bowdler's Legacy* (London, 1970) is largely concerned with the particular problem of expurgation.
3. C. R. Decker in *The Victorian Conscience* (New York, 1952), who attributes *Griffith Gaunt* to Charles Kingsley on his first page, provides an adequate specimen of this popular view which tends to lump together all Victorians as prudes; Perrin tends to do the same.
4. W. E. Houghton in *The Victorian Frame of Mind* (London, 1957), pp. 353–72, and 394–424, and Richard Stang in *The Theory of the Novel in England, 1850–1870* (London, 1959), pp. 191–224 give excellent preliminary discussions, although the former is more interested in the Victorian attitude to sex and to hypocrisy in general than in specific prudery, while Stang is principally interested in the period of his title. L. Stevenson in *Virgina Quarterly Review*, 13 (1937), pp. 257–70 provides some interesting information about the 1820s and 1830s which he regards as a battlefield between the prudish popular annuals and the less prudish literary periodicals.
5. 'French Novels', *Quarterly Review*, Vol. LVI (1836), p. 65 and Brimley, *Essays* (London, 1858), p. 233.
6. Professor Tillotson rejects hostility to the French novel to footnotes, pp. 7, 8 and 63. Houghton, pp. 359–64 gives a longer account.
7. *The Autobiography and Letters of Mrs M. O. W. Oliphant*, ed. Coghill (London, 1899), p. 447. Quoted by Stang, without reference to Mrs Oliphant, p. 191.
8. There is a good summary of Thackeray's attitude towards France in C. Campos, *The View of France* (Oxford, 1965), pp. 69–89. Thackeray's irony of course makes it difficult to ascertain whether his Podsnappish attitude is itself an attack on Podsnappery.
9. See Campos, pp. 13–48 for Arnold's mixed feelings towards France.

10. Compare *The Letters of Mrs Gaskell*, ed. Chapple and Pollard, pp. 410, 417 for *The Professor* with p. 227 for *Ruth*.
11. See Waugh, *A Hundred Years of Publishing* (London, 1930), pp. 145–6, for Meredith, and Gettman, *A Victorian Publisher* (Cambridge, 1960), p. 204–5 for Miss Jewsbury. For many other examples of authors adopting an inconsistent attitude see Stang, pp. 191–207.
12. Ibid., p. 47.
13. Ibid., pp. 46–51, for the breakdown of the earlier prejudice against the novel as a serious art form. Stevenson, p. 261 quotes an interesting passage from the *The New Spirit of the Age*, written by R. H. Horne in 1844, in which it is said that people are no longer ashamed to read a novel because the novel has become sensible and useful. There is some additional evidence for the growing respectability of the novel of the '20s, and '30s in *Vorstufen zum Victorianischen Realismus* (Vienna, 1969) by H. Foltinek.
14. See Houghton, p. 366, note 74.
15. Factual articles advocating free love or birth control were severely frowned upon. See Houghton, pp. 361–4.
16. *Quarterly Review*, Vol. LVI (1836), p. 75.
17. Ibid., LXIV (1839), pp. 83–102.
18. *Autobiography* (London, 1891), pp. 375–6. Quoted by Ian Jack, *English Literature, 1815–1832* (Oxford, 1963), p. 435.
19. The preface to the second edition of *The Tenant of Wildfell Hall* and the letter to W. S. Williams of 16 August 1849 are the best expressions of the Brontës' view. For the opinion of their critics see Chapter 7.
20. Quoted by Haight, *George Eliot* (Oxford, 1967), p. 268.
21. Tillotson, p. 57.
22. Ibid., p. 15. Professor Tillotson quotes Trollope in a different context.

NOTES TO CHAPTER 6

1. See Hewish, *Emily Brontë*, pp. 27–45, 118–135, and Gerin, *Emily Brontë*, pp. 11–50, 213–19, F. S. Dry in *The Sources of Wuthering Heights* (Cambridge, 1937), and *The Sources of Jane Eyre* (Cambridge, 1940), goes too far in tracing detailed parallels; it is unconvincing to derive Rosamund Oliver's name from Oliver Twist.
2. In Charlotte's letter to Ellen Nussey recommending books.

(S.H.L.L., Vol. I, p. 122). See also The Clarendon Press, *Jane Eyre*, pp. 581–609 for frequent citations from Scott, Shakespeare and the Bible.

3. Ibid., p. 599.

4. *The Letters of Mrs Gaskell*, p. 881. In Mrs Gaskell's *Life of Charlotte Brontë*, p. 124, this rather bleak picture is softened as we hear of standard works of a solid kind to be found up and down the house, and most biographers have chosen to follow this account rather than that suggested by this letter.

5. We can again compare *The Letters of Mrs Gaskell*, p. 881 with *The Life of Charlotte Brontë*, p. 125. Bentley, *The Brontës*, p. 27 follows Mrs Gaskell in talking of a circulating library at Keighley. Lock and Dixon in *A Man of Sorrow*, p. 264, say that Charlotte frequently visited the lending library of Mr Hudson in Keighley, and Margaret Lane, in *The Brontë Story*, p. 94 further confuses the issue by talking of a library at Keighley and the Haworth Mechanics' Institute.

6. S.H.L.L., Vol. II, p. 227. For the important differences between the circulating libraries full of novels and frowned upon by earnest Evangelicals and the libraries of Mechanics' Institutes full of improving literature see Altick, *The English Common Reader* (Chicago, 1957), pp. 188–239.

7. I. Dewhirst, in B.S.T. 75 (1965), pp. 35–7, is sceptical, but there seems no very good reason to doubt the version of C. Whone, in B.S.T. 60 (1950), pp. 344–58.

8. Gerin, *Branwell Brontë*, pp. 43–4. Hewish, *Emily Brontë*, pp. 34–5, is more sceptical, although producing additional evidence for a connection between the Heatons and Emily.

9. *Jane Eyre*, p. 121 and *Agnes Grey*, p. 533.

10. *Jane Eyre*, pp. 3 and 53, *The Professor*, pp. 64 and 248, *Shirley*, p. 410, and *Villette*, p. 253.

11. I have not been able to trace many of the tempting eighteenth century titles, although *Fashionable Follies*, by T. Vaughan (London, 1781) with its account of the successive cuckoldings of the Marquis D'Illois is hardly a very moral work. Also in the library were the works of Middleton, of whom Mrs I-S. Ewbank sees echoes in *The Tenant of Wildfell Hall* (*Notes and Queries*, N.S. 14 (1967), pp. 449–50), Jonson, Wycherley, Etherege, Vanburgh and Aphra Behn.

12. S.H.L.L., Vol. II, p. 61 for Fielding and Smollett and Ibid., p. 166 for Fielding and Thackeray. Other references to Fielding, such as those connected with Thackeray's lectures, are too late to count as evidence of formative influence.

13. *The Autobiography of Mark Rutherford* (London, 1888), p. 31.
14. Compare Altick, *The English Common Reader*, p. 116 with *Blackwood's Magazine*, Vol. XIV (September, 1823), p. 283.
15. 'Hartley Coleridge and the Brontës', by Fran Carlock Stephens, in T.L.S. 14.5.70. Hewish, op. cit., p. 149, and Craik, op. cit., pp. 234–5, compare Richardson and the Brontës; see also Chapter 8.
16. Mayo, *The English Novel in the Magazines* (Evanston, 1962) is an invaluable guide to such novels.
17. For these and other examples of eighteenth century prudery see Ford K. Brown, *Fathers of the Victorians*, pp. 41–2, Stevenson, p. 259 and J. S. M. Tomkins, *The Popular Novel in England, 1770–1800* (London, 1932), pp. 125–6.
18. Quoted by Quinlan, p. 1, Jack, p. 434, and Brown, p. 41 from *Letters of Sir Walter Scott* (London, 1936), Vol. X, p. 96. Perrin in *Dr Bowdler's Legacy*, p. 9 dates this incident to the 1790s.
19. Quinlan, p. 119 for the Evangelical Spiritual Barometer with novel reading valued at –40.
20. I. Williams, *Sir Walter Scott on Novelists and Fiction* (London, 1968), pp. 59, 72 and 150.
21. Jack, p. 239 gives some hostile comments on *Adam Blair*. The *Edinburgh Review* Vol. XXXIX (October, 1823), pp. 185–9, praises the book, though saying it is 'neither very pleasing nor very moral'. *Blackwood's* Vol. XI (1822), pp. 349–58 and 466–7, gives more praise, though saying it is indelicate and that a few paragraphs might be omitted. Neither review hesitates to describe the nature of what is improper, and *Blackwood's* comments upon Mrs Campbell's nakedness in almost as much detail as Lockhart.
22. In addition to Croker's article on French novels in 1836 and Ford's review of *Oliver Twist* in 1839 there is an article on Beaumont and Fletcher in 1848, mentioning in italics 'specimens fit for young people'. Lockhart himself wrote a reproving if sympathetic article on Theodore Hook in 1843.
23. S.H.L.L., Vol. II, p. 169.
24. Jack, P.M.L.A. 72 (1957), pp. 122–46.
25. S.H.L.L., Vol. II, p. 136.
26. *Studies in Early Victorian Literature* (London, 1895), p. 153. See also Hewish, *Emily Brontë*, pp. 35–6.
27. S.H.L.L., Vol. II, p. 136.
28. Ibid., Vol. I, p. 122, and I-S. Ewbank, *Their Proper Sphere* (London, 1966), pp. 146–7, and Mrs Gaskell, *The Life of Charlotte Brontë*, p. 85.
29. S.H.L.L., Vol. I, pp. 133–4. Hogg also appears in Charlotte

Brontë's *The History of the Year*. See F. Ratchford, *The Brontës' Web of Childhood* (New York, 1964), p. 27.

30. See the preface to *The Confessions of a Justified Sinner*, ed. J. Carey (Oxford, 1969), p. xxvi for these bowdlerisations. The Brontës presumably, if Branwell's remarks mean anything, read the unexpurgated version if they read the book at all. Hogg's contributions to the short-lived *Spy* (1811–12) were also shocking, but there is no evidence that the Brontës read these.

31. Branwell's letter to *Blackwood's* mentions Wilson's contribution, and Christopher North was chosen by Charlotte as one of her characters in *The Play of the Islanders*. One of the first issues of *Fraser's*, also taken by the Brontës, was dedicated to Wilson.

32. Wilson, *Works*, ed. Ferrier (Edinburgh, 1858), p. 353.

33. See Ewbank, op. cit., pp. 20–1. I have not been able to trace two titles in the Keighley library, *Hope on, Hope ever*, and *Poor Rich Man, Rich Poor Man*, but they presumably belong to the same highly moral tradition. Nor can we find anything to offend prudish readers in the five volumes of Mrs Barbauld's *British Novelists* or in the eleven volumes of Fenimore Cooper, an author mentioned in the letter to Hartley Coleridge as writing like a boarding-school miss.

34. See the introduction to the Bentley's edition (London, 1832), pp. iv–v.

35. Warren wrote in *Blackwood's*, and his book was in the Keighley library. In addition he is mentioned in the letter to Hartley Coleridge as writing like a boarding-school miss, and a copy of *The Diary of a Physician* is in the Brontë Parsonage Museum, although there is no indication of anything to justify its inclusion.

36. Compare *The Tenant of Wildfell Hall*, pp. 455–6, with *Passages from the Diary of a Late Physician* (5th edition, London, 1837), p. 95.

37. Ibid., p. 98.

38. *Tom Cringle's Log* (London, 1900), p. 230. There is a rape on the same page.

39. *Peter Simple* (London, 1874), p. 170.

40. Compare the Methodist meeting in *Peter Simple*, pp. 267–8, with the meeting at Sanctification Chapel in *And the Weary are at Rest* (London, 1924). The name of the sinister black character Quashia Quamina in the latter work may derive from 'quashie' used as a general name for a black person in both Marryat and Scott.

41. *Blackwood's* and *Fraser's* have a mixed record with regard to

prudery, hostile to the new annuals, but denouncing Bulwer for his immorality. *Blackwood's* apart from the work by Warren and Scott published Galt's *Ayrshire Legatee* (1820–1), and Moir's life of *Mansie Wauch* (1824–7). In December 1839, *Fraser's* published a poem expressing confidence that Prince Albert will chase from the royal palace 'The scribe of the luscious novel'.

42. Stevenson, op. cit., p. 257.
43. Altick, *The English Common Reader*, pp. 320–1, 332–8.
44. Mayo, *The English Novel in the Magazines*, pp. 183–90, for the racy periodicals and pp. 190–208, for the more sober reviews. Though not approving of immoral works the reviews gave a fair insight into them, and it is perhaps worth remembering that many of the reviews in the *Monthly* were contributed by John Cleland, the author of *Fanny Hill*.
45. *Shirley*, p. 400.
46. S.H.L.L., Vol. I, p. 122.
47. See the poem *Winter Night Meditations* in the Rev. Patrick Brontë's *Collected Works*, ed. Horsfall Turner, pp. 37–43.
48. See Annette B. Hopkins, *The Father of the Brontës*, pp. 63, 148.
49. Blondel, *Emily Brontë*, p. 47.
50. S.H.L.L., Vol. I, p. 109, 'the great Sir Walter', and Vol. II, p. 255, 'even the greatest (novelist), even Scott'.
51. *Agnes Grey*, p. 469, 'a fashionable novel', *Jane Eyre*, p. 286, and *The Tenant of Wildfell Hall*, p. 283, 'the last new novel'. *Jane Eyre* also likens (p. 283) the life of Georgiana Reed to a volume of fashionable life, but the description of the Ingrams in this novel would suggest little acquaintance with the Silver Fork school, and this is confirmed by a letter to Mrs Gore of August 27th, 1850 (S.H.L.L., Vol. III, p. 150). Charlotte does seem to know Disraeli, bracketed with Bulwer Lutton as inferior to G. H. Lewes (S.H.L.L., Vol. II, p. 207).
52. *Blackwood's*, Vol. XI (1822), p. 633 probably speaks for the Brontë household when it says 'that our Magazine is read by a great number of very respectable people, who never think of buying books at all, far less of buying novels, and least of all novels that cost £1.11.6d'.
53. S.H.L.L., Vol. II, p. 150.
54. Ibid., p. 288.
55. Ibid., p. 156.
56. *Jane Eyre*, p. 453.
57. For the curiously ambiguous attitude of Thackeray see Chapters 5 and 8.

58. Compare S.H.L.L., Vol. II, p. 27, for *The Chimes*, with Vol. II, pp. 146, 184, etc. for the selection by Charlotte of Dickens and Thackeray as typical great novelists.

59. The extent of Charlotte's debt to the early Thackeray is discussed in Chapter 8. Dickens joins Bulwer, Cooper, and Warren as an author who can write like a boarding-school miss in the letter to Hartley Coleridge, and S.H.L.L., Vol. II, pp. 146, 184, 329, Vol. III, p. 20, 254, do show some knowledge of Dickens as a novelist; this knowledge seems to have come mainly after the publication of *Jane Eyre*. There is a general resemblance between Lowood and Dotheboys Hall, but no proof that the latter influenced Charlotte in depicting the former. I have not been able to trace in any published juvenilia a curious reference to Mr Squeers in a juvenile manuscript sold at Mr Nicholls's death (see *Book Prices Current, for* 1907, p. 682).

60. S.H.L.L., Vol. I, p. 215.

61. See Campos, p. 169.

62. Blondel, pp. 121–5, gives the best account of French literary influence , although he does not mention Rousseau. The influence of German literature is well discussed by Mrs Humphrey Ward in her preface to *Wuthering Heights*, and by Hewish, *Emily Brontë*, pp. 125–8. B. Gilbert and D. C. Cross in B.S.T. 80 (1970), pp. 412–16 dispute Hoffman's influence. Although Hannah More disapproved of German influences, and *Wilhelm Meister* was thought by some to be an immoral work, it is hard to find much licentiousness in German literature of this period.

63. S.H.L.L., Vol. II, pp. 29, 37, 41, 57, etc. Writing to M. Heger on 24 July 1844, Charlotte says that she learns half a page of French each day from a book written in a familiar style.

64. Ibid., Vol. III, p. 172.

65. Ibid., Vol. IV, p. 44.

66. T.L.S. 13.3.69, p. 267. Sir Tresham Lever is persuaded by Charlotte's praise of Sue to call Eugene Sue eminent and celebrated. For a more accurate estimate of Sue's sensational style see L. James, *Fiction for the Working Man* (London, 1963), pp. 138–141.

67. As in the articles by Hepworth Dixon in the *Daily News* of 1847 cited by M. Dalziel in *Popular Fiction 100 Years Ago* (London, 1957). Dalziel and James give an excellent account of the sub-literary fiction of this period.

68. See Dalziel, op. cit., p. 29, for Reynolds as the translator and imitator of Sue.

69. S.H.L.L., Vol. II, pp. 210–11.

70. Ibid., p. 184.
71. Stevenson, op. cit., pp. 261–2.
72. Sadleir in *Bulwer and His Circle* (London, 1931), pp. 185–207, shows how Bulwer's reputation as an immoral novelist stemmed largely from his unwise first novel *Falkland*, and from the personal animosity of the *Blackwood's* coterie. See also Stang, op. cit., pp. 196–9.
73. B.S.T. 61 (1951), p. 15.
74. S.H.L.L., Vol. II, pp. 197, 329.
75. Ibid., p. 288.
76. Ibid., p. 207. Other references to Bulwer's inferiority to Burns (S.H.L.L., Vol. II, p. 319), and to Sidney Dobell (Vol. III, p. 175) refer presumably to Bulwer's poetry.
77. *The Cornhill Magazine*, N.S. Vol. IX (1900), p. 792.
78. S.H.L.L., Vol. II, pp. 206–11.
79. This is suggested by F. Gary in his article on 'Charlotte Brontë and George Henry Lewes' in P.M.L.A. 51 (1936), pp. 518–42. Apart from this suggestion Gary has little to say about *Rose, Blanche and Violet*, except for remarking that it is not such a bad novel as the title would suggest.
80. Ibid., p. 535.
81. S.H.L.L., Vol. II, p. 207.
82. *Rose, Blanche and Violet*, 3 volumes (London, 1848), Vol. I, pp. 51–3.
83. Ibid., pp. 92–6.
84. Ibid., p. 291.
85. Ibid., p. 292.
86. Ibid., Vol. II, pp. 45–7.
87. Ibid., pp. 213–17.
88. S.H.L.L., Vol. II, p. 209.
89. Compare *Rose, Blanche and Violet*, Vol. II, p. 279, for Mrs Vyner's wickedness with the mild treatment of Marmaduke on p. 272.
90. Ibid. Vol. III, p. 275.
91. Ibid., pp. 308–16.
92. Ibid., p. 236.
93. I have not been able to find any review hostile to Lewes in the same way as some of the reviews which denounced the coarseness of the Brontës' novels. The *Dublin University Magazine*, Vol. XXXII (1848), pp. 89–100 was not very favourable to *Rose, Blanche and Violet*, as it had been to *Jane Eyre*, although it did say that the moral tone of Lewes's book might be of a more elevated standard.

94. For 'bitch' and 'devil' see 'A Census of Brontë Manuscripts in the U.S.A.' by Miss Mildred G. Christian, published in the *Trollopian*, 2, 3, 1947–8, referring to letters of 14 November 1844, and 21 August 1846 respectively. For 'chemises' see S.H.L.L., Vol. IV, p. 11, note.
95. *The Letters of Mrs Gaskell*, p. 228.
96. Ratchford, *The Brontë's Web of Childhood*, p. 102.
97. It is hard to distinguish flirtation from adultery, and certainly Zamorna is flirtatious in *High Life in Verdopolis* (1834). In *The Spell*, written in the same year, Miss Laury is deeply in love with Zamorna, but there is no acknowledgement that she is his mistress.
98. Mary Percy's death is bewailed in *Zamorna's Exile*, but she is restored to life and her title in *Mina Laury*. Note also the youthful marriages of Zamorna and his first wife Marian Hume (Ratchford, *The Brontës' Web of Childhood*, pp. 85–88), and of yet another wife, this time black, for Zamorna, and another for Northangerland in *A Leaf from an Unopened Volume*, printed in *Derby Day and Other Stories*.
99. Notably in *Percy*, written in 1837, for a summary of which see Gerin, *Branwell Brontë*, pp. 134–7. In *Charlotte Brontë: The Evolution of Genius*, p. 119, Miss Gerin finds traces of Branwell's influence in the masculine cynical tone of *The Duke of Zamorna*.
100. For a brief description of these manuscripts see *The Trollopian*, Vol. II (1947), pp. 195–7, and for Wrenn's purchase see Wise's *Letters to John Henry Wrenn* (New York, 1944), p. 162.
101. For these two stories see S.H.C.B.M., Vol. II, pp. 280–314, and 348–401. Miss Ratchford does not mention either story in *The Brontës' Web of Childhood*; it is not clear whether this is due to doubts about the authorship or the absence of the manuscripts or to the fact that neither story is easy to fit into the Angrian cycle. In *The Return of Zamorna* Mary Percy is apparently unmarried to Zamorna.
102. The strongly religious element in Anne's poetry precludes it from being very passionate. Thus in a poem of October 1837 (S.H.E.A., p. 195) we read:

> And day and night I've thought of him,
> And loved him constantly,
> And prayed that Heaven would prosper him
> Where ever he might be.

103. *The Brontës' Web of Childhood*, p. 102.
104. For arguments against this view see Chapter 4.

105. A.G.A.'s desertion of Lord Alfred for Julius Brenzaida depends on the indentification of A.G.A. with Rosina Alcona.
106. *Agnes Grey*, p. 542.
107. *Villette*, pp. 391, 413.
108. Charlotte M. Yonge, *The Heir of Redclyffe* (London, 1909), p. 311.
109. For these alterations see 'The Manuscript of the Professor', by M. M. Brammer, in R.E.S., n.s. 11 (1960), pp. 157–70.
110. *The Letters of Mrs Gaskell*, p. 417.
111. The conjectured reading of a description of Hunsden's appearance as 'more the result of an amour between Oliver Cromwell and a French grisette', is more comic than coarse.
112. *The Professor*, p. 70.
113. Ibid., p. 192.
114. Ibid., p. 121.
115. Ibid., p. 233.
116. Ibid., p. 103.
117. The *Athenaeum* review of *The Tenant of Wildfell Hall* (July 1848), and the *Quarterly* review of *Jane Eyre* (December 1848), comment on these features, but reviewers were handicapped, as was pointed out in *Sharpe's London Journal* (September 1848), by that fact that they could hardly mention coarse features without themselves being coarse.
118. Hewish, *Emily Brontë*, p. 150, suggests that Cathy may be Heathcliff's child, but not very seriously.

NOTES TO CHAPTER 7

1. The reviews of Anne and Emily Brontë's work are very scanty, and no effort is made to make any kind of list of reviews in newpapers. The list in Poole's *Index of Periodical Literature* (London, 1891), Vol. I, pp. 166–7 is very similar, and is probably Butler Wood's main source. There is a good bibliography for reviews of Emily Brontë's work in Hewish, *Emily Brontë*, pp. 188–9, a useful list of reviews of *Shirley* and *Villette* by R. L. Brooks in *Bibliographical Society of America* (1959), pp. 270–1, and I have been fortunate enough to see the reviews collected by Dr Miriam Allott for her forthcoming work on the Brontës in the *Critical Heritage* series.
2. See Appendix C for a list of such reviews as I have not been able to trace.

3. This letter, dated 29 March 1853, is printed in B.S.T. 65 (1955), p. 409 and says 'I am indebted to my publishers for all I know of the favourable notices of *Villette*. The hostile notices have been the care of my friends.'
4. See Appendix C.
5. *The Dublin University Magazine*, Vol. XXXIV (December 1849), pp. 680–9. A summary of this review is given below.
6. S.H.L.L., Vol. III, p. 35.
7. B.S.T. 66 (1956), pp. 13–18, 'The Brontës and The North American Review', by K. J. Fielding, and B.S.T. 74 (1964), pp. 39–44, 'First American Reviews of The Works of Charlotte, Emily and Anne Brontë' by Jane Grey Nelson.
8. B.S.T. 57 (1947), pp. 89–96, 'Contemporary Reviews of the Brontë Novels', by Edith M. Weir. The reviews in Emily's desk are discussed in sufficient detail by C. Simpson in *Emily Brontë* (London, 1929), pp. 171–9, and there is an excellent discussion of the critical reception of Emily's work in Hewish, *Emily Brontë*, pp. 157–72.
9. C. K. Shorter in revising Mrs Gaskell's *Life of Charlotte Brontë* for the Haworth edition adds on pp. 334–5 a very favourable extract from *The Spectator's* review of *Jane Eyre* although Charlotte herself says that the review is a hostile one. Winifred Gerin in her life of Charlotte quotes the publisher's selection from *The Times* review of *Shirley*, as if to show that the review was a favourable one. The new Clarendon edition of *Jane Eyre* gives the extracts from the reviews that appeared in the third edition.
10. *Sharpe's London Journal*, Vol. XI (June 1850), p. 371.
11. *The Athenaeum*, 13 June 1857, p. 755.
12. *The Christian Remembrancer*, Vol. XV (April 1848), pp. 396–409.
13. *The Leader*, 28 December 1850, p. 953. G. H. Lewes was the editor of *The Leader*. For a discussion of reviews of the second edition of *Wuthering Heights* see A. R. Brick, 'Lewes's review of *Wuthering Heights*, in *Nineteenth Century Fiction* (1960), pp. 355–9.
14. *The Wellesley Index to Victorian Periodicals* (London, 1966), is invaluable for tracing the authors of reviews, and sometimes has suggestions for the date of composition. Unfortunately it only covers a limited amount of periodicals.
15. For details of these reviews, all published in the last three months of 1847, see Appendix C.
16. *The Economist*, 27 November 1847, pp. 1376–7.

17. *The Literary Gazette*, 23 October 1847, pp. 748–9.
18. *The Athenaeum*, 23 October 1847, pp. 1100–1.
19. *The Spectator*, 6 November 1847, pp. 1074–5.
20. *The Mirror*, 4th series, Vol. II (December 1847), pp. 377–80. The author of this review was George Searle Phillips.
21. S.H.L.L., Vol. II, pp. 161, 200.
22. *The Sunday Times*, 5 December 1847.
23. *The Church of England Quarterly Review*, Vol. XXIII (April 1848), pp. 491–2.
24. *The Christian Remembrancer*, N.S. Vol. XV (April 1848), pp. 396–409.
25. Extracts from these reviews may be found in C. Simpson, *Emily Brontë* (London, 1929), pp. 172–9.
26. *The Athenaeum*, 25 December 1847, pp. 1324–5.
27. *The Spectator*, 18 December 1847, p. 1217.
28. *The Athenaeum*, 8 July 1848, p. 671.
29. *The Spectator*, 8 July 1848, pp. 662–3.
30. *The Rambler*, Vol. III, September 1848, pp. 65–6. *The Rambler* was a Catholic paper, but this hardly explains the degree of its hostility.
31. *Sharpe's London Magazine*, Vol. VII (September 1848), p. 181. The editor at this time was F. E. Smedley.
32. *Fraser's Magazine*, Vol. XXXIX (April 1849), pp. 423–6.
33. I am indebted for this information to the editor of *The Wellesley Index of Periodicals*.
34. *The Quarterly Review*, Vol. LXXXIV (December 1848), pp. 162–76.
35. *Blackwood's Magazine*, Vol. LXIV (October 1848), pp. 473–474.
36. Reviews of *Shirley* in *The Dublin Review, Edinburgh Review, Fraser's Magazine* and *The North British Review* all appear to take up points made by the *Quarterly* and to argue against them. For the history of Charlotte Brontë's *Word to the Quarterly* see S.H.L.L., Vol. III, pp. 12, 15–18.
37. *The North British Review*, Vol. XI (August 1849), pp. 475–93. The reviewer was James Lorimer.
38. *The Dublin Review*. Vol. XXVIII (March 1850), pp. 209–223. As an Irish Catholic paper *The Dublin Review* would have grounds for hostility to a novel which attacks both Anglo-Catholics and Irishmen.
39. *The Spectator*, 3 November 1849, pp. 1043–5.
40. *Fraser's Magazine*, Vol. XL (December 1849), p. 694. The reviewer was W. G. Clark.

41. *The Dublin University Magazine*, Vol. XXXIV (December 1849), pp. 680–9.
42. *The Edinburgh Review*, Vol. XCI (January 1850), pp. 153–73.
43. The editor of *The Edinburgh Review* at this time was Jeffrey's son-in-law, William Empson, who had written a very prudish account of Spindler's novel, *The Natural Son*, in *The Edinburgh Review*, Vol. LXI (April 1835), pp. 71–81.
44. *Sharpe's London Journal*, Vol. XI (June 1850), pp. 370–3.
45. *The Morning Call, A Table Book of Literature and Art*, 4 vols. (London, 1850–2). Quoted with some other criticisms of the Brontës' coarseness in B.S.T., 72 (1962), pp. 20–2.
46. The details of these reviews, all appearing in the last two months of 1849 are to be found in Appendix C.
47. *Britannia*, 10 November 1849, pp. 714–15.
    The Economist, 10 November 1849, pp. 1251–3.
48. *The Daily News*, 31 October 1849, p. 2.
49. *The Nonconformist*, 15 December, 1852, p. 992; the *Sunday Times*, 2 January 1853, p. 22 and the *Globe*, 6 December 1852, p. 1.
50. *The Atlas*, 3 November 1849, pp. 696–7; *The Examiner*, 3 November 1849, pp. 692–4; *The Morning Herald*, 16 November 1849, p. 6, and *The Times*, 7 December 1849, p. 3.
51. *The Leader*, 28 December 1850, p. 953, and *The Athenaeum*, 28 December 1850, pp. 1368–9.
52. *The Eclectic Review*, N.S. Vol. I (February 1851), pp. 223–7.
53. *The North British Review*, Vol. XV (August 1851), pp. 422–3.
54. *The New Monthly Magazine*, Vol. XCV (July 1852), pp. 295–305.
55. S.H.L.L., Vol. IV, p. 80 and Vol. II, p. 319.
56. *The Christian Remembrancer*, Vol. XXV (April 1853), pp. 423–43.
57. *Letters of the Rev. J. B. Mozley*, edited with biographical introduction by Anne Mozley (London, 1885).
58. S.H.L.L., Vol. IV, p. 58.
59. *The Guardian*, 23 February 1853, pp. 128–9.
60. For the best description of this phenomenon see Newsome, *The Parting of Friends*.
61. For an example of High Church prudery in opposition to Broad Church laxity see Newsome, op. cit., p. 165, where Henry Wilberforce is shown attacking Dr Arnold for allowing his son and daughter to bathe together.
62. *The Daily News*, 3 February 1853, p. 2.
63. *The Athenaeum*, 12 February 1853, pp. 166–8.

64. *The Literary Gazette*, 5 February 1853, pp. 123–5.

65. *Bell's Weekly Messenger*, 12 February 1853, p. 6.

66. *Blackwood's Magazine*, Vol. LXXVII (May 1855), pp. 554–68. Compare also the important article 'The Licence of Foreign Novelists' in *The Edinburgh Review*, Vol. CVI (July 1857), pp. 124–56.

67. *Fraser's Magazine*, Vol. LV (May 1857), pp. 569–82. The author of this review was John Skelton.

68. *The Critic*, Vol. XVI (15 April 1857), pp. 168–71.

69. *The Oxford and Cambridge Magazine* (June 1856), pp. 328–35.

70. *Revue des Deux Mondes*, t. X (1857), p. 459. French reviews of Charlotte's novels were consistently favourable, just as American reviews were almost uniformly hostile. For a useful summary of French opinion see M. G. Devonshire, *The English Novel in France* (London, 1967), pp. 375–84, and a short article by E. Langlois, 'Early Critics and Translators of *Jane Eyre* in France' in B.S.T. 81 (1971), pp. 11–18.

71. *The Westminster Review*, N.S. Vol. XXVI (1864), pp. 48–9.

72. Quoted in B.S.T. 59 (1949), p. 247, but the citation from '*The Letters and Journals of Queen Victoria*, edited by G. E. Buckle and A. C. Benson' is inaccurate.

73. For both these remarks see *The Cornhill Magazine* Vol. LXXXII (December 1900), pp. 778–95.

74. In 1854 Mrs Gaskell wrote to her daughter Marianne, aged twenty, 'I am afraid I never told you that I did not mind you reading *Jane Eyre*.' (Chapple and Pollard, p. 860). Mrs Gaskell was also worried about *The Professor*, and admitted some coarseness in her *Life of Charlotte Brontë*.

75. S.H.L.L., Vol. III, p. 23.

76. Ibid., pp. 74–5, 77–8. Charlotte's indignation is of course a very important factor in assessing the reaction of the reviews on the novels.

77. Both Dean Merivale and Mrs Browning are cited in B.S.T. 72 (1962), pp. 20–5. Professor Tillotson, op. cit., p. 258n. cites Dean Merivale, as well as other less ambiguous tributes, as one of the people to acclaim *Jane Eyre*.

78. *Jottings on Currer, Ellis and Acton Bell* (London, 1856).

79. Ibid., pp. 26–7.

NOTES TO CHAPTER 8

1. C. H. Rolph, *The Trial of Lady Chatterley* (London, 1961), p. 17.

2. O. Christie, *The Transition from Aristocracy* (London, 1927), pp. 66–101, gives a good account of this.
3. The completely different verdicts on *Wuthering Heights*, given by Arnold Kettle in *An Introduction to the English Novel* (London, 1951), vol. I, pp. 138–54. T. K. Meier in B.S.T. 78 (1968) and, most notably, by Q. D. Leavis, in *Lectures in America* (London, 1969), pp. 84–152 show how hard it is to ascribe a fixed view to Emily Brontë. There are also some brief but valuable insights into the sociological aspects of *Wuthering Heights* and *Jane Eyre* in Raymond Williams's *The English Novel: from Dickens to Lawrence* (London, 1970), pp. 60–74. R. Faber in *Their Proper Sphere* (London, 1971) has a few useful points to make clear about snobbery in general, and the Brontës' attitude to it in particular, but in general is disappointingly superficial.
4. *The Tenant of Wildfell Hall*, pp. 481–7.
5. *The Professor*, pp. 5, 55, 202, 270.
6. W. A. Craik, *The Brontë Novels*, p. 167. Not only does Mrs Craik declare that Lucy 'begins quite destitute', but she is also impressed by the Comte de Bassompierre's title into thinking him aristocratic, apparently forgetting that he began life in the novel as plain Mr Home, like Lucy a friend (and in addition a relation by marriage) of Mrs Bretton, who is despised by Ginevra Fanshawe for not being aristocratic enough.
7. *Villette*, p. 48.
8. Marsh, *The Changing Social Structure of England and Wales* (London, 1965), p. 195.
9. *Locksley Hall*, l. 60. *Edwin Morris* (1851) and *Maud* (1855) are other poems showing Tennyson's interest in this subject.
10. Ruskin, *Works*, ed. Cook and Wedderburn (London, 1904), vol. 12, p. 342. Quoted by Houghton, *The Victorian Frame of Mind*, p. 168.
11. For an analysis of this uncertainty see Asa Briggs, *Essays in Labour History* (London, 1967), pp. 43–73.
12. *The New English Dictionary* (Oxford, 1919), Vol. IX, p. 325.
13. There is a good summary of the Irish problem in Annette B. Hopkins, *The Father of the Brontës*, pp. 1–11, to which Lock and Dixon in *A Man of Sorrow*, pp. 1–13, add little. Earlier accounts like W. Wright's *The Brontës in Ireland* are extremely fanciful. See also J. Horsfall Turner's postscript to *The Rev. Patrick Brontë: His Collected Works and Life*, pp. 267–304.
14. Mrs Gaskell's *Life of Charlotte Brontë*, pp. 36, 38 for the noble ancestry and the acquaintance with Lord Palmerston. The best account of the name Brontë is to be found in J. Erskine Stuart's article, *Brontë Nomenclature*, in B.S.T. 3 (1895).

15. For the difference see Mr Brontë's letter to Miss Burder (S.H.L.L., Vol. I, p. 61).
16. *The Last Chronicle of Barset* (London, 1961), p. 777.
17. S.H.L.L., Vol. I, pp. 209, 213, 278.
18. See note 8 in Chapter 6 and letters between Mr Brontë and the Heatons also in Lock and Dixon, p. 337.
19. For the Ferrands of Bingley see S.H.L.L., Vol. III, p. 149, and Vol. IV, pp. 80–1.
20. S.H.L.L., Vol. I, p. 104, and Vol. III, p. 23.
21. After 1838, there is one reference to Miss Outhwaite trying to find a job for Charlotte (S.H.L.L., Vol. I, p. 250.) and two to her legacy to Anne Brontë, but that is all.
22. S.H.L.L., Vol. I, pp. 121, 145, 214, Vol. III, pp. 204, 224, 338. Amelia was the niece of the Atkinsons, and the first cousin once removed of Elizabeth Firth, who married the Rev. J. C. Franks. From Mrs Franks's diary we learn that on their wedding tour they visited the Brontës at Cowan Bridge, and it is just possible that Charlotte has used this incident to form a basis for the visit of Mrs and the Misses Brocklehurst to Lowood in *Jane Eyre.* Certainly there is a constrained air in Charlotte's letters to Mrs Franks at Roe Head (S.H.L.L., Vol. I, p. 87) and it is clear from Mr Brontë's letters to Mrs Franks (Vol. I, p. 85, 130) that he was receiving financial help from his old friend at Thornton.
23. *Jottings on Currer Ellis and Acton Bell*, p. 41.
24. S.H.L.L., Vol. I, pp. 213–4, Vol. III, pp. 280–1. See also B.S.T. 64 (1954), pp. 299–300, for a letter to a Branwell cousin from Charlotte.
25. See B.S.T. 33 (1923), 49, (1939) and 70 (1960) for accounts of the Branwells at Penzance.
26. *Jane Eyre*, pp. 52–4, 72–5. See note 17 above.
27. The Atkinsons who were friends of Mr Brontë are assumed by the editors of the *Shakespeare Head Brontë* to be a different family from the Mrs Atkinson, friend to Ellen Nussey, who unexpectedly gave birth in 1850, and neither is likely to be related to Mr Atkinson, a dentist in Leeds. The Misses Brooke, fellow pupils of Charlotte at Roe Head, would seem, as they were considering being governesses, to have nothing to do with Mrs Thomas Brooke, a prospective employer of Charlotte's. For the two families of Carrs, see B.S.T. 79 (1969), pp. 334–5. There is a more obvious gap between the Greenwoods of Haworth and the Greenwoods of Swarcliffe, the Sugdens of the Talbot Inn, Halifax, and Isabella Sugden of Roe Head, and the Taylors of Gomersal

and James Taylor of Smith, Elder Co., but the Carter and Walker family connections are extremely obscure.

28. See the articles by J. T. M. Nussey, in B.S.T. 78, (1968) and 79, (1969) for the Healds, Carrs and Walkers, and S.H.L.L., Vol. I, 83, and 123 for the Allbutts, Carters and Brookes.

29. Phyllis Bentley, *The Brontës and their World* (London, 1969), p. 37. Winifred Gerin, in *Charlotte Brontë: The Evolution of Genius*, pp. 70–4, confuses fact and fiction too readily in her account of both Nussey and the Taylor families.

30. For the identification of Thornfield with Rydings, and indeed of Caroline Helstone with Ellen Nussey see H. E. Wroot, 'The Persons and Places in the Brontë Novels', B.S.T. (1900). For the old family Halls and the visits to London and Bath, see S.H.L.L., Vol. I, pp. 119, 120, 122, 162.

31. For information about the Nussey family I am greatly indebted to a privately printed history of the family by J. T. M. Nussey.

32. There is no comparable history of the Taylor family, although some interesting information about them can be gleaned from H. A. Cadman, *Gomersal, Past and Present* (Leeds, 1930) and an article by Joan Stevens in B.S.T. 79 (1969), pp. 301–13.

33. Winifred Gerin, *Charlotte Brontë: The Evolution of Genius*, p. 63, says that an uncle of Ellen's married a cousin of Mary's but does not state the source of this information. S.H.L.L., Vol. II, pp. 33, 62, 89, 178, records the courtship of Isabella Nussey.

34. See Appendix D.

35. The cousinship of St John Rivers and Jane Eyre, Caroline Helstone and the Moores, and the fact that Ginevra Fanshawe is the niece of Mr Home play little part in the plot of *Jane Eyre*, *Shirley*, and *Villette*.

36. B.S.T. 79 (1969), pp. 333–4.

37. Gerin. op. cit., p. 142.

38. S.H.L.L., Vol. I, 230–1.

39. Compare S.H.L.L., Vol. III, p. 240, 'admiring Duchesses and Countesses' and Ibid., p. 251, 'we had to go to Lord Westminster's' with Vol. I, p. 120, about Ellen 'withdrawing from the world . . . bringing with you a heart as unsophisticated, as natural, as true, as that you carried with you'.

40. S.H.L.L., Vol. III, pp. 155, 199, and Vol. IV, p. 67. There are some interesting observations on the Kay Shuttleworths after Charlotte's first meeting with them (Ibid., Vol. II, p. 87). They are not a parvenu family; on the other hand Lady Shuttleworth is excused of aristocratic pretension.

41. S.H.L.L., Vol. II, p. 292, for Mrs Gaskell's comment that Char-

lotte has seen no one but her father from July to November 1851. This comment would seem to be based on a remark by Charlotte herself.

42. Charlotte had read and not approved of *Yeast* and *Alton Locke* (S.H.L.L., Vol. III, p. 268) by August 1851, apparently receiving the latter in October 1850 (S.H.L.L., Vol. III, p. 174), and she read both *Mary Barton* and *North and South* shortly after publication. See however S.H.L.L., Vol. II, p. 184, for Charlotte's alleged reluctance to handle social themes which she did not understand.

43. For a penetrating analysis of Richardson's interest in class differences see W. M. Sale, Jr., 'From Pamela to Clarissa', in *The Age of Johnson*, edited by F. W. Hilles (New Haven, 1949).

44. For some interesting examples of class conflict in Scott, see A. O. J. Cockshut, *The Achievement of Sir Walter Scott* (London, 1969), pp. 38–41.

45. *The Waverley Novels* (Edinburgh, 1831), Vol. V, pp. 274–5.

46. Ibid., pp. 85–6.

47. In March 1848, Charlotte refers to the last number of *Vanity Fair*, and her words 'The more I read Thackeray's works' suggests some knowledge of other works by Thackeray. On the other hand she claims to have written *Jane Eyre* before reading any of *Vanity Fair* (S.H.L.L., Vol. II, pp. 201 and 314).

48. The two most obvious examples of social climbers being mocked by another kind of snob, *The Book of Snobs* and *Cox's Diary*, were not published in *Fraser's*. But there is plenty of the same kind of thing in *The Memoirs of Charles J. Yellowplush* (*Fraser's*, 1837, 1838 and 1840), *The Great Hoggarty Diamond* (*Fraser's*, 1841), *The Fitzboodle Papers* (*Fraser's*, 1842–3), *The Luck of Barry Lyndon* (*Fraser's*, 1844) and *A Shabby Genteel Story* (*Fraser's*, 1840).

49. S.H.L.L., Vol. II, p. 15.

50. See the conflicting accounts of Miss Ratchford, in *Gondal's Queen*, and W. D. Paden, in *An Investigation of Gondal*. It is not certain whether A.G.A. is one character with many titles, or more than one character, although in general we can say that the characters of Gondal rival those of Angria in the quantity and splendour of their titles. It is unfortunate however that in spite of such tantalising hints as the reference to the Republican-Royalist wars in the birthday notes of 1845, we do not know enough about the Gondal story to draw any conclusions from it about the attitude of Emily and Anne to the problems of class.

51. *The Spell* (Oxford, 1931), p. 106.

52. Quoted from *Julia* by Miss Gerin, in *Charlotte Brontë: the Evolution of Genius*, p. 132. See also the description of Zamorna's bedroom in *The Spell*, p. 71.
53. S.H.C.B.M., Vol. II, p. 4.
54. *The Spell*, pp. 46–7.
55. Ibid., p. 44.
56. Ibid., p. 47. In 'The Green Dwarf' (*Legends of Angria*, p. 45) Mr Leslie the painter turns out to be the Earl of St Clair, not 'a low-born son of drudgery', but from a 'line of ancestors as illustrious as any whose brows were ever encircled by the coronet of nobility'. This looks like straightforward snobbery, but it is as Mr Leslie that St Clair wins the heart of Lady Emily Chatsworth.
57. *The Brontës' Web of Childhood*, pp. 131–2, 142–4, 147–50. There seems no reason to doubt Miss Ratchford's general conclusion, even allowing for the possibility that Branwell may have written some of the more realistic stories.
58. Even in Angria Sir William Percy has to work for his living as an Army Officer, although he is the brother-in-law of the King. Miss Ratchford's account of his metamorphosis, via William Ashworth in the Yorkshire fragment, *Mr Ashworth*, into William Crimsworth (*The Brontës' Web of Childhood*, pp. 191–3) is a convincing one, and a useful reminder of Crimsworth's aristocratic ancestry.

NOTES TO CHAPTER 9

1. *The Professor*, Preface, p. 3.
2. *The Professor*, Introduction, p. xv.
3. It is perhaps significant that Charles, whom Miss Ratchford relates to Charles Townsend or Charles Wellesley, takes up a government appointment in one of the colonies, although there is nothing to suggest that the colony is Angria.
4. *The Professor*, p. 26.
5. Ibid., p. 28.
6. Ibid., p. 38.
7. Ibid., p. 86.
8. As in the remarks about the Flemish ushers (Ibid., pp. 92, 93), and pupils, (p. 98).
9. Ibid., p. 256–7.
10. Crimsworth's success in doubling his salary is mentioned in parenthesis (p. 252) perhaps because Charlotte felt it inappropriate that her modest hero should blow his own trumpet.

11. Ibid., p. 130, 'Her present position has once been mine, or nearly so'.
12. Ibid., p. 197.
13. Ibid., p. 238. Not many peers do have a genuine claim to Norman race or conquest-dated title, but Charlotte is presumably not being sarcastic about Hunsden's claim.
14. Ibid., p. 241.
15. Compare Ibid., p. 6, and 52. It is of course possible that the Hon. John Seacombe should have been a privy councillor as well as the younger son of a peer; alternatively the mistake, a small one, may have been Hunsden's rather than Charlotte's.
16. *Quarterly Review*, Vol. LXXXIV (December, 1848), p. 168.
17. *Jane Eyre*, p. 213. Charlotte would also seem to err in making Blanche's mother both the Dowager Lady Ingram and Baroness Ingram of Ingram Park. These two titles would only be possible if Lord Ingram had both a wife and another ancestral seat, of which we hear nothing.
18. Ibid., p. 241.
19. Ibid., p. 223.
20. Ibid., p. 270.
21. Ibid., p. 23.
22. Ibid., p. 22.
23. Ibid., p. 107. The editors of the Clarendon Press *Jane Eyre* (p. 596) suggest that Mrs Reed calling her husband Reed may be a hint of vulgarity.
24. Ibid., p. 108.
25. Ibid., p. 288.
26. Ibid., p. 358.
27. Ibid., p. 107.
28. Ibid., p. 81.
29. Ibid., p. 15.
30. Ibid., pp. 103, 146, 269, 270. Mr Rochester's omniscience is all the more surprising because he has spent much of his life abroad.
31. Ibid., p. 393. Judging by the time taken for all journeys this would seem to be the longest distance travelled by Jane.
32. Ibid., p. 424. St John Rivers does not (p. 464) know Rochester and Jane seems surprised by this.
33. Ibid., p. 123.
34. Ibid., p. 189.
35. Ibid., p. 351.
36. Ibid., p. 418.
37. Ibid., p. 452. Rosamund Oliver despises the young knife-grinders

and scissors merchants of the neighbourhood, and eventually marries the grandson and heir of Sir Frederick Granby.

38. *The Professor*, p. 251. 'We were working people, destined to earn our bread by exertion, and that of the most assiduous kind'. But we hear little of this work and even less of the less pleasant work in Edward Crimsworth's mill.

39. *Jane Eyre*, p. 416, where Hannah suggests that after being at a boarding school for eight years Jane should be able to keep herself, and p. 451, where more pointedly Rosamund Oliver declares that Jane is clever enough to be a governess in a good family.

40. Ibid., pp. 434, 438.

41. Ibid., pp. 435, 439.

42. Ibid., p. 341.

43. The word 'plebeian' is also used when Jane is comparing herself to Blanche Ingram (p. 192).

44. The high Tory clergyman is a figure who has a long innings in English literature, appearing as the Rev. Esau Hittall, in *Friendship's Garland* (1866), and Frank Greystoke's father in *The Eustace Diamonds* (1871). For the very different historical picture of the Yorkshire clergyman see J. C. Gill, *The Ten Hours Parson* (London, 1959).

45. This criticism is of course just as true both of Mrs Gaskell when it comes to providing solutions and of Disraeli when it comes to providing sympathetic insight. Kingsley comes closest to supplying this combination, but his working-class heroes are a little too good to be true.

46. *Shirley*, p. 453.

47. The man who shoots at Robert Moore is half mad, and most of the leaders of the riot were not 'members of the operative class; they were chiefly down-draughts, bankrupts'. Nevertheless it is hard to make much of the sympathy of Charlotte for the working Classes when they are represented in her books by such characters as Moses Barraclough and Noah o'Tims.

48. *Shirley*, pp. 297, 363.

49. Ibid., p. 364.

50. Ibid., p. 4.

51. Ibid., p. 117.

52. Ibid., p. 314.

53. Ibid., p. 480.

54. Ibid., p. 172.

55. This rather bleak picture does look like a condemnation of the modern capitalistic system, and is taken as such by many critics,

such as Robert Martin, in *The Accents of Persuasion*, p. 135. But it is possible to exaggerate the sociological implications of this passage and to forget the personal and autobiographical note.

56. *Shirley*, pp. 65, 595.
57. Ibid., p. 380.
58. Ibid., p. 480.
59. Branwell was paid £20 a quarter, whereas Anne for better service and harder work was paid £10.
60. *Shirley*, p. 386.
61. Ibid., p. 387.
62. Ibid., p. 480, when Sam Wynne is rejected, because, among other things, 'his intellect reaches no standard I can esteem', and p. 565 when Mr Sympson takes up her words in pressing the claims of Sir Philip Nunneley's intellect, although unfortunately they are not good enough for Shirley.
63. Ibid., pp. 567, 568.
64. Ibid., pp. 565, 636.
65. Ibid., pp. 208, 209.
66. Ibid., pp. 226, 227.
67. Ibid., p. 377.
68. Ibid., p. 571.
69. *The Life of Charlotte Brontë*, p. 619
70. See the reviews in *The Dublin University Magazine* (December, 1848), *The Edinburgh Review* (January 1850), *The Times* (7 December 1849), and *Sharpe's London Journal* (June 1850), all of which are discussed in Chapter 7.
71. *Villette*, p. 52.
72. Ibid., p. 1.
73. Ibid., pp. 208, 324, 521.
74. Ibid., p. 468, for Paul Emanuel's wealthy father. There is a pleasant egalitarianism in M. Paul's behaviour to even the most aristocratic, best shown in the concert scene, but little is made of this.
75. Ibid., pp. 57–8.
76. Ibid., p. 61.
77. Ibid., p. 170.
78. Ibid., p. 174.
79. Ibid., p. 265.
80. Ibid., pp. 320, 321, although the first comparison between Dr John and a bear is made by Lucy Snowe when she likens him (p. 164) to the Ours or sincere lover playing opposite to her at the fête.

81. Ibid., p. 89. See Dunbar, 'Proper names in Villette', *Nineteenth Century Fiction*, Vol. 15 (June 1960), pp. 77–80.
82. *Villette*, p. 93.
83. Ibid., p. 256.
84. Ibid., p. 513.
85. Ibid., p. 369.
86. Ibid., pp. 369–70.
87. B.S.T. 68 (1958), p. 242.
88. See J. Malham Dembleby, *The Confessions of Charlotte Brontë* (Bradford, 1954), pp. 198–217. for resemblances between the Whites and the Birdwoods. Mrs White's maiden name was Robson.
89. Winifred Gerin, *Branwell Brontë*, pp. 216–26. But see Chapter 3 for differences between Thorp Green and Horton Lodge.
90. Mr Hatfield appropriately marries a rich but elderly spinster (*Agnes Grey*, p. 536).
91. *Branwell Brontë*, p. 252.
92. *Agnes Grey*, p. 408.
93. Ibid., pp. 368, 423.
94. Ibid., p. 432.
95. Ibid., p. 429.
96. Ibid., pp. 356–7.
97. Ibid., p. 356. We may compare the very different attitude shown by Mr Oliver to St John Rivers, although Mr Oliver is not a squire, but a self-made manufacturer.
98. Ibid., p. 436.
99. See the reviews in *Sharpe's London Magazine* and *Fraser's Magazine*, cited in Chapter 7.
100. *The Tenant of Wildfell Hall*, pp. 1, 401.
101. Ibid., p. 485–7.
102. Ibid., p. 448.
103. Ibid., p. 235.
104. Anne seems almost relieved to get rid of her characters, and this is one more indication that she was a reluctant novelist.
105. Her four years at Thorp Green as a sociable and fairly amiable family are in marked contrast to Charlotte's short career as a governess. Charlotte did of course spend time away from home, but only in the unworldly atmosphere of Miss Wooler's school and M. Heger's Pensionnat.
106. See Chapter 8 for the way in which Ellen Nussey's friends are also her relations.
107. The difference between calm and storm, suggested by Lord

David Cecil in *Early Victorian Novelists*, pp. 147–93, is the most obvious example of such a metaphysical difference.

108. C. P. Sanger in *The Structure of Wuthering Heights* (London, 1926) is the pioneer here.

109. *Wuthering Heights*, p. 229.

110. Ibid., p. 3.

111. Ibid., p. 47.

112. Ibid., p. 7.

113. Ibid., p. 8.

114. Ibid., pp. 318–9.

115. Fire is also mentioned at Thrushcross Grange, when Caroline throws a key into the fire (p. 119), when she says she does not want to light another fire (p. 98), when Catherine is wheeled to the fire on her first arrival (p. 50), and when Lockwood returns from his second visit to Wuthering Heights almost unable to enjoy the fire (p. 31).

116. Ibid., p. 108.

117. Ibid., p. 140.

118. Ibid., p. 45. The different attitudes to servants at Wuthering Heights and Thrushcross Grange have caused critics to make strange mistakes. T. K. Meier, in B.S.T. 78 (1968), thinks that both Joseph and Nelly rise above their station in life, and Nelly's peculiar position may be partly the reason for the celebrated and misguided contention of James Haffley (*Nineteenth Century Fiction*, 13 (December 1958), pp. 199–215) that Nelly Dean is evil.

119. Ibid., p. 147, ' "*Parlour!*" ', he echoed sneeringly, "*parlour!* Nay we've noa *parlours*. If yah dunnut loike wer company there's maister's; un' if yah dunnut loike maister, there's us!" '

120. Ibid., pp. 10, 315, 329.

121. Ibid., p. 169.

122. Ibid., p. 117. Nelly describes these men as underlings, indicating her position as an upper servant, the means of communication between Edgar and the other servants.

123. Ibid., pp. 132, 133.

124. Ibid., p. 98.

125. Ibid., pp. 13, 15.

126. Ibid., p. 29.

127. Ibid., p. 218.

128. *Lectures in America*, pp. 102–3.

129. For the best account of the significance of this move to Thrushcross Grange, see '*Wuthering Heights*: The Rejection of Heath-

cliff?' by Dr Miriam Allott in *Essays in Criticism*, 8 (1958), pp. 27–47. This article is a useful corrective against too narrowly a sociological approach to *Wuthering Heights*.

130. *Wuthering Heights*, p. 4.
131. Ibid., p. 153.
132. The dispute between Arnold Kettle in *An Introduction to the English Novel*, and T. K. Meier in B.S.T. 78 (1968) is an unreal one, as both parties ignore the change in Heathcliff.

Select Bibliography

For reviews of the Brontë novels see Appendix C above.

Allott, M., *Novelists on the Novel* (London, 1959).

——, 'Wuthering Heights: The Rejection of Heathcliff?'. In *Essays in Criticism*, VIII, pp. 27–47.

Altick, R. D., *The English Common Reader* (Chicago, 1957).

Andrews, W. L., 'The *Times* Review that made Charlotte Brontë Cry'. In *Transactions of the Brontë Society*, 60, pp. 359–69.

——, 'A Challenge by Anne Brontë'. In *Transactions of the Brontë Society*, 75, pp. 25–30.

Baker, F. E., *William Grimshaw, 1708–1763* (London, 1963).

Bentley, P., *The Brontës* (London, 1947).

——, *The Brontës and Their World* (London, 1969).

Birrell, A., *Life of Charlotte Brontë* (London, 1887).

Blondel, J., *Emily Brontë: Expérience Spirituelle et Création Poétique* (Paris, 1955).

Brammer, M. M., 'The Manuscript of *The Professor*'. In *Review of English Studies*, N.S., XI, pp. 157–59.

Brick, A. R., 'Lewes's Review of *Wuthering Heights*'. In *Nineteenth Century Fiction*, XIV, pp. 355–9.

Briggs, A., 'Private and Social Themes in *Shirley*'. In *Transactions of the Brontë Society*, 68, pp. 203–19.

——, *Essays in Labour History* (London, 1967).

Brimley, W., *Essays*. Edited by W. G. Clark (Cambridge, 1858).

Brontë family, *The Life and Works of Charlotte Brontë and her Sisters*, Haworth edition, 7 volumes. Edited by Mrs H. Ward and C. K. Shorter (London, 1899–1900).

——, *The Shakespeare Head Brontë*, 19 volumes. Edited by T. J. Wise and J. A. Symington (Oxford, 1931–8).

Brontë, C., *The Story of the Brontës: Their Homes, Haunts, Friends and Works. Part Second – Charlotte's Letters*. Edited by J. Horsfall Turner (Bingley, 1885–9).

Brontë, C., *The Adventures of Ernest Alembert: A Fairy Tale*. Edited by T. J. Wise (London, 1896).

——, *The Four Wishes: A Fairy Tale*. Edited by C. K. Shorter (London, 1918).

——, *The Twelve Adventurers and Other Stories.* Edited by C. K. Shorter (London, 1925).

——, *The Spell: an Extravaganza.* Edited by G. E. Maclean (Oxford, 1931).

——, *Legends of Angria: compiled from the Early Writings of Charlotte Brontë.* Edited by F. E. Ratchford and W. C. De Vane (New Haven, 1933).

——, *Jane Eyre.* Edited by J. Jack and M. Smith (Oxford, 1969).

Brontë, E. J., *The Complete Poems of Emily Jane Brontë.* Edited by C. W. Hatfield (Oxford, 1941).

——, *Five Essays Written in French by Emily Jane Brontë.* Translated by L. E. Nagel. Edited by F. E. Ratchford (Austin, 1948).

Brontë, P., *The Rev. Patrick Brontë A.B., His Collected Works and Life. The Works; and the Brontës of Ireland.* Edited by J. Horsfall Turner (Bingley, 1898).

Brontë, P. B., 'And the Weary are at Rest' (London, 1924).

Brooke, S., 'Anne Brontë at Blake Hall: An Episode of Courage and Insight'. In *Transactions of the Brontë Society*, 68, pp. 239–50.

Brooks, R. L., 'Unrecorded Newspaper Reviews of Charlotte Brontë's *Shirley* and *Villette*'. In *Bibliographical Society of America*, LIII, pp. 270–1.

Brown, F. K., *Fathers of the Victorians: The Age of Wilberforce* (Cambridge, 1961).

Cadman, H. A., *Gomersal Past and Present* (Leeds, 1930).

Campos, C., *The View of France: From Arnold to Bloomsbury* (Oxford, 1965).

Carter, J. and Pollard, G., *An Enquiry into the Nature of Certain Nineteenth Century Pamphlets* (London, 1934).

Chadwick, E. A., *In the Footsteps of the Brontës* (London, 1914).

Christian, M., 'A Census of Brontë Manuscripts in the U.S.A.' In *The Trollopian*, II and III.

——, 'The Brontës'. In *Victorian Fiction: A Guide to Research.* Edited by L. Stevenson (Cambridge, Mass., 1964).

Christie, O., *The Transition from Aristocracy, 1832–1867* (London, 1927).

Cortazzo, E. H., 'The Reminiscences of Emma Huidekoper Cortazzo'. Edited by H. H. G. Arnold. In *Transactions of the Brontë Society*, 68, pp. 220–31.

Craik, W. A., *The Brontë Novels* (London, 1968).

Dalziel, M., *Popular Fiction 100 Years Ago* (London, 1957).

Decker, C., *The Victorian Conscience* (New York, 1952).

Devonshire, M. G., *The English Novel in France, 1830–1870* (London, 1929).

Dewhirst, I., 'The Rev. Patrick Brontë and the Keighley Mechanics Institute'. In *Transactions of the Brontë Society*, 75, pp. 35-7.

Dry, F. S., *The Sources of Wuthering Heights* (Cambridge, 1937).

——, *The Sources of Jane Eyre* (Cambridge, 1940).

Dunbar, G. S., 'Proper Names in *Villette*'. In *Nineteenth Century Fiction*, XV, pp. 77-80.

Erskine Stuart, J., 'Brontë Nomenclature'. In *Transactions of the Brontë Society*, 3 (1895), pp. 14-18.

Ewbank, I-S., *Their Proper Sphere: A Study of the Brontë Sisters as Early Victorian Novelists* (London, 1966).

Faber, R., *Proper Stations: Class in Victorian Fiction* (London, 1971).

Fielding, K. J., 'The Brontës and The North American Review'. In *Transactions of the Brontë Society*, 66, pp. 14-18.

Foltineck, H. *Vorstufen zum Viktorianischen Realismus* (Vienna, 1969).

Froude, J. A., *Shadows of the Clouds*, by Zeta (London, 1847).

Gary, F., 'Charlotte Brontë and George Henry Lewes', In *Publications of the Modern Language Association of America*, LI, pp. 518-42.

Gaskell, E. C., *The Letters of Mrs Gaskell*. Edited by J. A. V. Chapple and A. E. Pollard (Manchester, 1966).

Gerin, W., *Anne Brontë* (London, 1959).

——, *Branwell Brontë* (London, 1961).

——, *Charlotte Brontë: The Evolution of Genius* (Oxford, 1967).

——, *Emily Brontë* (Oxford, 1971).

Gettman, R. A., *A Victorian Publisher: A Study of the Bentley Papers* (Cambridge, 1960).

Gilbert, B. and Cross, P. C., 'Farewell to Hoffman'. In *Transactions of the Bronte Society*, 80, pp. 412-16.

Haffley, J., 'The Villain in *Wuthering Heights*'. In *Nineteenth Century Fiction*, XIII, pp. 199-215.

Hanson, L. and E. M., *The Four Brontës* (Oxford, 1949). Revised edition (Hamden, Conn., 1967).

Harrison, A., and Stanford, D., *Anne Brontë: Her Life and Work* (London, 1959).

Harrison, F., *Studies in Early Victorian Literature* (London, 1895).

Hewish, J., *Emily Brontë* (London, 1969).

Hinkley, L., *Charlotte and Emily: The Brontës* (New York, 1945).

Hopewell, D., 'New Treasures at Haworth'. In *Transactions of the Brontë Society*, 61, pp. 18-26.

Hopkins, A., *Elizabeth Gaskell: Her Life and Work* (London, 1952).

——, *The Father of the Brontës* (Baltimore, 1958).

Houghton, W. E., *The Victorian Frame of Mind* (New Haven, 1957).

——, ed., *The Wellesley Index to Victorian Periodicals* (Toronto, 1966).

Jack, I., 'De Quincey Revises His Confessions'. In *Publications of the Modern Language Association of America*, LXXII, pp. 122–46.

——, *English Literature, 1815–1832* (Oxford, 1963).

James, L., *Fiction for the Working Man, 1830–1850* (London, 1963).

Kettle, A., *An Introduction to the English Novel*, Volume I (London, 1951).

Knies, E., *The Art of Charlotte Brontë* (Ohio, 1969).

Lane, M., *The Brontë Story: A Reconsideration of Mrs Gaskell's Life of Charlotte Brontë* (London, 1953).

Law, A., *Emily Brontë and the Authorship of Wuthering Heights* (Altham, 1925).

Leavis, Q. D., 'A Fresh Approach to *Wuthering Heights*'. In *Lectures in America* by F. R. and Q. D. Leavis (London, 1969).

Leyland, F., *The Brontë Family: With Special Reference to Patrick Branwell Brontë*, 2 vols. (London, 1886).

Lock, J., and Dixon, W. T., *A Man of Sorrow: The Life, Letters and Times of the Rev. Patrick Brontë* (London, 1965).

Maison, M., *Search Your Soul, Eustace: A Survey of the Religious Novel in the Victorian Age* (London, 1961).

Malham Dembleby, J., *The Confessions of Charlotte Brontë* (Bradford, 1954).

Marsh, D. C., *The Changing Social Structure of England and Wales, 1871–1961* (London, 1965).

Martin, R., *The Accents of Persuasion: Charlotte Brontë's Novels* (London, 1966).

Maurice, F. D., *Theological Essays* (London, 1853).

Maurier, D. du, *The Infernal World of Branwell Brontë* (London, 1960).

Mayo, R., *The English Novel in the Magazines, 1740–1815* (Evanston, 1962).

Moore, V., *The Life and Eager Death of Emily Brontë* (London, 1936).

Nelson, J. G., 'First American Reviews of the Works of Charlotte, Emily and Anne Brontë'. In *Transactions of the Brontë Society*, 74, pp. 39–43.

Newman, J., *Apologia pro Vita Sua: Being a History of his Religious Opinions*. Edited by M. J. Svaglic (Oxford, 1967).

Newsome, D., *The Parting of Friends* (London, 1966).

Newton, A. E., *Derby Day and Other Stories* (Boston, 1934).

Nussey, J. T. M., 'Rydings-Home of Ellen Nussey'. In *Transactions of the Brontë Society*, 78, pp. 244–9.

——, 'Notes on the Background of Three Incident in the Lives of the Brontës'. In *Transactions of the Brontë Society*, 79, pp. 331–335.

Nussey, J. T. M., *Nussey Family History* (privately printed at Chester, 1969).

Oliphant, M. O., *The Autobiography and Letters of Mrs Oliphant*. Edited by A. L. Coghill (London, 1899).

Oram, E. A., 'Emily Brontë and F. D. Maurice'. In *Transactions of the Brontë Society*, 67, pp. 131–40.

——, 'A Brief for Miss Branwell'. In *Transactions of the Brontë Society*, 74, pp. 28–38.

P.,W.P., *Jottings on Currer, Ellis and Acton Bell* (London, 1856).

Paden, W. D., *An Investigation of Gondal* (New York, 1958).

Partington, W., *Thomas Wise in the Original Cloth* (London, 1946).

Perrin, N., *Dr Bowdler's Legacy* (London, 1970).

Prescott, J., 'Jane Eyre: A Romantic Exemplum with a Difference'. In *Twelve Original Essays on Great Novelists*. Edited by C. Shapiro (Detroit, 1960).

Quinlan, M. J., *Victorian Prelude: A History of English Manners 1760–1830* (New York, 1941).

Ratchford, F. E., *The Brontë's Web of Childhood* (New York, 1941).

——, *Gondal's Queen: A Novel in Verse* (Austin, 1955).

Reid, T. W., *Charlotte Brontë: A Monograph* (London, 1877).

Robinson, A. M. F., *Emily Brontë* (London, 1883).

Sadleir, M., *Bulwer and His Circle* (London, 1931).

S(anger), C. P., *The Structure of Wuthering Heights* (London, 1926).

Scruton, W., 'Reminiscences of the Late Miss Ellen Nussey'. In *Transactions of the Brontë Society*, 8 (1898), pp. 23–42.

Shepheard-Walwyn, C. C-W., *Henry and Margaret Jane Shepheard – Memorials of a Father and Mother* (London, 1882).

Sherry, N., *Charlotte and Emily Brontë* (London, 1970).

Shorter, C. K., *Charlotte Brontë and her Circle* (London, 1896).

——, *Charlotte Brontë and her Sisters* (London, 1905).

——, *The Brontës: Life and Letters*, 2 volumes (London, 1908).

——, *The Brontës and Their Circle* (London, 1914).

Simpson, C., *Emily Brontë* (London, 1929).

Sinclair, M. *The Three Brontës* (London, 1912).

Solomon, E., 'The Incest Theme in *Wuthering Heights*'. In *Nineteenth Century Fiction*, XIV, pp. 80–3.

Stang, R., *The Theory of the Novel in England, 1850–1870*. (London, 1959).

Stevens, J., 'Woozles in Brontëland: A Cautionary Tale'. In *Studies in Bibliography*, XXIV, pp. 99–105.

Stevenson, L. 'Prude's Progress'. In *Virginia Quarterly Review*, XIII, pp. 257-77.

Sugden, K. A. R., *A Short History of the Brontës* (Oxford, 1929).

Thrall, M. M. H., *Rebellious Fraser's, 1830–1840* (London, 1934).

Thompson, P., *The Victorian Heroine* (London, 1956).

Tillotson, K., *Novels of the Eighteen-forties* (Oxford, 1954).

Tompkins, J. S. M., *The Popular Novel in England, 1770–1800* (London, 1932).

Utter, R. P., and Needham, G. B., *Pamela's Daughters* (New York, 1937).

Visick, M., *The Genesis of Wuthering Heights* (Hong Kong, 1958).

Watson, M. R., 'Wuthering Heights and the Critics'. In *The Trollopian*, III, pp. 243–64.

Weir, E. M., 'Contemporary Reviews of the First Brontë Novels'. In *Transactions of the Brontë Society*, 61, pp. 88–96.

Whone, C., 'Where the Brontës Borrowed Books'. In *Transactions of the Brontë Society*, 60, pp. 344–58.

Williams, R., *The English Novel: From Dickens to Lawrence* (London, 1970).

Wills, I. C., *The Brontës* (London, 1933).

——, *The Authorship of Wuthering Heights* (London, 1928).

Wilson, R., *All Alone: The Life and Private History of Emily Jane Brontë* (London, 1928).

Winnifrith, T. J., 'Charlotte Brontë and Calvinism'. In *Notes and Queries*, 1970, pp. 17–18.

——, 'Charlotte Brontë's Letters to Ellen Nussey'. In *Durham University Journal* LXIII, 1, pp. 16–18.

Wise, T. J., *A Bibliography of the Writings in Prose and Verse of the Brontë Family* (London, 1917).

——, *A Brontë Library: A Catalogue of Printed Books, Manuscripts and Autograph Letters by the Members of the Brontë Family* (London, 1929).

——, *Letters of Thomas J. Wise to John Henry Wrenn*. Edited by F. E. Ratchford (New York, 1944).

Woolf, V., 'Jane Eyre and Wuthering Heights'. In *The Common Reader*, first series, (London, 1925), pp. 196–205.

Wood, B., "A Bibliography of the Works of the Brontë Family'. Part I of the *Transactions of the Brontë Society* (1895). Supplement in Part 6 (1897).

Wright, W., *The Brontës in Ireland* (London, 1893).

Wroot, H. E., 'The Persons and Places in the Brontë Novels'. Volume III of the *Transactions of the Brontë Society* (1906).

Index